Cynthi

BE THY LIGHT

KIM CHRISTIN

BE THY LIGHT

Daily Intentions
for
Mindful Living

ISBN: 978-0-9600169-2-1

Acknowledgements

I continue to send out heartfelt gratitude to the following individuals that continue to be a priceless support system in my inspirational writing and personal journey.

Russ McKnight, Ruby McCall,
Sandra Marshall, Velda Shelby, and Carol Schloegel.

Be thy Light would not have come to fruition without the following contributors. Their commitment to their passion has elevated this project to touch the lives of all those who are open to the message of intention.

Book Cover Designer

Ana Grigoriu~ Owner of Books-Design.com, Ana has a natural talent for taking powerful ideas and translating them into stunning visual art.

Editor

Becky Holland Fuller~ A mother of five children, architectural graduate, world traveler, writer, and editor. This woman knows no boundaries. She is committed to touching and creating that which she is passionate about, and her life reflects that in every way.

Photography and Logo

Suz Gossett (SG)~ A deeply honest, committed, hard-working, and spiritual person who is dedicated to using her communication skills to help people connect with themselves, other people, and the world at large. Suz is dedicated to inspiring and motivating others to build more aligned and connected lives by showing them the beauty that not only surrounds us but lies within each one of us.

Photography

Tim Chinn (TC)~ Tim resides in western Colorado, where he captures the beauty of the outdoors through photography. He and his wife have several acres where he finds many of his photographic subjects. He enjoys exploring assorted camera lenses that allow him to capture his subjects in a creative way that the human eye cannot.

Steve McCall (SM)~ A retired biologist that worked for 30 years for the Department of Interior. He has assisted in preserving the water, land, and fish and wildlife habitat of the Colorado Rockies. Steve is now a volunteer committed to various organizations that sustain the health, diversity, and productivity of our planet for the enjoyment of present and future generations. His photography captures the passion that he has for nature and the creatures that reside there.

When we heal ourselves,
the world heals with us.
~Kim Christin

You are here to shine your Light upon the world. You are a unique being with thoughts, experiences, and gifts that only you can give to those that witness your journey.

Be thy Light is your day-to-day guide to living a life of intention for 365 days through conscious awareness and connection.

As your days unfold with various experiences, the following tools will be there to guide and assist you in balancing your heart, mind, and soul:

- Weekly Themes
- Word of the Day
- Daily Intentions built around the Word of the Day
- Daily Blessings
- 'I Am' Affirmations

The words within will support you to live a compassionate life of intention. They will bring you hope when all appears deep in despair, bring you guidance when all seems lost, and assist you in becoming the highest version of yourself.

Be thy Light provides spiritual tools to incorporate into your journey to help you overcome life's obstacles, embrace forgiveness, and create a more mindful way of living through your awakened consciousness.

We are One, truly connected to all things, a family here on this beautiful planet. Let us come together and create a life of intention, leading to a world of compassion and joy for all.

When you and I shine our unique Light in all that we do,
we create a world of compassion for all.

~Kim Christin

Kim Christin is the creator of *365 Intentions to Inspire App*. She is a spiritual healer and inspirational writer, supporting others in their journey to true awareness and connection through her inspirational words of Light. She lives with her significant other and their three dogs near San Diego, California.

Also by Kim Christin

365 Intentions to Inspire App
Available on Android and Apple

Daily Inspiration
Facebook - @kimchristin.kc
Instagram and Twitter - @kc_kimchristin

Website
www.kimchristin.com

Table of Contents

Introduction   **1**

Flowing with Possibilities **4**
Aligned.................................6
Balance.................................6
Flowing 7
Focusing 8
Imagination 8
Nature..................................9
Possibilities 9

Attitude of Abundance **12**
Carefree.............................14
Admiration 15
Abundance 15
Attitude 16
Glory 17
Lessons...............................17
Living 17

Awakening to Greatness **20**
Awakening 22
Choices...............................22
Expansion............................23
Goodness.............................23
Meaningful..........................24
Awaken 24
Powerful..............................25

Liberty of Awareness   **27**
Acknowledge 29
Awareness...........................29
Feel.....................................30
Instinctively........................31
Liberty.................................31
Listening 31
Manifesting 32

Aspire to Just Be   **35**
Just Be................................36
Aspire..................................37
Be..38
Greatness.............................38
I Am 39
Reflect.................................39
Sparkle 40

Inspired Transition   **43**
Believe 44
Inspired...............................45
Power 45
Step by Step 46
Supported 46
Transform............................47
Transition 48

Glorious Blessings   **50**
Blessed 51
Given...................................52
Glorious...............................52
Inspiration 53
Moonbeams..........................53
Praise 54
Rejoice 54

Supported Purpose   **57**
Purpose................................58
Guide...................................59
Mystery 59
Reflection............................60
Release 61
Renew..................................61
Shift....................................62

Catalyst in Compassion **64**
Be Fulfilled 66
Catalyst...............................66
Compassion.........................67
Emotions 67
Empower..............................68
Forgiveness 68
Kind....................................69

Consciously Creating   **72**
Incredible 74
Infinitely.............................74
Conscious............................75
Intention 75
Meaning 76
Movement 76
Our-Self...............................77

Courageous Action   79

Courage 80
Bold 81
Brave 81
Conquer 82
Courageous 83
Fearlessness 83
Persistence 84

Art of Creativity   86

Adventurous 88
Creative 88
Masterpiece 89
Music 89
Pleasure 90
Creativity 91
Poetry.......................91

Destiny Rising   94

Destiny.....................96
Narrating...................96
Persevere 97
Destination...............97
Realization 98
Recognize 98
Rising.......................99

Dreams Aligned   101

Vitality....................103
Voice 103
Whispers..................104
Within......................104
Worthy.....................105
Yield 106
You 106

Empowered Freedom   109

Empowered...............110
Freedom...................111
Initiative...................111
Resilience 112
Responsible 112
Rise..........................113
Thrive 114

Encouraging the Hear   116

Appreciated...............117
Encouraging...............118
Forever......................119
Magnificent................119
Narrator....................120
Smile.........................120
Spark.........................121

Nurturing thy Being   123

Gift...........................124
Insightful...................125
Loved........................125
Nurturing 126
Passion......................126
Perfect.......................127
True 127

Expanding Growth   130

Evolving 131
Experience 131
Flow...........................132
Growth........................133
Expanding...................133
Life-Giving..................134
Open 134

Resilient Faith   137

Faith...........................139
Achieve.......................139
Fears 140
Guided 140
Inner Voice 141
Lean In........................142
Resilient.......................142

Beauty within Grace   145

Beauty.........................146
Grace 147
Serenely 147
Twilight 148
Everything 148
Graciously....................149
Unstoppable..................149

Attention to Gratitude 152
Gratitude.................................153
Attention 154
Circumstance.........................154
Colors....................................155
Contribution 155
Generosity 156
Reach.....................................156

Certainty of Guidance 159
Guidance 160
Always 161
Answers.................................161
Ask 162
Certainty................................163
Challenge 163
Confidence 164

Harmonious Moments 166
Beliefs 167
Harmonious...........................168
Uncertainty............................169
Undoing.................................169
Union.....................................170
Harmony 171
Unique...................................171

Embracing Intention 174
Embrace 175
Arising...................................176
Beginning..............................176
Clarity 177
Desire 177
Heart......................................178
Intentions..............................178

Reflection of Hope 181
Hope......................................182
Clarify 182
Envision 183
Feelings.................................184
Focus 184
Fulfillment.............................185
Aspiration..............................185

Renewing the Song 188
Enriched 189
Insight....................................189
Inspire....................................190
Renewed.................................191
Seeds 191
Song 192
Spontaneity............................192

Positive Perspective 195
Breath 196
Passion 197
In Sync 197
Openness................................198
Perspective 198
Positive..................................199
Spontaneous 199

Receptive Change 202
Receptive...............................203
Blossoms 204
Allowing................................204
Change...................................205
Contemplate 206
Effortless 206
In Tune 207

Journey of Joy 209
Acceptance.............................210
Joy...211
Enthusiasm 211
Excitement 212
Exhileration...........................212
Enjoy 213
Giggles 213

Mantra of Kindness 216
Kindness.................................217
Manifestation 218
Mantra 218
Preciousness...........................219
Triumph..................................219
Lovingkindness 220
Truly......................................220

Essence of Bliss   223

Essence 224
Authenticity 225
Awakened 225
Aware 226
Bliss 226
Brilliance 227
Light 228

Mirror of Love   230

Love...232
Activate 232
Eternity 233
Interpreter 233
Loving 234
Mirror 234
Vibrant.....................................235

Manifesting Prosperity 237

Creator.....................................238
Divine 239
Limitless 239
Manifest...................................240
Master......................................240
Proactive..................................241
Prosperity.................................242

Mysterious Miracles   244

Miracle.....................................246
Capable....................................246
Conviction 247
Magic..247
Mysterious...............................248
Perception................................248
Sacredness 249

Rejuvenating Laughter 251

Cradle 252
In the Beginning 253
Fascination...............................253
Laughter...................................254
Narrator 254
Nurture.....................................255
Rejuvenate 255

Union of Peace   258

Peace..260
Calmness..................................260
Happiness 261
Potential...................................261
Similarities...............................262
Story 262
Together....................................263

Actions of Perseverance 265

Achieving 266
Accountability 267
Action.......................................267
Bravery.....................................268
Empowering 268
Integrity 269
Perseverance.............................269

Intuitive Presence   272

Appreciate.................................273
Witness 274
Present 274
Complete...................................275
Deliverance...............................275
Intuitive....................................276
Thankfulness.............................276

Legacy of Relationships 279

Family.......................................280
Gathering 281
Harmoniously 281
Inseparable................................282
Interpret 283
Legacy 283
Relationships 284

Genuine Self   286

Creation 287
Higher Self................................288
Extraordinary............................288
Faithful 289
Genuine.....................................290
Inquisitive.................................290
Self..291

Listening in Silence   293
Silence................................294
Listen.................................295
Favorite 295
Quietude............................296
Synchronize.......................296
Listener 297
Quiet..................................298

Shining thy Light   300
Facets 301
Grateful 302
Happily...............................302
Phenomenal.......................303
Progress.............................304
Radiate 304
Shine 305

Soul Communication   307
Communication...................308
Interpretation.....................309
Playful 309
Reaching............................310
Soul 311
Special...............................311
Spirit..................................312

Sacred Stillness   314
Stillness.............................315
Well-Being.........................316
Intuition.............................316
Sacred...............................317
Solitude 317
Time 318
Soothe 319

Releasing Resistance   321
Letting Go 322
Releasing...........................323
Resistance.........................323
Reveal 324
Surrender...........................324
Teachings 325
Unboundedness 325

Remembering Thankfulness 328
Happy.................................329
Joyful.................................330
Perfection 330
Others................................331
Remember 331
Thankful 332
Value 332

Trusting in the Process 335
Divinity 336
Honesty 336
Process 337
Promise..............................338
Reassured 338
Honor 339
Trust..................................339

Authentic Truth   342
Knowing..............................343
Truth..................................344
Authentic............................344
Declare 345
Devotion.............................345
Enlightenment 346
Truthful 346

Unity Collaboration   349
Arise...................................350
Blessed Be..........................351
Collaboration......................351
Connection 352
Differences.........................352
Unique................................353
Unity...................................354

Warrior Strength   356
Adventure............................357
Declaration.........................358
Explore...............................358
Overcome 359
Strength 360
Strive 360
Warrior...............................361

Honoring Wisdom 363

Adaptation 364
Honored 365
Becoming................................365
Experiences 366
Patience 366
Honoring..................................367
Wisdom 367

Witness of Wonder 370

Example...................................371
Moments.................................371
Observer 372
Storyteller 372
Today......................................373
Validate 374
Wonder...................................374

Bonus 377

Peace......................................377

Shine Brilliantly 378

Additional Notes 380

Index 386

Introduction

You are here to shine your Light upon the world. You are a unique being with thoughts, experiences, and gifts that only you can give to those that witness your journey.

The words that follow will help guide you to live a compassionate life of intention. They are here to bring you hope when all appears deep in despair, to bring you guidance when all seems lost, and to assist you in being the highest version of yourself.

How many of us are attempting to live each day in inspiration, awakening in a state of gratitude and hope for the day ahead, only to encounter, time and time again, a floundering day where the plan or goal has wavered once more.

My life began to change when I started living with intention. It did not lead to perfection, because we all know that life can be messy, but it guided me into a more profound presence to create the compassionate life I longed to be living.

Be thy Light is your day-to-day guide to live a life of intention for 365 days. It includes 52 weekly themes with 365 daily intentions and empowering I Am affirmations. It will discuss various tools that you can mindfully incorporate into your life through your thoughts, words, and actions.

Struggles will not disappear; but you will begin to understand how to feel fully and to move through the emotions of disappointment, heartache, and anger into awareness instead of avoidance.

Relationships will begin enriching your journey, instead of depleting you, as your perception shifts into a compassionate way of being. It is in this space that you will be able to create the life that you came here to share with others.

Below are a few suggestions to assist you with your daily practice. Try one, a few or create your own customs that resonate with your desire to find more sacred moments of true connection.

- Essential oils (Element of air and water)
  I use a variety of scents based upon my intuitive guidance for the day. I diffuse them in my home and wear them as my personal perfume.

- Crystals (Element of Earth)
  A wonderful spiritual tool to assist you in your journey. Crystals can be used in meditation, as well as worn in your jewelry, to support you in what you are concentrating upon while promoting healing within your mind, body, and soul. I also place crystals into the essential oils that I wear on my skin.
- Light a candle (Element of fire)
  I use a tealight candle to set my daily intention. I envision the Earth, my home, relationships, and my body surrounded in this light as I begin my day.
- Meditate/ Pray (Element of Spirit)
  I have found that if I begin and end my day with prayer and meditation practice, the 24 hours has more moments of inner peace. What is the difference between prayer and meditation? Prayer is talking with the Divine. Meditation is listening to the guidance and answers that await all of your questions.
- Journal
  Writing is a powerful tool to bring more of that which you desire into your life. It assists in releasing that which no longer serves us. Always end your journaling in a moment of gratitude and hope.
- Grounding or Earthing
  Place your bare feet or hands into the grass or soil. This simple action will restore and harmonize your basic biological rhythms. Studies have shown that grounding will boost your body's self-healing, and reduce inflammation and pain.

We are unique beings and what resonates with my journey will not always be the same for you. Do that which you are drawn too. If one process doesn't work, try something else until you find a pattern to begin your day with mindful intention.

If each of us takes the time to find peace within ourselves, we will bring more peace and compassion into the world. May the words that follow inspire your journey to be and share your true essence with the world.

Be thy Light.

Image captured by Susan Gossett.

Week 1
Flowing with Possibilities

~~~~~~~~

Blessings of Hope are sent to you today. May your heart be open to the Flow and alignment with the ever-expanding Possibilities of unconditional love and compassion.

~~~~~~~~

Often in our lives, we notice patterns that no longer contribute to the life we came here to experience. It is when we become consciously aware of our past hindering the endless possibilities for the future, that it is time to heal these areas and create the *Flow of Possibilities* for our tomorrows.

It is in the act of forgiveness that we remove the barriers of yesterday, and that which no longer serves our journey, discovering the pathway to honor where we have been and the direction we are guided to move towards.

We cannot heal that which has not been spoken or remains hidden in secret. Avoidance and denial will never lead us to oneness or the feeling of being whole and complete. It is through our awareness that our actions can move into the vulnerability to discover our strength and validate the wounds and scars of yesterday.

This is when the healing begins and the compassion for one another, and ourselves, is needed more than ever. One becomes open to the feelings and emotions, often feeling overwhelmed by the memories of yesterday and leading us to shut down once again.

It is in this space of raw emotion and vulnerability that I personally use a sacred Hawaiian tool called Ho'oponopono. It is a ritual of reconciliation and forgiveness that was traditionally practiced by indigenous Hawaiian healers, who repeat the following phrases:

> *I am sorry.*
> *Please forgive me.*
> *I love you.*
> *Thank you.*

No matter the situation or place one can use this tool. It is not uncommon in the beginning to say the phrases and to *not* feel connected to what you are speaking. I promise that somewhere in the process of denial, hurt, disappointment, betrayal or anger a shift will begin.

Repeat the phrases with each thought or memory that crosses one's mind, with every emotion that comes through the body, and with the abundance of tears that may accompany each revelation

Many years ago I used Ho'oponopono when a long-term relationship was on the rocks. We were not speaking, and honestly, there was nothing to discuss at that time because we weren't ready to hash out the ins and outs of what was and was not working.

I had an old rock garden that was in disarray. I wanted to refurbish the area and decided that the labor of moving each stone would be completed with the intention of unburdening my heart.

Each stone, whether small or large, round or jagged, dark or light, I repeated the phrases *I am sorry* that my actions were not always from the highest version of myself, *Please forgive me* if I did not hear or correctly interpret the words that you spoke to me, *I love you* for all that you are and have been in this journey thus far, and I *Thank you* for this experience to know my true self even more.

Each time I would place different phrases behind the Ho'oponopono words of I am sorry, Please forgive me, I love you, and Thank you. In the beginning, I did not feel love, only anger and disappointment, but somewhere the resentment faded and love began to emerge. My heart felt lighter and oh so bright once again.

There is magic that takes place when using Ho'oponopono, and I will personally testify that it assisted me in aligning my heart, body, and soul when I thought it was impossible.

When we heal ourselves, we heal the world for we are One. When you and I are FLOWING WITH POSSIBILITIES, we are in alignment with one another and our blessed planet that each of us call home.

Be thy Light.

Day 1
ALIGNED~ When we are ALIGNED with our highest self and functioning from a place of love, synchronicities multiply and doors open where there were once only walls. You are a miracle, and when your heart, mind, and soul are ALIGNED, there are no boundaries to the possibilities. The distance between you and your dreams is a barrier that you have placed before you through your perceptions. Knock down the wall of doubt, be ALIGNED with the hope and love of the Universal Light, and watch your dreams unfold before you with all the endless possibilities.

~ I AM ALIGNED with my heart, mind, and soul.

~~~~~~~~~

Blessings of Alignment are sent to you today. May your inner wisdom be ALIGNED with your heart, mind, and soul in this journey that you are experiencing.

~~~~~~~~~

Day 2
BALANCE~ As we walk along this path of life there are moments of intense joy but also of deep sadness. You and I must be aware of the innate endeavor within our souls to create a BALANCE; a BALANCE between our spirituality, relationships with others, responsibilities to ourselves and the

world around us, and our efforts to bring our dreams into reality. The community, the tribe, the family that we create can assist our journey to find BALANCE; it is all in the perception of what you and I may or may not be witnessing. Let us consciously choose to embrace the thoughts, words, actions and, relationships that bring BALANCE to our world.

~ I AM aware of my choices, and I choose to live a life of BALANCE and love.

~~~~~~~

Blessings of Balance are sent to you today. May you consciously choose that which brings BALANCE into your life.

~~~~~~~

Day 3

FLOWING~ As we experience life in difficult moments, the emotions that you and I feel can be manifesting in our physical bodies as ailments or injuries. This does not have to be our reality if we are in tune to that which is happening internally and externally. Let us feel the emotions as a wave FLOWING through us, always moving around us as we breathe in and breathe out. Let us not swallow the pain or the hurt of the negative energy. This will prevent our well-being from FLOWING effortlessly with the Universe. Let us remember, all that you and I experience are but moments. The tears, laughter, anger, and sadness take place, and we acknowledge the wave of emotions; but then we must release these emotions from our being, allowing the stream to continue FLOWING in and around us in the course of the experience. These moments are only a grain of sand on the white beach that we walk upon during our journey.

~ I AM one with the journey of life, FLOWING effortlessly along the path.

~~~~~~~

Blessings of being in the Flow are sent to you today. May your heart be open to releasing and FLOWING through the emotions that move through you today.

~~~~~~~

7

Day 4

FOCUSING~ Each of us has dreams that are precious jewels waiting to be discovered and experienced. To manifest our dreams into reality, we must spend a moment each day FOCUSING on what we desire. Dreams need to be nurtured with thought and action. Just as the seeds are nurtured in a garden, so must we tend to our dreams. FOCUSING on our dreams will raise our vibrations, attract more joy to our day, and facilitate the movements that will align our purpose with the life we are leading. You and I are never too young or old to have a dream and bring it to fruition by FOCUSING on that which we came here to share with the world.

~ I AM FOCUSING on the thoughts and actions that will bring my dreams into reality.

~~~~~~~~

Blessings of Clarity are sent to you today. May you be open to FOCUSING on that which you came here to share with the world.

~~~~~~~~

Day 5

IMAGINATION~ It is in the world of IMAGINATION that you and I can take steps towards our goals and dreams. In this alternate reality, we are living the life of our passion, creating relationships and beauty, sharing our gifts with the world. The world of IMAGINATION is filled with guidance and support to assist us in bringing the essence of each of us to its highest vibration. In this space we are one with everything around us, attracting all the things that are needed to raise our consciousness as a planet. This world is not imaginary, for you and I need only believe and to take steps of actions to bring it into the realm of possibility. It is through our faith that the Universe sprinkles its magic, aligning people and places in ways that you and I cannot fathom. Let us take a few moments today to visualize all that we dream of and take a single step toward making our IMAGINATION our reality.

~ I AM using my IMAGINATION to create a compassionate world where I share my Light with others.

8

Blessings of Creativity are sent to you today. May you be inspired to use your IMAGINATION and use your unique gifts to share with all those around you.

Day 6

NATURE~ It is important for each of us to spend time in NATURE and to be open to its wisdom by observing the ebb and flow of life's natural changes. When the moment arrives for the seasons to change, NATURE does not argue that it is too soon or too late; it just unfolds in the perfect timing of the Universe. On occasions that we feel drained or depleted, let us take a walk in the beauty that surrounds us; to touch the leaves, to place our toes in the dirt or grass, and to reconnect to our foundation with the intent to raise our energy to a new level. Bringing NATURE inside with a plant or cut flowers can lift our spirits at home or the office. It is up to each of us to be in tune with what our body, mind, and soul need. Let us be responsible for taking the time to raise our vibrations today.

~ I AM taking the time to raise my vibrations by being in tune with Mother NATURE and my surroundings.

Blessings of Peace are sent to you today. May you be in tune to NATURE and all the lessons and wisdom it gives to your daily journey.

Day 7

POSSIBILITIES~ The rays of sun peak over the horizon, and the darkened sky is filled with a prism of light. The morning welcomes us with the joy of all that is, with the love that constantly surrounds us, and with the peace that is ours if only we open our hearts to the POSSIBILITIES. This moment is ours for the taking; to experience, to learn, and to grow. The POSSIBILITIES are endless. We need only to be open to what may seem impossible and believe that through the power of trust, the doorways will open into the POSSIBILITIES.

~ I AM aligning my mind, heart, and soul with the ever-expanding POSSIBILITIES of love.

~~~~~~~~

Blessings of Hope are sent to you today. May you be inspired by all the POSSIBILITIES of hope and love that surround each and every situation.

~~~~~~~~

Lord. I ask that you show me
the Task Moment by Moment

Notes

As I start to be Thy light. The first thing
that comes to Mind is My gratitude
for this book. Thank You Holy Spirit
who dwells. Thank You Toni for
being inspired to share Thy light
with Me. This book comes at a
perfect time. I just had a conversation
with My Mom and My heart hurts. I
truly love her and yern to share
light. I will not give up on her.
Dear Lord help Me and forgive Me
where I fall short. Help me to find
Balance, Help My being flow.
Focus. I pray to be a blessing for
God and a becon of light from God.
I hope to be fruitful and to be a
good servant and steward to shepra
My children Cole, Taly Cal and
Sren Guer ♥

11

Image captured by Susan Gossett.

Week 2
Attitude of Abundance

~~~~~~~~

Blessings of Unconditional Love are sent to you today. May you bring an
Attitude of Abundance to every moment and conversation you experience.

~~~~~~~~

There is a direct correlation between one's belief in their worthiness and
their capacity to manifest abundance. You and I desire to create a life of
prosperity, not only financially, but in regards to spiritual, physical and
overall well-being.

It is through conscious awareness of our thoughts and belief patterns that we
are able to shift that which is no longer serving our journey. When you and I
tune into our limiting beliefs of worthiness, we can counteract those with
new thoughts and words of love and compassion, creating a well-rounded
life of unity and balance in every way.

When we are in sync with our essence, our connection with others is from a
state of compassion and love. It is here that we begin to live in a state of
Oneness and abundance can be for all. Competition is no longer what drives

12

society, but unity for each other, for the Earth, and for all that inhabits her.

As you and I become more and more in tune with our attitude towards the present moment we raise the consciousness of our world.

In this conscious awareness of our limiting thoughts, you and I can replace the negative self-talk with affirmations of positivity, leading us to an attitude of abundance. Here is one of my favorites that I have created and placed a melody too. I often sing my affirmations because music raises my vibration and elevates me into a more joyful state of being.

> *I am whole.*
> *I am perfect.*
> *I am strong and powerful.*
> *I am loveable and harmonious.*
> *I am happy to be me, and I am what I will to be,*
>   *to visualize is the key.*
> *I believe the Universe is this to me.*
> *I believe the Universe brings this to me.*

Affirmations have personally changed my life, and I believe they have assisted in manifesting positive outcomes in stressful situations.

Many years ago, while I was traveling by myself to foreign lands, I became lost due to incorrect decisions on the commuter train system. The signs were not in English, and I became very disoriented, unsure of which direction I needed to go. Time appeared to be rushing by, and I had a flight to catch to my next destination.

I was in a high state of stress and was feeling vulnerable and afraid. I began repeating the following affirmation:

> *Only good and amazing things happen to me.*
> *Only good and amazing things happen to me.*
> *Only good and amazing things happen to me.*

The repetition assisted in limiting my thoughts of negativity by focusing on the words that I envisioned in my mind.

A young man asked in English with such kindness if I was going to the airport. 'Yes,' I replied with gratefulness. He attempted to explain what I needed to do but must have seen that I did not comprehend all that he was saying. He got off at the next exit with me and personally showed me the

13

train to catch.

Once I was back to the original place of error, I was attempting to find the correct train yet again. I was still repeating the phrase to alleviate the stress. *Only good and amazing things happen to me. Only good and amazing things happen to me.*

As I was looking at the trains and signs for some clue, a sweet silver-haired woman yelled across the tracks. 'Are you going to the airport?' 'Yes.' I said enthusiastically. 'You want to be on this side of the tracks, my dear.'

Two complete strangers were brought to me without uttering or inquiring one word aloud. The Universe allied these kind individuals to me, assisting and guiding my journey to my ultimate destination. A stressful situation was corrected and morphed into a moment of sincere gratitude and connection with two strangers.

You and I can choose to bring the Light of our essence to each of our experiences through our conversations and actions.

In moments of darkness should appear, let us not lose our hope. Let us instead choose to bring kindness and compassion to each situation, even to those circumstances that we may not understand or agree with. It is through communication that we create bridges. You and I have the responsibility to be the example of that which we wish to see in the world.

Together we can create a home, relationships, communities, cities, countries, and a planet surrounded in an ATTITUDE OF ABUNDANCE for all.

Be thy Light.

Day 1
CAREFREE~ As children we played with no barriers. We possessed a CAREFREE attitude towards all things around us as we giggled loudly for all to hear. Let us remember the childhood games of Hide and Seek; Tag, You're It; and Red Rover, Come on Over. Let us recall the smiles on our childhood faces. Let us see once again through the eyes of a child. Let the wonder and bewilderment come through our thoughts and envision that which surrounds us as a CAREFREE and loving world. When was the last time we giggled with one another until our belly hurt, or we spread our arms spinning around and around until falling to the ground in absolute delight? Let us be CAREFREE today, nurturing the childlike being inside of each of us.

~ I AM CAREFREE and unburdened as I approach my day. A child of the Universe, with eyes filled with curiosity and wonder.

Blessings of Love are sent to you today. May you remember your CAREFREE nature and explore each moment with curiosity and wonder.

Day 2

ADMIRATION~ Let us visualize the rays of sun touching the ripples upon the water. Let us see the beauty, feel the warmth on our skin, and soak in the blessing of this moment. Let each of us feel the ADMIRATION for the beauty that surrounds our world. Let us listen with the utmost ADMIRATION to each precious note as the birds share their melody with the world. May we take this moment to send blessings to the planet and all that she continues to provide to you and me; that we may be in awe of all that she is today, was yesterday, and the possibilities of her tomorrows. In this ever-present moment, let us think of one another and all that you and I have to offer each other through our talents and gifts. Let us sit in complete ADMIRATION of our essence and what we can do together. May we shine our Light upon the world.

~ I AM in complete ADMIRATION of the world in which I live, and of the blessings, I have been given to share with the world.

Blessings of Hope are sent to you today. May you see the blessings that are in every moment and be in ADMIRATION of the miracles in life.

Day 3

ABUNDANCE~ You and I are surrounded by ABUNDANCE in all things. Let us feel the joy as we awaken to this morning that we have been given. This gift is an amazing moment to experience all things through our unique perceptions. May you and I experience laughter as we go through our day; for humor lightens the load of the burdens we may carry. May you and I unconditionally love who we are and are striving to be. May the

ABUNDANCE abound in all aspects of our lives and may we have the wisdom knowing that life is unfolding perfectly. We may not see the future at this moment, but we have all looked back and experienced how the 'imperfect' moments of yesterday, which later gave us the insight into what we needed today. May our day be blessed in every way, and may we feel the ABUNDANCE of love, joy, and laughter throughout.

~ I AM living every moment with an attitude of ABUNDANCE.

Blessings of Faith are sent to you today. May you see the ABUNDANCE of love and support that surround you in this journey of life.

Day 4

ATTITUDE~ It is in our ATTITUDE that a moment is perceived as good or bad. It is within our perception and how we look at the world that determines if the glass is half full or half empty. Let us choose to drink of the world with a smile, knowing that somehow in someway everything is happening for a reason, even when we do not have the wisdom to see the future outcome. It is not our responsibility to understand the hows or whys. Our task is only to have a compassionate ATTITUDE toward one another. It is through compassion that our world can live in harmony, that the appearance of lack becomes abundant, and that we can come together to create a planet that is of grace and peace, not greed and war. Let us change our perception and priorities to an ATTITUDE of gratitude for the beauty in one another and all the inhabitants of this planet we call home.

~ I AM embracing an ATTITUDE of gratitude and grace.

Blessings of Compassion are sent to you today. May you approach every moment with an open heart and an ATTITUDE that will bring Light and hope to the world around you.

Day 5

GLORY~ As the sun rises, his rays shine their GLORY upon the leaves of green. It is as if the rays are the fingers of heaven touching down upon the Earth. The morning dew that blankets the grass sparkles with GLORY in the crisp air of the rising day. "Good morning!" says the meadowlark. The echoing coo of the dove seems to say, "What a glorious morning it is!" May we greet our day in the GLORY of all that is and will be.

~ I AM rising to the moment of greatness and give GLORY to this day.

~~~~~~~~~

Blessings of Wisdom are sent to you today. May you take the steps that lead you closer and closer to your highest essence witnessing the GLORY of Oneness.

~~~~~~~~~

Day 6

LESSONS~ The worry that we allow to rest upon our shoulders only hinders the LESSONS in our life. The doubt that things will not turn out in the way that we desire resides within these feelings of worry. When you and I worry about the "what if's" in life, it feeds our doubt, and the hope within us begins to wane, disrupting the speed in which the Universe can resolve life's scenarios. This journey is about giving and receiving, but in the middle of that exchange are the LESSONS. When we begin to embrace the LESSONS, the worry will subside, the hope will be abundant in our lives, and joy will flow through our world.

~ I AM open in every way to the LESSONS that life is teaching me.

~~~~~~~~~

Blessings of Hope are sent to you today. May you embrace the LESSONS that enter into your life, there are always blessings when we are expanding into the highest version of ourselves.

~~~~~~~~~

Day 7

LIVING~ Each day we choose, with intention, how we portray our lives. You and I can choose the good things by seeking the positive or we can view life with a negative perception. How are you LIVING your life, your days, weeks and years? When you and I look back on our yesterday, is it with an open heart, filled with love? When we envision our tomorrows, do we get excited about the possibilities? Let us choose to see the beauty, hear the music, feel the love, taste the goodness, and smell the sweetness of life today. We have a choice regarding the attitude that we bring to life's experiences. LIVING a life of joy and happiness can happen at any point in time; the choice is ours. Let us not wait for things to be perfect. The moment is now. Let us choose to be LIVING joyfully every day.

~ I AM LIVING a life of love and sharing that love with the world around me.

~~~~~~~

Blessings of Joy are sent to you today. May your life be a witness of LIVING in joy and love.

~~~~~~~

Notes

Image captured by Tim Chinn.

Week 3
Awakening to Greatness

~~~~~~~~

Blessings of Conscious Expansion are sent to you today. May you Awaken into your Greatness. Together we can create a world of unity and compassion.

~~~~~~~~

You and I can become more aware through our conscious awakening. It is in this awareness that we can transform the habits that no longer serve us into actions that create a life of compassion for everyone.

Together we can create the change we wish to see in the world. It begins in our home and relationships; when you and I start to personally take responsibility for the peace we want in the world by addressing it in our own lives.

The vibration that we bring to every experience is connected to our neighbors, and to the city in which we live, and ultimately to the world's consciousness.

Every conversation, perception, and judgment of what we are witnessing affects not only our personal lives, but also the planet we live on. We are One, and each of us can choose to bring love, compassion, and a deeper understanding into every conversation. Together we can assist in shifting that which is not serving the highest good.

Often this concept is difficult, and we may ask how one person can make such an impact. It is through our example in the midst of a conflict that others witness the hope and love they wish to see in themselves.

We have such great examples even in our lifetime of individuals that made a strong impact through adversity, such as Mahatma Gandhi, Nelson Mandela, and Martin Luther King.

It is when we learn to love without conditions that we begin to understand that every human should have their basic needs met. Such as clean water, nutritious meals, a place to call home, clean clothes, healthcare, to feel and know love, to experience education and safety, but to also have the opportunity and freedom to share their unique gifts with the world.

Often when I speak or write of these things, I am asked how I incorporate these concepts into my own life. How does one bring more peace into the world, let alone into their own lives?

My beliefs are often not reflected back to me. The majority of my family and friends have opposite viewpoints to mine. We have differences of opinions on taxes, gun control, war, healthcare, and government, wide ranges that span from conservatism to liberalism.

It is not always easy to discuss sensitive topics with my loved ones, but we do because we need to understand one another and all our different perspectives. We do not discuss these subjects to change one another's opinions, but through thoughtful conversations, each party may consider other viewpoints or become clear about their beliefs and why they believe them.

Would life be more comfortable to have only relationships that mirror my perspective? Possibly; but we are here to grow and expand. Sometimes it is the problematic conversations that bring our passions to the forefront and show us what we want to create in the world.

These are the ways we awaken into our greatness in the world, by learning to love unconditionally and respectfully, and by communicating with one another to create a world that is compassionate to all.

Let us deliberately choose the words that we speak from a place of wisdom and love, creating actions that are sharing Light with the world.

Let us AWAKEN to our GREATNESS in all that we do.

Be thy Light.

Day 1

AWAKENING~ As the sun rises and the hues of colors are bright and vivid to the eye, it caresses the shadows of the night, AWAKENING everything to a new day. The shadows that cross our paths bring clarity of what we may or may not want in our world. Once the shadows are recognized, each of us chooses to let them linger or to bless them as they continue their journey. It is when we let go of the places, the things, and even relationships that no longer serve us that we embrace the AWAKENING within our souls. Find the lesson in each experience, witness the clarity as we receive guidance from the Universe, and shine our inner Light upon the shadows that linger in the mind. Let our hearts be open, our minds fluid, and our spirits blessed with goodness, AWAKENING to the essence of our entire being.

~ I AM AWAKENING to the essence of my being. My soul awaits to be united with my heart.

Blessings of Openness are sent to you today. May you discover the AWAKENING of your true essence.

Day 2

CHOICES~ We are presented with many CHOICES throughout our lives. We make them every day and in every moment. You and I create our lives through our decisions. Let us choose to be empowered by that thought. Every morning as we awaken, let our CHOICES be conscious and emanate from the essence of who we are striving to be. Only you and I can make the decisions that bring us closer to the life we want to be living. You and I are the creators of our lives, our world, and our destiny through the CHOICES that we make each and every day.

~ I AM making empowered CHOICES as I create the life of my dreams.

~~~~~~~

Blessings of Wisdom are sent to you today. May your CHOICES be conscious in all that you say and do.

~~~~~~~

Day 3
EXPANSION~ The EXPANSION of you and I occurs every day whether we are aware of it or not. We live in an ever-expanding Universe; therefore, you and I cannot be stagnant in our journey. When the feelings of sadness, regret, anger, dissatisfaction, depression, etc. enter into our lives, it is a sign that life is expanding and we are not keeping up with our highest self. Let us reach for thoughts of hope and gratitude. The EXPANSION of our experience will shift into a higher gear where we are centered and balanced once more. We are the creators of our Universe; let us enjoy the journey and the EXPANSION of all that it is.

~ I AM embracing the EXPANSION of my being upon this unique and glorious journey.

~~~~~~~

Blessings of Openness are sent to you today. May you awaken into the EXPANSION of all that you are in this journey of life.

~~~~~~~

Day 4
GOODNESS~ As we awaken to this day and witness the sun rising before our eyes, let us see the GOODNESS in this present moment. As we peer into the essence of who we are, let us see the endless possibilities that surround us. As we watch the birds fly, the fish swim, the horses run, the bees buzz, and the hummingbirds' hum, let us see the GOODNESS in all things. Life blesses us with similarities as well as differences in the world in which we

live. The contrast will lead us to GOODNESS when our hearts are open to expanding into greatness.

~ I AM expanding into greatness. The wisdom of GOODNESS flows through me.

~~~~~~~

Blessings of Awareness are sent to you today. May you see, feel, and be the GOODNESS in every moment of your journey.

~~~~~~~

Day 5

MEANINGFUL~ As we awake and embrace the world around us, let us make the choice to live a MEANINGFUL life in each and every moment. You and I can choose to see the possibilities in all things that we touch, feel, and imagine. We can share the essence of who we are with the world around us by choosing thoughts of love, peace, and joy. Let us choose to give each of our journeys a MEANINGFUL existence. Let us embrace the impossibilities of today and choose to see them as opportunities to change the world into a more MEANINGFUL place. The only thing that makes positive change appear impossible is our limiting thoughts. Let us open our minds and hearts to all that is and will be.

~ I AM living a MEANINGFUL life filled with love and compassion, for all to witness.

~~~~~~~

Blessings of Love are sent to you today. May you awaken and witness the most MEANINGFUL moments in your journey.

~~~~~~~

Day 6

AWAKEN~ Let us AWAKEN from our slumbering position for we are often sleepwalking through this journey of life. Can we not see the beauty that surrounds us and has been laid before us as a blessing? Can we not hear the songs that are sung in the name of hope? Let us find our voices, and together we shall sing in sweet harmony. We are encouraged to walk towards the future with a promise that together we can make great changes in our world. The Universe pleads with us to be receptive to the joy and Light that waits to open our hearts. AWAKEN to the hope and compassion that has been given to each of us to live unconditionally through this journey. Embrace the higher thought, the higher vibration, and the higher essence of you and I. Hear the whispers of love that are spoken in our dreams of slumber. Rise to the mountaintops, shine upon all that witness this journey, and AWAKEN to the love in all things!

~ I AM open to all possibilities. I AWAKEN to my life's experiences with an open heart and soul.

Blessings of Joy are sent to you today. May you AWAKEN to the endless possibilities that greet you in every moment and letting go of the veil that hinders your journey.

Day 7
POWERFUL~ Let us awaken to a new day and set forth our POWERFUL intentions as we embrace this glorious opportunity. Let us be the Light in the darkest of moments and shine our essence upon the world. You and I can choose to be the beacons of Light and to live a POWERFUL example of love and compassion. Each of our lives can contribute to a more conscious planet. We are more POWERFUL when we are filled with Light and grow brighter with each thought of love, each word of gratitude, and each song of praise. Shine as brightly as the sun!

~ I AM using my Light of consciousness as a POWERFUL example of love and compassion.

Blessings of Wisdom are sent to you today. May your thoughts, words, and actions be from a POWERFUL conscious state of being.

Notes

Image captured by Susan Gossett.

Week 4
Liberty of Awareness

~~~~~~~~

Blessings of Awareness are sent to your conscious choice of Liberty today.
May you be in tune with the instincts that will lead you to create the life you
came here to share.

~~~~~~~~

As we begin our 4th week of intentions, let us take a moment to define
liberty and what that may look like to each of us. Siri defines liberty as, "the
quality or state of being free, the power to do as one pleases, freedom from
physical restraint or control, and/ or the power of choice."

Often we may associate liberty with the freedom a country gives its citizens,
but indeed it is the present we give ourselves. My words today are speaking
of freedom as a state of mind and the contribution of our unique voice and
sharing of our distinct gifts to the world.

No matter where we reside, our limiting thoughts and beliefs can restrict us from creating the life that we know should be ours. The reason we came here is to shine our Light through this human experience.

It is in the restrictions of our thoughts and beliefs that we may be hindering all that we came here to share with others. We often give fear the power to immobilize our creative genius and shut down our intuitive thoughts and guidance by numbing ourselves through addictions, obsessions, and/ or habits that do not serve the essence of who we are.

It is in the awareness and understanding that we are here to create, contribute, and give the best version of ourselves that we enrich our human experience. When we allow fearful thoughts of perfection, comparison, and judgment to paralyze this creation of our dreams, we become unmotivated, we feel depressed, or we busy our lives with the completion of tasks that are unfulfilling.

It is in our awareness of liberty that we have the opportunity to utilize fear as a motivator and a tool to build a fulfilling and meaningful life. Let us choose to befriend the nervous energy, not as a negative, but to instead use it as a tool to give us the adrenaline rush to create a masterpiece.

Many years ago when I began to entertain on stages, other performers would speak of butterflies and stage fright, but I never felt the fear, only excitement to entertain the audience.

I told this to my mother, and she summarized a story of long ago when, instead of being fearful of the butterflies, she allowed them to fuel her. She wanted to fit in though, and so she validated the other entertainers by 'pretending' she was nervous also. She, unfortunately, manifested her words into existence, and the feeling of empowerment soon morphed into fear.

This was a valuable lesson in my young life, helping me to understand that it is the perception and interpretation of our experiences that defines our outcome.

As my mother shifted her empowerment into fear, we can also choose to transform our feelings of limitation through fear into the unlimited possibilities of our liberty within our mind, body, and soul.

Let us choose to be conscious of the belief systems that dictate our thoughts, words, and actions. We can shift that which is no longer serving our journey; choosing to create a life of AWARENESS through the power of our conscious LIBERTY.

Be thy Light.

Day 1
ACKNOWLEDGE~ Let us take a moment to sit and be present, aware of the heart that beats within the chest, and the rise and fall as the air enters into and out of the body. Let us ACKNOWLEDGE the miracle of this capsule in which you and I reside. Let us think about our personal journey and the spiritual tools that assist us in the decisions that we choose. Let us ACKNOWLEDGE the past, present, and the future of our individual path. Let us visualize our home that we call Earth and send love to the ocean and all the creatures within. Let us send love to each tree and the flora that covers the ground, to the birds that fly in the sky and the animals that roam. Let us send love to all things big and small; to each of us on this glorious day. Let us ACKNOWLEDGE our journey together upon this planet, validating where we are headed. May the love surround you and me in this beautiful experience.

~ I AM one with the world. I ACKNOWLEDGE the miracle of you and I.

~~~~~~~

Blessings of Wisdom are sent to you today. May you ACKNOWLEDGE your inner wisdom and choose consciously in every moment.

~~~~~~~

Day 2
AWARENESS~ Our lives are filled with stimuli such as the outside chatter of television, radio, computers, smartphones and, let us not forget, the noise

of our inner thoughts. All of these forces are clamoring for our undivided attention. Unfortunately, everything we hear, see, and think is not one with our highest of vibrations. They do not come to us in a vibration of love and truth. It is our responsibility to bring AWARENESS to the presence of now and to filter out of our lives that which is not one with our truth. Our intuition will guide us as the essence of who we are is striving and longing to be conscious. Let us be in tune with the AWARENESS of the Universe that is always guiding us. Our journey is not about the perceived perfection; it is about the AWARENESS of each and every moment through a filter of love and compassion for ourselves and the world around us.

~ I AM conscious of the AWARENESS within my thoughts, words, and actions.

~~~~~~~~~

Blessings of Insight are sent to you today. May you awaken to the inner wisdom and AWARENESS hat resides within you for all your personal conscious choices.

~~~~~~~~~

Day 3

FEEL~ Today is a new day to begin that which we have delayed, to finish that which we have not completed, and to take a step toward bringing our dreams into reality. It is a day to love one another through all of the experiences we encounter. It is an opportunity to FEEL the joy within and to see how truly blessed we are as we walk this journey. Let us take the time to FEEL the love and let it wash over us, encompassing all that we are. Now let us send that wave of love back into the world and FEEL the grace and peace that remains.

~ I AM the love, grace, and peace that I choose to FEEL throughout my journey.

~~~~~~~~~

Blessings of Love are sent to you today. May you FEEL the support and love of the Universe that surrounds you in every moment.

~~~~~~~~~

30

Day 4

INSTINCTIVELY~ The smallest of flowers with its tiny white petals stretched out does not ask, "What will I be?" From the beginning, it knew INSTINCTIVELY and proceeded to effortlessly flourish into the most beautiful creation that it could be; a mere seed, nourished by soil and moisture, that expanded into its essence for all to see. May we take the time to learn from the world around us to live INSTINCTIVELY by our truth. May we strive to be all that we INSTINCTIVELY know is our destiny.

~ I AM INSTINCTIVELY living my truth in all aspects of my life for I am always guided and supported.

~~~~~~~~~

Blessings of Intuition are sent to you today. May you INSTINCTIVELY live your journey from your truth in every aspect of your life for you are always guided and supported.

~~~~~~~~~

Day 5

LIBERTY~ You and I have the LIBERTY to choose our thoughts and words and to stay in the Light rather than gravitate towards the dark. We have the LIBERTY to make choices every day to spend a moment to bring our dreams just a bit closer to reality, one step at a time. Let us embrace the LIBERTY within us, choosing to shine our Light and surround ourselves in the positivity of all things.

~ I AM embracing the LIBERTY of choice today through my inner wisdom and Light.

~~~~~~~~~

Blessings of Inner Wisdom are sent to you today. May you awaken to shine your Light and words of LIBERTY to all those you encounter.

~~~~~~~~~

Day 6

LISTENING~ Let us take a moment, quietly LISTENING to the sound of our breath entering and exiting our body, and to the heart beating a steady rhythm that never falters. The regular cadence of these natural functions provides a lesson that each of us can learn from - to begin our day steadily and with purpose. Let us start this day with our intentions, LISTENING to and sifting through the words around us, gathering only words of truth for our lives and allowing the rest to drift away. Today we are LISTENING to the harmony of the melody; the rhythm that is in tune with the words of our hearts will accompany our journey.

~ I AM LISTENING for the harmony of the melody that is in tune with my heart and will accompany my day.

~~~~~~~~

Blessings of Openness are sent to you today. May you be in tune to the guidance that surrounds you, always LISTENING with an open heart.

~~~~~~~~

Day 7

MANIFESTING~ You and I have the ability to be continually MANIFESTING the life that we dream of through our thoughts, words, and actions. We send our energy out into the world each and every moment. Focusing on the things in the world that are negative will not assist us in achieving the life of which we dream. In every moment, we are MANIFESTING, and the majority of the feelings that surround our being are what we are attracting into our life. Notice that what I said was the 'majority'… because we all have moments of negativity. It is just how long you and I stay in the negative state of mind that hinders the world we create. Many of us, when we hear of this knowledge, begin to fear our thoughts, but may we allow the knowledge to empower our beings. When a negative thought or situation seems to encompass the mind, let us focus on the things, people, events, beliefs, and situations that bring hope. Hope in the present moment, and our future assists us in MANIFESTING that which we desire in life. You and I have the knowledge and the power to manifest that which we dream.

~ I AM MANIFESTING a world that is filled with compassion and love for the planet.

32

~~~~~~~

Blessings of Faith are sent to you today. May you align your heart, mind, and soul in MANIFESTING inner peace.

~~~~~~~

Notes

Image captured by Susan Gossett.

Week 5
Aspire to Just Be

~~~~~~~~

Blessings of Wisdom are sent to you today. May you consciously Aspire to Just Be the highest version of you and to shine brilliantly upon the world around you.

~~~~~~~~

Others are witnessing each of our unique journeys. They are a reflection of our current priorities, what we have learned from the past, and where we want the future to lead us. They show others how we handle success and stress in life's experiences. Yes, our journey is a reflection of our inner Light and how brilliantly we shine our uniqueness out into the world. Each of us sincerely is Aspiring to Just Be themselves.

In our youth, we may not understand who we are, and often we are inspired to become one of our heroes when something they did or said sparks an interest in mirroring their journey. We begin witnessing, shifting, and trying on verbiage or undertaking new passions. Through this process, something resonates, and we place it in our tools of life.

35

At this time, our world embraces uniformity and sameness more than uniqueness. The idea of beauty appears to be in one box, and if one does not fit in that space, beauty and grace are lost in the judgment. It is quite ironic since not one of us is precisely the same as another. We are as unique as the snowflakes that fall from the sky, and yet we do not pick them apart and judge that one is more beautiful.

When you and I attempt to mold ourselves into what society considers perfection, we limit our possibilities to bring the brilliance of our individual gifts to others. We have all witnessed someone that has lived a life that influenced our journey; mine was my grandfather's path.

He and I did not agree on all things, and at times anger would flare in our conversations. These emotions would come and go, but always led us back to the love and respect that we had for one another.

His voice was powerful, whether speaking, singing, or preaching. He chose the life of a minister, serving others within the framework of his chosen religion. His youth was far from this path, a bruiser and boxer when in the ring and a hothead that often found himself in trouble, but war changed all of that. It redefined his priorities and how he viewed the world. It is not uncommon that difficult experiences will either soften or harden one's heart and in his case, it created a path to more love and closeness with the Higher Power.

He was a great teacher to me. I watched how he handled his relationships with others, the Divine, and money, as well as his generous service to the world. Discipline, perseverance, and determination intertwined through all that he did, and I am sure that he had no idea what an impact he would make on my life.

This is not uncommon; one never knows how their unique Light is changing and influencing others. Each of us is special, and yet we witness other's paths when they affect our own, leading us to the highest version of ourselves.

Let us ASPIRE TO JUST BE all that we uniquely are with the understanding that our journey is a Light to all that witness this path of life.

Be thy Light.

Day 1
JUST BE~ Let us take this moment to connect with the essence of who we came here to be. JUST BE here, present and in the now. Let us take this time

to center ourselves with a visualization of sitting upon a rock, next to a stream and watching as the water cascades down the stones of a bubbling brook. The leaves rustle above as we witness the water's journey as it gently caresses the pebbles of the creek bed. At this moment, let us allow our hearts to be present and ourselves to JUST BE. Let the worries of yesterday and the anxieties of tomorrow melt away. Our essence longs for the nourishment of connection with the Universe, which allows for the renewal of our souls. Life brings us many choices and paths, but the lesson is always to be present and living in the now. Today let us choose to be connected to the essence, unified with all that is, and to JUST BE.

~ I AM the essence of the Universe that resides in every cell of my being. I choose to JUST BE in this blessed moment.

~~~~~~~~

Blessings of Unconditional Love are sent to you today. May you JUST BE your true essence in all that you think, say, and do.

~~~~~~~~

Day 2

ASPIRE~ Today let us ASPIRE to share more with the world just as the birds awaken enthusiastically singing or as the rosebuds gloriously bloom to share their beauty or as the sun brightly shines upon you and I. As we embrace our day let us ASPIRE to be all that we are meant to be. A being of Light, joy, compassion, peace, balance, grace, strength, and love! We must ASPIRE to be our best selves. It is when we function from a place of higher consciousness and inspiration that we will have more joy, love, and fulfillment in the journey of life. By raising our personal energy and Light, we are contributing to raising the consciousness of the planet. Together we can ASPIRE to a world of love, Light, hope, joy, and abundance to all that share this world. In each and every moment let us ASPIRE to be the best version of ourselves!

~ I AM all that I ASPIRE to be. I AM the highest version of myself in all that I do.

Blessings of Hope are sent to you today. May you ASPIRE to be the highest version of you in your thoughts, words, and actions.

~~~~~~~

Day 3

BE~ Too often in life we spend our time fitting in with the norm or just existing by living in the manner in which others expect. When you and I do not follow our hearts and allow fear to keep our gifts hidden from the world, we become dissatisfied and restless. The Light within us becomes stifled and our passion lifeless. We came here to thrive, not just exist and watch as the time passes. Let us not wait to start pursuing our dreams tomorrow. Let us take steps today toward the life through which we are sharing our gifts with the world. Let us BE the courageous soul that we are, bold in our actions to achieve our dreams. Let us BE the Light when all that surrounds the world is dark, for we will show the way to hope and grace. Let us BE the unique beings that we are and show the world our radiant Light and genuine nature.

~ I AM the Light when all is dark. I am present and conscious of my choices to BE me.

~~~~~~~

Blessings of Light are sent to you today. May you BE the hope and compassion in all that you think, say, and do. The world needs your unique and authentic essence to shine brilliantly.

~~~~~~~

Day 4

GREATNESS~ Each of us should be aspiring to GREATNESS in our lives; using our talents, and abilities, and sharing them with the world. It is through these actions that we will inspire others to strive for their GREATNESS. Let you and I avoid hiding in the shadows of life and instead, shine as if we were the sun that brightens the world. There is no one like you or me. The uniqueness of who we are is a blessing to this world; so let us share our individual gifts and talents with all those around us. Let us be inspired to aspire to our GREATNESS!

~ I AM aspiring to GREATNESS through the thoughts, words, and actions that I place into the world.

~~~~~~~~

Blessings of Inspiration are sent to you today. May you aspire to your GREATNESS in your thoughts, words, and actions that you place into the world.

~~~~~~~~

Day 5

I AM~ Two of the most powerful words that we can say are 'I AM.' The thoughts and words that follow this phrase are crucial to the life that we are creating. If you or I had to describe ourselves to a stranger, would our words be ones of kindness and love? Even though we have many roles in life, let us take a moment and ask ourselves this question: "Who am I?" Each of us is a powerful creator residing in a miracle body, creating a life filled with experiences through our thoughts, words, and actions in every moment. Yes, we are creating our destiny through that which we do or don't do. We choose in every moment what follows that phrase, 'I AM.' We make that choice, but, more importantly, you and I can *change* those words today to be more empowering. We can opt for words such as I AM love, joy, peace, hope, Light, grace, inspired, or compassionate. Let us choose words of wisdom.

~ I AM consciously empowering my being through my thoughts, words, and actions.

~~~~~~~~

Blessings of Wisdom are sent to you today. May you be inspired to create your world from a conscious state of being. I came from love, therefore; I AM love.

~~~~~~~~

Day 6

REFLECT~ We are like a mirror as we walk through this journey of life. You and I are always sending out energy to the world, and that same energy will REFLECT back into our lives. It is important that the things, people, and places in our world are serving the highest good. If the world is reflecting something in our lives that we dislike, then we must look within us to see how we can improve this portion of our lives. We must understand that if one wants less negativity, they cannot change this reflection with more of the same thing. We must counter-balance with the opposite feelings such as hope, love, kindness, and joy. We must REFLECT that which we want in our lives out into the world. Let us be that which we want more of, and the Universe will REFLECT that back into our lives.

~ I AM choosing the thoughts and actions that I want to REFLECT back into my world.

~~~~~~~~~

Blessings of Inner Wisdom are sent to you today. May your thoughts, words, and actions REFLECT that which you came here to be and share with the world.

~~~~~~~~~

Day 7
SPARKLE~ You and I are the SPARKLE in the star, the rays of light in the sunshine, the moon that casts its glow on the Earth, and the shimmer in the water that cascades over the stones. We are the SPARKLE in the rare and precious jewel. We love and experience life uniquely, and our dreams can only be fulfilled through us. Let us love ourselves for all that we have experienced thus far, having gratitude for the moments of learning that have molded us into who we are becoming. Each of us is surrounded and supported by love. Let us not contain the SPARKLE within our hearts, but allow it to radiate with love for one another without conditions, for the world needs our Light.

~ I AM unconditional love as I SPARKLE my Light upon the world around me.

~~~~~~~

Blessings of Light are sent to you today. May you SPARKLE and shine brilliantly in the world today. Be uniquely you, always.

~~~~~~~

Notes

Image captured by Tim Chinn.

Week 6
Inspired Transition

~~~~~~~~

Blessings of Inspiration are sent to you today. May you be Inspired by all of life's Transitions to be the highest version of you.

~~~~~~~~

As the Greek philosopher, Heraclitus of Ephesus said, 'The only thing constant is change.'

Life is always moving and shifting in various directions. Change happens to everything that we witness, whether it is in nature, in our bodies, or in the relationships of our lives. These transitions can be difficult at times, especially when we are holding on tightly to that which is moving away from us.

How do we find acceptance of all that we cannot control and ultimately find the inspiration in these transitional moments?

The old saying, 'Everything happens for a reason,' doesn't always make one feel better during a wave of change. Often the only thing that gives us insight into the situation is time.

Time is what gives us the perspective to understand our lessons and how the unexpected outcomes assisted in our evolution. Until that insight unfolds the most critical thing that we can do is not to resist. Let the emotions flow through you, the tears fall from your eyes, and keep the faith that time will ease the discomfort of the current circumstances.

The world around us is such an excellent teacher when it comes to transitional moments. There is no hesitation when the waves of the ocean crash to the shore, or the clouds float across the sky, or the tree blows in the wind. There is no resistance, only surrender into the movement. When the seasons change, flora and fauna do not stand still, but uses their energy to move in preparation for the change.

Let us begin to shift our perspective about a transition from fearful to hopeful, and remember that we are always supported and guided by the Universe. We need only to listen for the INSPIRED TRANSITION that awaits us.

Be thy Light.

Day 1
BELIEVE~ It is important in the journey to BELIEVE that we each came here to do something amazing and unique. The Universe is striving to awaken the consciousness of the world. Each of us can contribute to that fulfillment by being conscious throughout our journey and fulfilling the purpose we came here to do and be. No one else can do what you came here to do, and if you do not fulfill it, sadly, the purpose dies with you. The essence of our spirit is abundant love, but often this becomes clouded because of our fears of the unknown. When you and I BELIEVE, we trump fear and doubt every time. Let us embrace the peace within our souls, which will assist us in overcoming the fears that prevent us from accomplishing our dreams. Let us BELIEVE that we are capable of great things and that together we can heal the damage and hatred in the world by loving ourselves and one another with unconditional compassion and grace.

~ I AM contributing the highest version of myself with the Universe. I BELIEVE that I came here to share my unique gifts with the world.

Blessings of Faith are sent to you today. May you BELIEVE that you are supported and guided to share your gifts with the world.

Day 2

INSPIRED~ The seeds of dandelions are blown out by the wind, floating on the breeze with a gentle ease that warms the heart. Their flight is INSPIRED by hopes and dreams of a world filled with more love. Let us emulate the wind by sending blessings of joy, peace, grace, and compassion to the world around us. May soothing music enrich our days and may we be INSPIRED with a passion for sharing our gifts with the world. Let us move toward making our dreams a reality with actions that are INSPIRED by our unique gifts.

~ I AM INSPIRED to share the uniqueness of me with the world. My gifts and talents are flowing freely.

Blessings of Inspiration are sent to you today. May you be INSPIRED to share your unique gifts with the world bringing more joy to your life and those around you.

Day 3

POWER~ You and I are capable of achieving all of that which we dream. We need only to believe that these words are true. Each of us has the POWER within us to accomplish the task at hand, as well as those that will lead us to the life that we desire for tomorrow. This POWER is within each cell of our being; in the chair upon which we sit, in the cat that rests on our lap, in the moon that bids us goodnight, and in the sun that we awaken to each day. You and I are one with all things. It is only our limited thoughts and beliefs that keep our dreams at bay. No one else has the POWER to keep us from achieving our dreams except you and me. Let us choose to take our POWER back and begin using it wisely in each and every moment.

~ I AM tapping into the POWER that resides within my being and sharing my gifts with the world.

Blessings of Inner Wisdom are sent to you today. May you create the life you came here to share by using the POWER within your being.

~~~~~~~

Day 4

STEP by STEP~ In every thought that we think, breath that we take, and word that we speak, we have the choice to move forward, STEP by STEP, toward a more fulfilling life. Let our movements be brave, courageous, and bold when we go out into the world. STEP by STEP, let us walk in faith and accomplish all the things the Universe is guiding us to do along the path of life. May we not take this day for granted, or live a life where we are not sharing our gifts with the world. When we take the time to do things that we love--whether it is singing, writing, drawing, sewing, cooking, gardening, dancing, running, or playing--we move in the direction of our truth and connect with the energy of creation. STEP by STEP, we can empower our journey by living a life of joy and giving our Light to the world.

~ I AM walking my truth, STEP by STEP, as the Universe continues to guide me through life.

~~~~~~~

Blessings of Faith are sent to you today. May you continue to use the guidance of the Universe to create a life of love, STEP BY STEP, along with your journey.

~~~~~~~

Day 5

SUPPORTED~ Often in our journey, it appears that we walk alone and that we are not SUPPORTED by our loved ones in the ways that we would hope. We long for things to be different--easier somehow-- as we grow and change toward the individuals we want to become. This contrast is also a part of the journey and process of evolving into the essence of who we are. Each of us is always SUPPORTED and loved by the Universe; we need only to believe and ask for the guidance as we move forward. It is only through time that we will look back on our journey and see that both the kind words from strangers, and the controversies that we faced, pushed us to become all that we are. We will realize that all along, these encounters were guidance from the Universe. We are always SUPPORTED in all things.

~ I AM SUPPORTED and guided by the Universe, always and in all ways.

~~~~~~~~~

Blessings of Unconditional Love are sent to you today. May you see how your life has been guided and SUPPORTED in every moment of joy and sadness. You are so loved dear one.

~~~~~~~~~

Day 6

TRANSFORM~ Let us choose to TRANSFORM into our highest selves and to live our lives from the heart; not allowing the mind to hinder us from following our truth. Let our decisions be made out of compassion and for the highest good, rather than based on what society dictates. When we begin to live and breathe from a place of love, we become a beacon of love to the world. Through this action, we will TRANSFORM this world into one that offers compassion to all. Instead of living in a world of lack and competition, abundance will surround us in every way, through cooperation with and support from the Universe. Together we will heal ourselves as well as the planet on which we live. Let us live our truth and watch the world around us TRANSFORM into a place of hope and possibility.

~ I AM choosing to TRANSFORM into my highest self and following my truth toward changing the world to one that is filled with compassion.

~~~~~~~~~

Blessings of the highest Truth are sent to you today. May you TRANSFORM each moment, day, and the life you are creating into a space of unconditional love.

~~~~~~~~~

47

Day 7

TRANSITION~ As we walk along our path, the one thing that we can be certain of is that we will have moments of TRANSITION. The Universe is always guiding us in ways that we are unable to conceive or imagine. Let us not hold onto yesterday or worry about tomorrow, for we have no control over these matters. May we have faith that we are supported throughout our journey and that by continuing to TRANSITION into our highest selves, we attract the life that we envision. Let us embrace today as we TRANSITION into a place of trust that everything is unfolding in the Universe's perfect timing.

~ I AM living in the present moment, as I continue to TRANSITION into my highest self.

~~~~~~~~~

Blessings of Faith are sent to you today. May you embrace the TRANSITION into the highest version of yourself as we create a world of love and compassion.

~~~~~~~~~

48

Notes

Image captured by Tim Chinn.

Week 7
Glorious Blessings

~~~~~~~~

Blessings of Inspiration are sent to you today. May you witness the Glorious Blessings that surround you in this very moment. You are loved.

~~~~~~~~

One of the beautiful things about getting older is awakening to the understanding of blessings. The things that we may have taken for granted in our youth, we now view through a heart filled with love and appreciation.

It is in our words and actions that we express adoration to those around us, to the Earth we reside on, to the body we are experiencing life through, to the sun that warms us, to the soil that bears fruit, to the seeds that burst forth from the ground, and to the water that gives life to it all.

When you and I choose to live consciously, we see the blessings and glory in this human experience. Let us remember to take moments of gratitude for that which brings a smile to our face.

It is in the little things such as the hummingbird that drinks from a flower, when you take just a moment to get some rays of the sun, the stranger that holds the door open for you, or the smell of rain that fills your nose. Simple, yet beautiful, they rejuvenate your soul.

These are the blessings that are always in front of us, waiting for us to awaken into the present moment. Let us honor that which we have neglected to see, hear, and feel with the business of life.

I love the saying, 'Count your blessings.' It is a wonderful tool that I use when my energy is low, focusing on all that is going right can lift your spirit. It can be done anywhere and anytime; while we are driving down the street, or walking into work, or standing in line at the grocery store. We can say something as simple as:

> *Thank you for this car that takes me from point A to B*
> *Thank you for the individuals who repair the roads I drive on.*
>
> *Blessings to the bees and plants that surround this walkway.*
> *Blessings to those that grow the food that nourishes my body.*
>
> *Thank you for this opportunity to witness life in this body.*
> *Thank you. Thank you. Thank you.*

Let us find the inspiration this week to create moments of grace and compassion for this amazing life we are witnessing. May you honor the GLORIOUS BLESSINGS that surround you.

Be thy Light.

Day 1
BLESSED~ The stars twinkle down upon us, and the sun shows its everlasting Light upon our world. We are BLESSED. The wispy clouds float before us in the bluest of skies as the air fills our lungs, giving us life. The laughter and the tears shared with those we love as we talk about the days gone by; even now we are BLESSED to have had them. Through the darkest of nights, each of us can choose to have love and hope; we can give compassion and grace, and together we can bless the world around us with our Light. We are BLESSED.

~ I AM giving of myself to the world around me because I am BLESSED.

~~~~~~~~~

Blessings of Compassion and Grace are sent to you today. May you see the gift of this moment and all you are able to witness. You are BLESSED.

~~~~~~~~~

Day 2

GIVEN~ Our past is filled with lessons that provide us with more clarity in the present moment. The present has GIVEN us the opportunity of today to be in awe of all that we are and are experiencing. The future has GIVEN us the possibility to bring our dreams into reality with effort and plans. The past, present, and future are gifts that we have received to expand into the essence of who we are. They have GIVEN us the blessings of what has come to pass, what is, and what will be.

~ I AM grateful for the past, present, and future. They have GIVEN me the possibilities to make all my dreams come true.

~~~~~~~~~

Blessings of Hope and Universal Insight are sent to you today. May you see this life as a gift that has been GIVEN to you to create loving and compassionate moments in all ways.

~~~~~~~~~

Day 3

GLORIOUS~ The air is filled with the scent of the jacaranda tree, the bumblebees are buzzing, the lizards are sunning, the hummingbirds are humming, and the crows are cawing. It is a GLORIOUS day. The summer heat floats through the air as the children run through the sprinklers, squealing with laughter. It is a GLORIOUS day. All of the experiences, including the smells and sounds, are here for the taking. Let us be willingly receptive of the love and joy with which we are surrounded. Let us open our hearts to this GLORIOUS moment that we have been given.

~ I AM basking in the gift of this GLORIOUS day.

~~~~~~~~~

Blessings of Love and Joy are sent to you today. May you create a world of GLORIOUS love in every thought, word, and action that you take.

~~~~~~~~~

Day 4

INSPIRATION~ When we give ourselves stillness, the Universe blesses us with INSPIRATION. It is a bolt of energy, which cannot be contained; a wave that comes into our world that must be explored and experienced. When we allow our life to be filled with INSPIRATION, our smiles cannot be restrained and each cell within our being is empowered by the endless possibilities. When the wave passes one is left breathless and grateful for the gift of astounding beauty. Let us choose to accept the priceless gift of INSPIRATION each and every moment that it enters our world.

~ I AM open to the INSPIRATION of the Universe, and I move forward into action the moment that I receive this precious gift.

~~~~~~~~~

Blessings of Creativity are sent to you today. May INSPIRATION surround you with insight to create a life of endless moments of love.

~~~~~~~~~

Day 5

MOONBEAMS~ As the MOONBEAMS shine their light upon the world, let us smile and give thanks for the beauty. The MOONBEAMS have guided humankind in the darkness of the night since the beginning of time, and yet their beauty does not fade. We are blessed to witness the beauty that surrounds the world. Let us be present and open our hearts to the guidance of the Universe, partaking in the beauty of the sun, moon, and stars. You and I are blessed to be experiencing all of life through our wonderful senses. We have the choice to express ourselves to the world through our words and actions toward one another. This life that we live is an amazing experience. Let us send the magic of MOONBEAMS to all those we encounter today.

~ I AM choosing to see the beauty of the world around me and send the blessings and light of MOONBEAMS to all I encounter today.

~~~~~~~~

Blessings of Universal Light are sent to you today. May you witness the magic of MOONBEAMS and the world's beauty in your everyday moments.

~~~~~~~~

Day 6

PRAISE~ Let us sing a song of PRAISE, and send it out with love and Light today. Let us sing a lullaby to the inner child within each of us. May we open our hearts to feel the support of the Universe and raise our voices in PRAISE to the opportunity of today. Let us sing a melody of PRAISE, simple and true; that it may fill our hearts with love for all that we are aspiring to be.

~ I AM singing a song of PRAISE, with a melody of love and words of compassion for all to hear.

~~~~~~~~

Blessings of Grace are sent to you today. May you sing a song of PRAISE for the love that surrounds you and the Light that supports you in every moment.

~~~~~~~~

Day 7

REJOICE~ You and I do not know what today will bring. We do not know what tomorrow has in store, or how many days we have on this planet. We only have this moment, and we can choose to REJOICE in all that is beautiful and hopeful. We can only control our reaction to the present situation. It is not our job to control others or the situations that unfold around us. Let us greet each day with love. Let us embrace each moment with the Light of who we are, and REJOICE in all that we are experiencing upon this amazing journey. Let our hearts REJOICE in the opportunity of now.

~ I AM choosing to REJOICE in this moment and send my love out to the world.

~~~~~~~~

Blessings of Hope are sent to you today. May you REJOICE in every moment you have been given, being the compassionate voice in every conversation, and the Light in moments of darkness.

~~~~~~~~

Notes

Week 8
Supported Purpose

~~~~~~~

Blessings of Faith are sent to you today. May you remember that you are always Supported in your unique Purpose in life.

~~~~~~~

Let us take a moment to remind ourselves that we are always supported in this personal journey. We need only to tune in to our inner guide, the gentle nudge that the Universe uses to assist us in the answers to our many questions.

You and I are guided towards fulfilling our purpose and all we came here to experience. When we take the time to connect and communicate our wishes, concerns, and gratitude, there will be more moments of synchronicity; where the impossible becomes possible, the answers or ideas take form in a dream, or the unexpected phone call brings the perfect opportunity. These are the moments of Universal magic and mystery that each of us witnesses.

When we take moments to be intentionally present, by sitting in silence, we become clear and aligned with the actions that will move us along on our path. You and I can shift our perspective, releasing that which no longer serves us and renewing our hope and passion for the purpose we came to fulfill.

I have found that often in life's conversations it is the terminology that can create barriers because of different interpretations or negative experiences around certain words.

When someone uses the term God, Universe, Divine, Higher Power, Jehovah, Allah, etc. All of these words define that which is higher than you and I. Sometimes those words can carry with them the baggage of centuries of dogma, yet I hold no judgment on the word that resonates with your soul.

Each of us is here to expand into our essence, and we need words to communicate that which we are experiencing. One of my favorite words, that I use often, is Light. It is because this is where we came from and it resides in each of us. It is why I place it at the end of each daily intention, and why this book has the same title, *Be thy Light*.

Other items that can cause misinterpretation are meditation and prayer. I define prayer as my questions to and communication with the Divine. I personally do this in silence, speaking, journaling, or in song. Meditation is my time to listen for the guidance and the answers to my questions or concerns. Both are needed to have a deep connection and understanding for clear guidance to a supported purpose.

You and I came here to embrace life fully, the movement of all that comes in and out of our world. We are here to be present in our journey and to witness the miracles of this lifetime. Let us not forget that we are always SUPPORTED in our PURPOSE.

Be thy Light.

Day 1
PURPOSE~ As we watch the creatures of the world, their every movement is with PURPOSE. We can learn so much by witnessing the hummingbird drinking the nectar from the flower. A tiny creature of grace and beauty, their movements are with PURPOSE and pure joy. Let us not waver nor procrastinate on the things that must be done to accomplish the PURPOSE of this lifetime. Let us move gracefully and lovingly in our actions and decisions throughout each day. Let us begin each morning with the certainty of our PURPOSE and that each of our steps will be taken with a joyful heart.

~ I AM living each moment with a loving heart filled with PURPOSE.

~~~~~~~

Blessings of Intention are sent to you today. May your steps be deliberate and with PURPOSE as your actions lead you to create a life of love.

~~~~~~~

Day 2
GUIDE~ Let us be open to the Universe serving as our GUIDE toward a better tomorrow. Let us observe the sun that rises in the sky, giving light to the world around us; may we learn from its example and freely share our Light with the world. Let us regard the rain that falls to nourish the Earth, sustain life and stimulate growth; may you and I be like the rain, nourishing our essence and sharing ourselves with the world. Let us also take note of the tree that sways in the wind, giving in to the elements, rooted and stable deep within the Earth; may you and I be as the tree swaying with the world around us, yet anchored in our love for ourselves and one another. This planet upon which we dwell serves as a constant GUIDE, providing examples each and every day of not only how to live, but how to thrive as we make this journey. Let us be open to the guidance and the wisdom, which the Universe provides to me in all that I witness.

~ I AM open to the wisdom and guidance, which the Universe provides to me as a GUIDE in all that I see.

~~~~~~~

Blessings of Wisdom are sent to you today. May you be open to the Universe and all that it provides to GUIDE and support you. You are so loved my friend.

~~~~~~~

Day 3
MYSTERY~ As children, we recognized the MYSTERY of the life surrounding us and asked many questions. "Why do birds fly, and why can't I? How does the rainbow appear in the sky? Why does everything eventually die? Why do people lie? Why are some people rich and others poor?" As

adults, we may know some of the answers to the MYSTERIES of life, yet we still find ourselves asking about things that appear unfair. It is important to realize that all we are witnessing is part of this experience to assist us in reaching a higher spiritual plane. It is through the contrast that clarity will be revealed. Let us step forth in faith without knowing the answers to the questions, for it is in our personal growth that the clarity will come shining through. Until this moment of clarity, let us embrace the magic and the MYSTERY of this wondrous journey.

~ I AM at peace with the MYSTERY of life and knowing that in the perfect moment, clarity will be found.

~~~~~~~

Blessings of Faith are sent to you today. May you find the peace with all that is known and unknown in the MYSTERY of life.

~~~~~~~

Day 4
REFLECTION~ Time is a gift that has been given to each of us. It allows for the REFLECTION of our past and how it has expanded our present moment. It is through a conscious and meditative breath that you and I experience the fullness of our love for the world around us. This moment allows for the REFLECTION of that which is for the highest good. There are times of both sadness and disappointment along our path, but each of these moments of contrast allows for our essence to shine through. Let us always appreciate the REFLECTION of life's lessons that bring us the wisdom to make the most of our time on this planet.

~ I AM encompassing the essence of who I AM through the REFLECTION of my experiences.

~~~~~~~

Blessings of Love are sent to you today. May your REFLECTION be from your true essence with love and compassion in all that you do.

~~~~~~~

Day 5

RELEASE~ You and I are here to experience life and to grow as a result of the things we see and do in our personal journeys. As we learn from our experiences, it is important to RELEASE things from our lives that no longer serve the path we are walking. The 'letting go' process can be for physical items, belief systems, coping mechanisms, or habits. Sometimes things have served us in the past, but we have outgrown them, and it is time to RELEASE them to let new things come into our lives. Let us take a moment to look at the world around us, as well as within ourselves, to see how we can let go of the things that are no longer of benefit. Let us RELEASE the things from our mind and body that we are no longer in need of, embracing the expansion of releasing the old and welcoming the new.

~ I AM embracing the expansion of me as I RELEASE the items from my life that no longer serve my highest self.

~~~~~~~~

Blessings of Reflection are sent to you today. May you RELEASE that which no longer serves you, expanding into all that you came here to be and do.

~~~~~~~~

Day 6

RENEW~ Today we RENEW our thoughts with clarity and purpose - the fogginess now gone from our world as the sun rises over the horizon. Today we send out feelings of love and hope to RENEW the energy that surrounds our journey. We walk with purpose in the rays of sun that shine upon our paths. We RENEW each morning as we rise to a new day. Each morning on this road that we are traveling, may the first thoughts that cross our mind be of love and compassion.

~ I AM allowing myself to RENEW my energy every day, and my heart expands as I go out into the world.

Blessings of Insight are sent to you today. May you RENEW the hope and compassion within your soul, awakening to the uniqueness of you.

Day 7

SHIFT~ Each of us can SHIFT our thinking from a negative perception to a positive, and open our hearts to the world around us. At this very moment, we can choose thoughts of love and gratitude for the body that we reside in, and through which we experience life. We can SHIFT our words to ones that are of encouragement and support for others in their personal journey. Each of us can brighten the world by seeing things through love; the grass will appear greener, the flowers will smell sweeter, all the things around us will begin to reflect a new perception. It is through this SHIFT that we will have more joy and peace within our beings, allowing our hearts to expand and shine in every moment.

~ I AM choosing to SHIFT my perception to that of compassion and love.

~~~~~~~~~

Blessings of Clarity are sent to you today. May your perceptions SHIFT into a space of unconditional love and compassion in all that you think, say, and do. Shine brilliantly.

~~~~~~~~~

Notes

Image captured by Susan Gossett.

Week 9
Catalyst in Compassion

~~~~~~~

Blessings of Insight are sent to you today. May you be the Catalyst of
Compassion in all that you think, say, and do.

~~~~~~~

If each of us lived a life of compassion, how different would our world be?
Would the air and soil be free of toxins? Would everyone have enough to
eat? Would the creatures of the world no longer be in danger?

When you and I awaken, we no longer have the luxury to support that which
does not align with our essence. It can feel like a burden at first, when the
understanding swoops into your consciousness, a knowing that we could do
better.

My awakened journey into compassion began more than 10 years ago. It is
always evolving just as I do, but at this point, it has infiltrated every area of
my life. My journey is far from perfect, just as the world we live in, but my
effort is strong and I am determined to be a catalyst of compassion in this
life.

It is why I place my inspirational words out into the world each day via Social Media. It is why I created the app 365 Intentions to Inspire. Indeed, it is the foundation of all that I do, from the words that I speak and write to the food that I eat, the clothes that I buy, and the businesses I support. All my actions are completed with the thought, 'Is this the most compassionate decision?'

Life is messy, but it is essential to choose consciously. Each of our actions is a pebble tossed into the water to create endless ripples. It touches places and people that we may never be aware of in this lifetime.

What will be your catalyst today to bring more compassion into the world? Are your actions in alignment with your values?

It is not always the easiest of choices. It can be inconvenient. For instance, a few years ago I began looking at my finances and where my retirement funds were located. I reviewed the 'values' of my bank to see what they were investing in and asked 'Is this what I want my money to support?'

I had to have tough conversations with my broker, letting him know that I was not willing to profit from companies or industries that didn't align with my essence. In the end, I closed my accounts and took my money elsewhere.

It's sometimes easy to hear or view a story of the world and think, 'Where is the compassion?' We have to begin with ourselves.

It begins with feeling fully, the discomfort of making difficult decisions, the disappointment that our favorite food is not the best decision for our body or the world, and, most importantly, the lack of understanding we have for those that do not agree with our choices and decisions. Wherever you may be in the moment, feel it, so you heal that which needs to be honored, forgiven, and shifted into alignment, knowing that we are all connected. We are One.

Society will not encourage or support you in this, but your awareness will bring you more joy and compassion in this journey of life and ultimately to the world. Let us show more kindness and forgiveness; these actions will be the CATALYST of COMPASSION that we can assist in bringing into our world.

Be thy Light.

Day 1

BE FULFILLED~ Let us nurture our souls with a vision of a beautiful
garden filled with flowers; the sound of the trickling water soothing our ears,
the feeling of the dirt sifting through our fingers as we touch the ground
beneath our feet. Each of us are caretakers of our personal journey; of the
body in which we reside and of the soul that came here to BE FULFILLED
in its undertaking of purpose. A caretaker nurtures and replenishes; knows
when to prune and when to fertilize. This role is not easy, but it is necessary
for the aligning of the heart, mind, and soul. Let us assist ourselves by being
compassionate toward ourselves, for we all need an inner voice of kindness
and love. Let us consciously choose times, places, relationships, and
experiences that fill us spiritually and mentally, rather than always depleting
our resources. Let us find the stillness to embrace gratitude and to ultimately
BE FULFILLED at this very moment. May you and I be the best caretakers
of this life we are creating, finding the moments that rejuvenate our beings.
Let us BE FULFILLED in all that we see, touch, hear and feel today.

~ I AM a compassionate caretaker of my journey, replenishing my every
need to BE FULFILLED in my blessed life.

~~~~~~~

Blessings of Wisdom are sent to you today. May you BE FULFILLED in all
that you see, touch, hear and feel throughout this journey of life.

~~~~~~~

Day 2

CATALYST~ There is always a lesson to be learned in each of our
experiences along this journey. The lessons that bring the moments of
insight are blessings for they may be a CATALYST to assist in our
continued expansion. You and I cannot cease to expand for we are in the
midst of an ever-changing Universe. Therefore, we are always evolving. Let
us embrace the CATALYST, knowing that it is the continuance of our
expansion; the expansion of the essence of you and me; the expansion into
the world in which we want to live. Let us embody the CATALYST that
creates a world of compassion and love.

~ I AM the CATALYST of compassion and love; embracing the moments to assist in my evolving being.

~~~~~~~~

Blessings of Openness are sent to you today. May the CATALYST moments bring you continued expansion along your personal journey.

~~~~~~~~

Day 3
COMPASSION~ Let us choose to live a life of COMPASSION and embrace all that we witness with an open heart. You and I have the opportunity to bring more Light into the world when we have no judgment of each other's journey. Let us support one another from the essence of our beings, for we know not what the other has experienced upon their path. When you and I share COMPASSION with one another, we raise up all of humankind through the expansion of our consciousness, assisting the Earth and all of its inhabitants. COMPASSION is a gift that we can give to one another through the simple action of opening our hearts to everyone and everything we witness.

~ I AM open to all that I witness with a heart of COMPASSION and grace.

~~~~~~~~

Blessings of Expansion are sent to you today. May your life reflect a journey of COMPASSION in your words and actions.

~~~~~~~~

Day 4
EMOTIONS~ The range of EMOTIONS that you and I feel over a lifetime is similar to an endless wave that moves along the ocean. One cannot hold them in place for they must move with the ebb and flow of life. Our EMOTIONS can be used as a tool, bringing us guidance on what we should do more of to feel joyful and hopeful. You and I have been given this opportunity to experience life in the fullest way possible. Let us expand our hearts to moments of great love, sharing our Light with those around us. Let us assist one another in creating compassionate EMOTIONS for one another in this journey of life.

67

~ I AM creating experiences to feel joyful and blissful EMOTIONS throughout my day.

~~~~~~~~

Blessings of Hope are sent to you today. May your EMOTIONS bring you closer to your essence for you are here to feel fully.

~~~~~~~~

Day 5

EMPOWER~ Unconditional love will EMPOWER our truth to come forth. It brings our world endless possibilities, because when freely given, miracles take place. Boundless hope will EMPOWER us to take affirmative action. It opens our heart to a compassionate world. You and I can create a world of higher vibrations by being responsible for raising our energy. It begins with each of us. Let us EMPOWER our hearts to guide us in the actions of love.

~ I AM love. My actions EMPOWER my compassionate soul to love unconditionally.

~~~~~~~~

Blessings of Hope are sent to you today. May your actions EMPOWER your journey to be of truth and wisdom.

~~~~~~~~

Day 6

FORGIVENESS~ We give the gift of FORGIVENESS to ourselves when we do not hold anger or bitterness, or treat those who believe differently than we do with indifference. Our world is full of opposites, but in the contrast comes growth and expansion in our personal journey. At the moment that the anger rushes through our body, we can feel the effects of fight or flight mode; the heart racing, the blood coursing through our veins at the temple, the stress that soars through the mind, body, and soul. This place is not where you and I want to live our lives. It is not a place of peace, love, or kindness; for us or one another. Let us take a moment to take in a deep breath and send a blessing to all those involved in the incident that has taken place. The blessing can be as simple as saying, "I am *thankful* for this experience to grow and expand. I *love* myself and those who have given me the experience to open my heart to those things/people that believe differently than I do. I *forgive* myself and others for the painful emotions that the experience caused each of us. I *release* the negative thoughts and feelings around the experience, as I move through to a place of FORGIVENESS and love." May each of us be brave and walk through to the other side of FORGIVENESS, for it is truly a gift to all of us on the planet.

~ I AM open to the gift of FORGIVENESS, surrounding all those involved with love and compassion.

~~~~~~~

Blessings of Inner Clarity are sent to you today. May your heart, mind, and spirit be aligned with the actions of FORGIVENESS.

~~~~~~~

Day 7
KIND~ Acts of kindness to all creatures and beings is the foundation of a better world. When we see these acts, such as an officer stopping traffic for a mommy duck and her ducklings to cross the road in safety, our spirit is nurtured by what we have witnessed. We know in our hearts that these acts of kindness should be the norm and not the exception. When you and I take the extra moment to place the garbage in the recycling, we know in our hearts that this one act is KIND to our planet that we call home. A KIND word or action to a complete stranger, or to the ones that we love, uplifts their spirits, enriching our connection with the world. Kindness comes from our higher selves - the part of us that is wise and acts with the knowledge that we are all connected. Let us go out into the world today in wisdom with KIND actions, words, and thoughts toward one another, the creatures and our planet.

~ I AM open to the wisdom of the Universe and all that I think, say and do is KIND to the world around me.

Blessings of Compassion are sent to you today. May your heart be open to being KIND and sharing words and actions of love with the world.

Notes

Image captured by Susan Gossett.

Week 10
Consciously Creating

~~~~~~~~

Blessings of Inner Wisdom are sent to you today. May you begin
Consciously Creating a world of compassion in all that you do.

~~~~~~~~

There are avenues upon avenues of ways that our lives prompt creativity. We
express our creative genius in many ways such as building, painting,
drawing, designing, writing, dancing, cooking or planting. The list goes on
and on.

I believe even if you are an accountant designing spreadsheets with numbers
and formulas, the communication to the audience aspires to be symmetric in
the presentation. The attorney, in performing their final arguments, is
weaving their words as a dance of persuasion. The engineer, in designing
within the many restrictions of city code, is creating perfection with each
piece that fits within the puzzle. Yes, even those that we consider analytical
are using their creative genius.

We are creative beings. If you have said, 'I am not creative,' it just isn't true. Each of us is creating unique paths and experiences with the time that we have here in this body.

It is when we consciously create that we have the opportunity to tap into the magic and power of the Universe. There is a beauty that conspires to bring your imagined concept into the world; let us call it the Universal Consciousness. It is a unified web of ideas, where we feed one another without even consciously knowing that we are doing so.

The ideas come from everywhere and yet appear to come from nowhere. The seed of an idea comes to you in a dream, or through a conversation, or while driving a car. It wasn't there just moments before, and then suddenly, it is.

By becoming aware of this concept, the Universe can assist you in creating pathways that were not there before. They may appear like magic, but it is the Divine's way of aligning all the stars to create that which you are here to bring to the world.

When we do not allow ourselves to create, it stifles the flow of our essence and all we came here to do. The movements that we make physically, emotionally, and spiritually unify our intention to bring our creations to others.

It is when we begin living and creating with intention, that we bring more meaning to our journey. Every movement starts to shift from the ego of my-self to a deeper understanding of our-self and our highest state of our awareness.

Let us begin creating an incredible journey of consciousness into the infinite possibility that together we can bring more Light to the world. It starts with you. It begins with me.

Together we can create miracles in hopeless situations by being the hope in every conversation and experience that we partake in. We are CONSCIOUSLY CREATING the Light that we came here to be.

Be thy Light.

Day 1

INCREDIBLE~ Today let us give thanks for the INCREDIBLE path we are experiencing in this lifetime. Let us find joy in the body in which we awoke this morning, for it is a gift through which we can witness and partake in this day. Let us feel gratitude for the loved ones who are in our lives, and the ways that they contribute to our journey. It is an INCREDIBLE and unique life that we are creating with every moment. Let us make the most of the moments, embracing the ebb and flow of that which we know and that of which we are not yet aware. Each and every day let us be mindful of this INCREDIBLE journey as we go out into the world to shine our love and Light upon all those around us.

~ I AM witnessing and partaking of the INCREDIBLE journey that I AM consciously creating.

~~~~~~~~

Blessings of Light are sent to you today. May you be in tune with the INCREDIBLE opportunity you have in every moment to shine brightly in the world.

~~~~~~~~

Day 2

INFINITELY~ Everything that we do, say, or think has an energy that goes out into the world. The energy that you and I put forth, consciously or unconsciously, reflects back upon our journey. The energy is INFINITELY powerful with or without this understanding. It is as if each of us is a pool of water capable of reflecting love or hate, joy or sadness, grace or anger, out into the Universe. Let us be a shimmering pool of Light and love. Just as darkness dispels when flooded with light, the hatred that we see in our world cannot survive when we surround it in love. It is INFINITELY impossible for darkness to overcome light; only light overcomes darkness. May we be a shimmering pool of Light that reflects all that is good, gracious, and kind, INFINITELY being a blessing upon the world around us.

~ I AM consciously aware of the energy that I place out into the world. I AM INFINITELY a blessing upon the world around me.

Blessings of Grace are sent to you today. May you shine your Light INFINITELY for all to witness your unique brilliance on the world.

Day 3

CONSCIOUS~ Let us live a CONSCIOUS life, one where you and I are awake and present to that which is happening around us. It is time to open our eyes to the choices and decisions that are no longer serving our world. How are you and I contributing to that which is not of our highest selves; and what can we do differently? Let us begin today to live a more CONSCIOUS life, to be present in our conversations with others, and to act lovingly toward those who are different than you or I. Let us not wait until tomorrow, for we can make a difference in this very moment. Let us send love to those involved in contrasting situations so that they may be surrounded by peace. Let us make a CONSCIOUS decision to live our lives in the present, knowing that the past cannot be undone and that our future can be a more loving place, filled with a higher state of being.

~ I AM living every moment in a CONSCIOUS state of being.

Blessings of Intuitiveness are sent to you today. May you live each moment from a CONSCIOUS state of being to create a world of love.

Day 4

INTENTION~ It is through our INTENTION that doors will open to that which we seek. Let us be mindful of our thoughts throughout each day, for they should be empowering our actions, not feeding our fears. Let our actions be completed with the INTENTION of greatness so that the outcome will mirror the same. Let our thoughts be with the INTENTION that you and I are creating the life of which we dream. Today let us make a conscious decision to place our attention on the INTENTION of our actions of greatness.

~ I AM placing my attention on my INTENTION of actions of greatness.

~~~~~~~~~

Blessings of Mindfulness are sent to you today. May your actions be empowered by INTENTION to create a life with all you came here to share.

~~~~~~~~~

Day 5

MEANING~ We give our lives MEANING in each and every moment. We define the MEANING through our perception of ourselves, of others, and of the present moment. In our judgment of the moment, we are either open to the experience, or we have closed our hearts to that which is taking place. Today, as we go out into the world, let us be fully present. May we see the sky in all its glory, with the clouds that appear to float gently without effort. Let us feel the warmth of the sun and the caress of the wind upon our skin. May we hear the words that others speak with our full attention, savor the taste of the food that is nourishing our bodies, and consciously inhale the aroma of the flowers blooming right outside the door. Let us give MEANING to our lives through an open and loving heart, and through the wisdom and kindness of our spirit.

~ I AM conscious of the MEANING that I give to the experiences of my life.

~~~~~~~~~

Blessings of Awareness are sent to you today. May you be conscious of the MEANING that you are placing on life's experiences.

~~~~~~~~~

Day 6

MOVEMENT~ Let each and every MOVEMENT of our life represent that which we are striving to be. Let the step that you and I are taking in this moment be from our highest selves. It is in the MOVEMENT of our steps that we are led to achieve our dreams. They are what others witness when they see our journey. May our movements represent the essence of who we are striving to be. Let us be conscious in our thoughts, words, and MOVEMENT as we share the uniqueness of who we are with the world.

~ I AM making conscious MOVEMENT towards achieving my dreams.

~~~~~~~

Blessings of Insight are sent to you today. May every MOVEMENT be from your true essence for the highest good.

~~~~~~~

Day 7

OUR-SELF~ We are spirits living within a human body and experiencing that which is around us through our senses. In our language, each of us refers to ourselves as "me," "myself," or "I," but the spirit within each of us is connected to the words "all as one," "we," or "us." When each of us functions from the ego "my-self," our choices do not raise our consciousness individually or as a united body. It is when we function from the higher state of the heart, which I call "OUR-SELF," that we are tapping into the vibrations that raise our level of consciousness as a whole. The key to living a life and making decisions from the OUR-SELF perspective is by living in the present and by doing all things with an open heart. Today as we go out into the world, let us make the conscious choice to be present and to assist our journey by living each moment from the OUR-SELF state of the heart. By doing so, we will soon see how our life will expand into a more loving and compassionate world.

~ I AM living each moment connected to the higher consciousness of the OUR-SELF state of heart.

~~~~~~~

Blessings of Awakening are sent to you today. May you be open to choices from the OUR-SELF state of being leading to a world of higher consciousness.

~~~~~~~

Notes

Image captured by Steve McCall.

Week 11
Courageous Action

~~~~~~~~

Blessings of Strength are sent to you today. May your movements be from a space of Courageous Action to create a better world.

~~~~~~~~

You and I make hundreds of choices each day, and those turn into actions. Sometimes they happen fast and without conscious thought as we go through the motions of our day. It is in our choices through consciousness that we can create an impact on the world around us by becoming aware of their influence and consequences.

What is it that fuels you and brings out your emotions? Where do your passions lie, making you want to put your resources behind the injustices? Often the issues seem overwhelming and untouchable, but it is through our focused awareness that the ideas will begin to whisper possibilities of courageous action that we can take today.

My passions are with the animals that cannot speak. It influences every aspect of my life from the food I eat to the clothes, makeup, and cleaning supplies I buy. It is how my footprint is a bit softer on the planet.

I have even asked the Universe to use me in assisting animals that are lost or hurt. One of my favorite stories was when a neighbor's dog came to my front door, literally. I think he would have knocked if he was physically able too.

It was not easy for him to come to my door as my three dogs were causing quite a ruckus inside. Intuitively he must have known, that I would assist him and we walked together side by side to his stressed-out mom who was searching for him.

When dogs aren't coming to my front door, I keep dog food and an extra leash in my car for those animals that have wandered off. I can't save every animal. I would if it were possible, but I can make actions from a courageous heart when the opportunity arises.

It is by tuning in to my intuition that I am given moments to assist whenever possible.

What are the passions that awaken your heart to action? If each of us does our small part, we can create a significant impact on the world.

It will take each of us to create change and to raise our vibrations to a higher consciousness of unconditional love for all. We have work to do my friends. Create your COURAGEOUS ACTION today.

Be thy Light.

Day 1
COURAGE~ We see the path before us as we walk toward our goals and dreams. It often appears intimidating from where we stand, but we should not fear, for all things are possible. Possibility comes from the faith that resides within us, knowing that we are guided. Let us take a deep breath and center our heart, mind, and soul, knowing that we are forever guided by the Universe. The COURAGE to accomplish that which we dream of is deep within each of our hearts as we walk our path of truth. We need only to believe that we are capable. Let us remember, even when we grow weary, and the voice of fear whispers thoughts of doubt, that we are forever supported. Take this moment and know that you have been given the COURAGE to be able to accomplish all that you envision. Follow your

truth, open your heart, walk forward in faith, and take action with the COURAGE of all possibilities.

~ I AM supported by the Universe, and the COURAGE is within me always to accomplish my dreams.

~~~~~~~~

Blessings of Alignment are sent to your heart, mind, and soul today. May your truth lead you to actions of COURAGE to share your gifts with the world.

~~~~~~~~

Day 2

BOLD~ Today is the day that we will be BOLD in our actions, creating a life of abundance in each and every way, awakening to the guidance that is being shown to you and I. Let us be in tune to that which opens our hearts more than before. Let us grasp the opportunities that are presented to us even when it is out of our comfort zone. We did not come here to be complacent on this journey, You and I came here to be BOLD, and to color outside of the lines. Let us embrace our unique path, sprinkling it with stardust and the jewels that we find along the way. Let us paint with the colors that fill us with joy, and plant the seeds that will become our favorite flowers, so that we may one day reflect on the path that we are now creating. Let our journeys sparkle as bright as the sun with all the Light that we came here to be. Let us be BOLD, brave and courageous today!

~ I AM courageous, brave, and BOLD as I go out, shining the uniqueness of me upon the world.

~~~~~~~~

Blessings of Awakened Guidance are sent to you today. May you be BOLD in your conscious actions as you bring more Light to the world.

~~~~~~~~

Day 3

BRAVE~ The fearful thoughts that cloud our minds are not the essence of you and I. Let us choose to be BRAVE, for we came here to do amazing things and to experience life to its fullest. The negative words that come from our mouths do not serve us nor the world in which we speak them. We are the brightest of lights shining on everyone around us. Let us allow the wisdom of the Universe to shine through us, guiding our way. Each of us must be BRAVE and bold in our actions to bring the impossible to reality, creating the miracles of love to abolish the fear. We are braver than we realize. The Universal wisdom, love, and Light are ours. Let us be BRAVE in our actions today to achieve a life filled with Light and love.

~ I AM BRAVE and do all that is needed to achieve the dreams of my life.

~~~~~~~~

Blessings of Courage are sent to you today. May your actions be BRAVE as you follow the guidance of the Universe in every moment.

~~~~~~~~

Day 4
CONQUER~ Is it fear that keeps you and I from accomplishing the goal or achieving the dream that appears out of reach? What would it take for us to overcome the fears and doubt and CONQUER that which is in our mind? Let us take a moment today and ask the Universe to assist us in letting go of the barriers and releasing the self-doubt. Let us ask for the guidance and wisdom to CONQUER that which we came here to achieve, and to share with the world. Let us become focused and clear as we walk forward with a renewed confidence that we are being assisted each step of the way to CONQUER that which we came here to do.

~ I AM open to the guidance of the Universe to CONQUER all of my doubts and fears.

~~~~~~~~

Blessings of Wisdom are sent to you today. May you CONQUER the doubts that keep you from creating the life you came here to share with the world.

~~~~~~~~

Day 5

COURAGEOUS~ May our thoughts, words, and actions come from a COURAGEOUS place deep within, from the space where you and I create the path to making our dreams a reality. Let us not focus upon our fear or negativity, for this keeps us from our destiny and from living the life of which we know we are capable. Let us instead concentrate on the positive and that all things are possible through our COURAGEOUS actions. It is through belief that the doors begin to open with possibility, and it is here that miracles will appear in our lives. Let us embrace who we are and who we are striving to be. Let us take one step at a time with a COURAGEOUS attitude toward the life that we dream of, for it is ours.

~ I AM COURAGEOUS in my journey to create the life of my dreams.

~~~~~~~

Blessings of Faith are sent to you today. May your actions be COURAGEOUS as you step into all the possibilities that await you.

~~~~~~~

Day 6

FEARLESSNESS~ Let us walk through this life with FEARLESSNESS, embracing the support and guidance of the Universe. We do not have to have all the answers in our journey. Let us seek direction from the Universe to break through to FEARLESSNESS. Our paths are assisted by intuition and thought. Let us grow wiser through our experiences, and not judge them as good or bad, but as lessons along this journey. Let us be open to the guidance and support, living from a place of FEARLESSNESS.

~ I AM guided and supported by the Universe. I walk with FEARLESSNESS along my path.

~~~~~~~

Blessings of Intuitiveness are sent to you today. May you take actions of FEARLESSNESS as you share your unique Light with all those around you.

~~~~~~~

83

Day 7

PERSISTENCE~ Today we shall awaken the fire within, breathing oxygen into our bodies and renewing the passion within our souls. Today our PERSISTENCE will drive the words that flow from our minds to our mouths and out into the world. Our actions will be bold as the Universal Light shines within us and out on the planet. Today our energy will be powerful and unstoppable. We will be wise with how we use our precious time. We will be focused and avoid giving into the things that do not serve us. Our passion will catapult us toward living life to its fullest. Today our PERSISTENCE will take us to moments filled with more joy, laughter, love, passion; more of the person that you and I came here to be. Let us live today with PERSISTENCE and with the awareness that this moment is a gift. May we approach this day with the desire to be the best version of ourselves.

~ I AM living each moment in the present, with determined PERSISTENCE.

~~~~~~~~

Blessings of Passion are sent to you today. May you be open to the PERSISTENCE that guides you to share your gifts with an open heart of love.

~~~~~~~~

Notes

Image captured by Steve McCall.

Week 12
Art of Creativity

~~~~~~~

Blessings of Openness are sent to you today. May you play at the Art of Creativity and bring new possibilities into your life.

~~~~~~~

You and I are powerful creators of our lives through our beliefs, thoughts, words, and actions.

Let us take a moment to reflect on our memories of childhood. During this time of discovery and adventure, reaching to touch all that we could with our fingers, our curiosity fueled every step, and our inquisitiveness led us to a deeper understanding of the world.

We thrive when we create and explore. This desire to understand and to become the highest version of ourselves should never falter. It is through our awareness that creating, being, or playing leads to more moments of joy, self-discovery, and connection with others.

Our actions of creativity lead to more creative moments, once it is turned on, the creative force has a consistent flow within the medium we are using. My experience with creativity reminds me of a childhood memory of irrigating fields on the farm.

It was in the early days before we had sophisticated pipes to water the crops. We would irrigate with 'S' shaped siphon tubes. One end went into the ditch with the water, and the other end was in the trench of the various rows. Dad or Mom would use their hands to create suction and, with just the right technique, water would flow through the tubes and out into the field.

This is how I nurture my relationship with creativity. I do certain things to get myself aligned for the flow to begin such as lighting a candle to set my intentions, diffusing essential oils to fill the room, and choosing a crystal for that I sit with at my computer. It is here, in this intentional space, that I begin to explore the art of my creativity.

The words move on to the page through my keystrokes, and I refine them by reading them aloud to hear their rhythm and cohesiveness.

Other art mediums, such as music or drawing, have similar approaches, but the stimulation and process vary through different senses. I am always recording when I am singing or playing music, listening for new ideas and harmonies to come through the inner ear. The medium of design on the page comes to life through various colors, shading, and textures perfecting the image from what is in my mind to the actual creation.

I think Elizabeth Gilbert said it best. 'It's all about curiosity, Dear Ones. Without curiosity, there is no journey. A willingness to trust and follow your curiosity is what links together creative exploration, spiritual exploration, psychological exploration, scientific exploration, travel adventures, and even the strange human journey of falling in love. None of these endeavors can be undertaken unless you make a practice of choosing your curiosity over fear — not just once, not just a few times, but consistently.'

Let us give ourselves permission to play and be creative. It will bring more energy into every area of your life. It will stimulate that which is no longer moving and where you have lost your motivation.

It is in the ART OF CREATING that we open ourselves up to the infinite possibilities and our answers to the unknown become clear. Let our lives blossom into the masterpiece that we came here to share in this beautiful journey.

Be thy Light.

Day 1

ADVENTUROUS~ Let us embrace the ADVENTUROUS part of who we are and share that with the world. Our creativity will thrive, and the possibilities will seem endless, when we feed the curiosity within our souls. Let us be a child in the world and see things from a place of wonder and awe, opening our viewpoints to new ideas. You and I do not have to be ADVENTUROUS by traveling the globe, for wherever our path may lead us; even in our own backyard, the world has much to teach us. As we look around, let us have an open heart, for this will allow acceptance of the diversity of that which we witness and compassion for all the unique journeys on this planet. Let us embrace that which is not similar or status quo. Let us bring the energy within ourselves to thrive and embrace the ADVENTUROUS ride of our wondrous journey.

~ I AM an ADVENTUROUS soul embracing the uniqueness of my path.

~~~~~~~

Blessings of Creativity are sent to you today. May your ADVENTUROUS actions lead you to all the wonder that awaits you.

~~~~~~~

Day 2

CREATIVE~ You and I are CREATIVE beings with every breath that we take into our body and every thought that crosses our mind. We have the ability to create that which we dream of and so much more. Let us place out into the world the CREATIVE part of ourselves, sharing our unique gifts with all those around us. The ebbs and flows of our journey are necessary for you and me to evolve. Let us not stifle that which is our CREATIVE side, or criticize that which does not appear as perfect, but let us embrace the hope, grace, and compassion of our beings. Let us raise our perception, narrative, definition, words, and our song to the highest vibration and share our CREATIVE being with the world.

~ I AM a CREATIVE being that shares my highest thoughts, words, and actions with the world.

~~~~~~~~

Blessings of Consciousness are sent to you today. May you feel your day with CREATIVE awareness as you share your Light with the world.

~~~~~~~~

Day 3

MASTERPIECE~ You and I have this lifetime to create our one and only MASTERPIECE. We have the opportunity to leave a legacy of love, kindness, hope, joy, compassion, and all the goodness that is within our hearts. Each of us is born with a blank canvas, and we create our unique journey with the experiences of colors, music, relationships, words, and actions. What each of us has in common is our limited amount of time on this planet and within these miracle bodies. Let us embrace the life that we know deep within our hearts we should be living. Our dreams are not our neighbors' or our parents'; they are unique to each of us. No one will live this life and give back to this experience as you and I. When we are not fulfilling the dreams, deep within our souls we know that we are not walking our unique and abundant path. Let us stay true to ourselves and create the MASTERPIECE that we came here to share with the world. The essence of who we are is beckoning to shine into the MASTERPIECE that is you and me!

~ I AM the creator of my MASTERPIECE, which is a life of love and abundance in all things.

~~~~~~~~

Blessings of Courage are sent to you today. May you awaken to the opportunities to create your unique MASTERPIECE.

~~~~~~~~

Day 4

MUSIC~ Our life is a symphony of MUSIC, a melody that lingers in our soul. The timing is to the beat of our heart, and the lyrics are the thoughts and words that we speak. Our life is as simple as a bird's song and as complicated as an orchestra, playing the timeless masterpieces of yesterday. This moment is the one that you and I have been given to create our unique song and to sing it to the world around us. Let us play the MUSIC that raises our vibrations high above the clouds in the sky. Let us shine with the colors of the rainbow, spreading the promise of hope. Let the gentle lullaby that soothes our spirit in trying times and the alluring song of love that brings passion flow from our fingers. Our lives are the chords of a favorite song, its melody rich with love, joy, and peace, and the hope that we can achieve all of our dreams. Let us share our song from the heart and play the MUSIC that is uniquely us to the world.

~ I AM creating and sharing the MUSIC that is within my soul with the world.

~~~~~~~~~

Blessings of Creativity are sent to you today. May your heart and mind be open to the MUSIC that inspires your journey.

~~~~~~~~~

Day 5

PLEASURE~ Let us take PLEASURE in the simple things today; such as the stranger that holds the door, a loved one that calls to say hello, the family pet that inches nearer, the sun that shines down upon us, the moon that glows, and our miraculous body that allows us to experience these blessings. It is easy to take PLEASURE in life when we look at the constant miracles of the world in which we live. Yes, each of us goes through moments that can be difficult, but there are always things that surround us that bring more joy into our day. Let us choose to be present and to see the PLEASURE in the blessings that surround us today and every day.

~ I AM seeking to find the PLEASURE in all aspects of my life.

Blessings of Awareness are sent to you today. May you be in tune to all that surrounds you and to the PLEASURE of life's beauty and your abundant blessings.

Day 6

CREATIVITY~ You and I are filled with the CREATIVITY of the Universe, and we are creating our experience through our thoughts and perceptions in every moment. We have the ability to hear the song of the bird outside our window or to listen to thoughts of yesterday. Let us choose to see the flower that has bloomed in the morning light, not to pass it by with thoughts of our busy day. Our CREATIVITY is waiting to be released through the senses. It thrives when surrounded by nature, a walk in the grass, the touch of a rose petal, and the sight of a butterfly. Let us choose to be present, not worrying about the past, where nothing can be done. Let us choose to live in the now, not fearing our tomorrows. Let us choose to be here, in the present, where our CREATIVITY can be one with all that we see, hear, taste, touch, and smell. Let us make our life more in tune with the love and Light of the Universe.

~ I AM living in the present moment, filled with the CREATIVITY of my being.

Blessings of Presence are sent to you today. May your CREATIVITY thrive as you create the life you were meant to experience.

Day 7

POETRY~ We are the writers of the POETRY that we give to the world. Our life is the movement of the ocean; the ebb and flow of the tides, in cadence with the cycles of the moon. Our life is a thousand trees connected; with the roots representing a sturdy foundation, and the limbs unlimited potential. You and I are the cry of a newborn babe and the scent that lingers from the honeysuckle. Our life is POETRY; the ins and outs, the give and take, the highs and lows, the ups and downs – this is the poem that is shared with the world. May our words be strong and powerful for others to hear and contemplate. May these words be filled with compassion and kindness as we speak them to others, and may love emanate from all that we see. You and I are writing our story each and every moment. We are POETRY in motion.

~ I AM POETRY in motion as I write my story with every thought, word, and action.

~~~~~~~~~

Blessings of Wisdom are sent to you today. May you see, speak, and share your Light with the world through the POETRY you are witnessing and being.

~~~~~~~~~

Notes

Image captured by Tim Chinn.

Week 13
Destiny Rising

~~~~~~~

Blessings of Faith are sent to you today. May you be open to your Destiny Rising into the true essence of all that you are.

~~~~~~~

There have been many thoughts and opinions of whether one's future is predetermined or free will has an influence on our tomorrows. The truth of the matter is that neither can be proven. The debate will continue long after today, and we can only move forward by making the best decisions with the understanding that we have at the moment.

What is most important is that we are evolving with life's experiences by moving through each emotion. Haruki Murakami said, 'Pain is inevitable. Suffering is optional.'

Each of us will experience pain in our lifetime because everything keeps moving and changing. The changes may catch us off guard, or tragic events may touch our lives. The longer we have the gift of living the more we will experience, and this includes joy, pain, and all the emotions in between.

94

It is when we can't let go of the pain that it can become part of our identity and it evolves into inner suffering.

It is why it is crucial to our journey to feel all emotions fully. You and I accomplish this by being in the present moment. For instance, when laughter and happiness surround the moment; move into that, not fearing when it will end or how one can make it continue.

It is the same for the painful moments. One must feel the sadness, cry the tears, and allow the disappointment or anger to flow through them completely.

These moments are not just minutes. They may be days, weeks, even longer depending on the situation. The important part is to keep recognizing the feelings, honoring and validating them in the moment, and trusting that eventually there will be fewer moments of sadness than the day before.

If we allow time to work its wonders, it can shift pain into a deeper understanding of our journey and ultimately we will be on the other side of the pain instead of sitting in the suffering of that which we can't control.

You and I are unique beings having a one of a kind experience. Therefore, what we create in this life will be like no other. There is so much that we cannot control in life but we can control our reaction to the experience.

The way you and I think and place our words together or share our gifts with the world with others is an opportunity to bring more love and compassion to each situation.

Sometimes we can get caught up in how big the problems are in the world but let us choose to focus instead on what we can bring to each moment. There is always the choice of adding more kindness and compassion in each conversation. We can make conscious decisions to support that which aligns with our values.

It truly begins every day with you and me creating and narrating our life's story. It is through a conscious realization that we must awaken and recognize the power of our actions. Let us persevere into the highest version of ourselves to create our RISING DESTINY.

Let us stop denying unconditional love because we are afraid. Let us stop doing nothing because we can't do it all. Time is of the essence. Your journey is important, significant, and worthy of all that you came here to do.

Be thy Light.

Day 1
DESTINY~ As the sun rises above our heads on this glorious day, let us sit in the moment, knowing that we are blessed with another day and opportunity to share our Light. Our DESTINY is to remember the essence of who we came to be and to share our gifts with the world. Let us create a reality of more compassion and hope to bring more Light into the world for the future. We must take steps in our thoughts, conversations, and actions to deliver truth to that which is in our hearts and that which we see around us. The Light of who we are is waiting and wanting to shine upon all that we do. This is the journey that we came to fulfill - our DESTINY, the story that we are creating each and every day. Let us not take this day, this moment or this incredible gift for granted. Let us instead embrace the joy and allow our heart to follow its DESTINY.

~ I AM fulfilling my DESTINY and truth with every breath and action that I take.

~~~~~~~~

Blessings of Courage are sent to you today. May you be brave in your actions to follow the path to your DESTINY.

~~~~~~~~

Day 2
NARRATING~ Each of us is NARRATING our life through the interpretation of what we experience. It is our choice to witness life with compassion or judgment. When the NARRATING voice is one of love, our heart can open to the possibilities of miracles. We begin to observe little actions of kindness and grace. The miracles were there all along; we just couldn't see them with our closed mind and heart void of hope. Let us rewrite our story, find the memories that bring us joy, and interpret the actions of others with understanding and gratitude. Each of our lessons has assisted in our evolvement. Let us begin NARRATING our stories with the

utmost love that we can imagine. Let us bring more compassion and peace into our world through our interpretation of the stories we witness.

~ I AM NARRATING the stories of my life through love and compassion.

~~~~~~~~

Blessings of Miracles are sent to you today. May your heart be open to life's many interpretations as you are NARRATING your story.

~~~~~~~~

Day 3

PERSEVERE~ We must PERSEVERE in the journey of life, in spite of the difficulties that may cross our path. We must learn from the discouraging moments and continue toward our purpose and goals, with determination. Today, if an obstacle seems too great, take a moment and ask the Universe for the guidance on how to overcome this barrier. The wisdom of the Universe will guide and assist you, encouraging you to PERSEVERE on your journey, as you contribute toward improving the world. Each of us must have the intention to become the best version of ourselves. It is our responsibility to keep striving, learning, developing, and persevering toward our greatness. May you and I PERSEVERE toward our destiny in every moment.

~ I AM guided by the Universe to PERSEVERE through all obstacles and to bring more Light into the world.

~~~~~~~~

Blessings of Universal Guidance are sent to you today. May you PERSEVERE through the obstacles that lead you to your true essence.

~~~~~~~~

Day 4

DESTINATION~ In moments where it appears that the world is spinning out of control, and we cannot find our DESTINATION, we must keep the faith that there is hope. It is in the heaviest of storms that the Light will show us the way to our DESTINATION. It may be when we least expect it, but a doorway will present a path for which we have longed. Let us raise our voice in a song of hope and lift up our hearts in gratitude for the experiences of our lessons. Our faith, hope, and belief will lead us to the answers and the way to our DESTINATION.

~ I AM following my heart to the DESTINATION of my dreams.

Blessings of Hope are sent to you today. May compassion guide you to your DESTINATION of love for all.

Day 5

REALIZATION~ Where we fall is also where we must get back up again. When you and I have the REALIZATION that this journey is our staircase and that we must not skip the building blocks towards our future, peace soon enters our path. We may stumble, and even take steps in the opposite direction, but we must journey one step at a time to see the REALIZATION of the perfection of our unique path. How we handle each step determines when the next one is taken. You and I each establish our own happiness and destiny. The peace comes from within, not from that which is outside of us. It is in this moment of REALIZATION that we will begin to see the ups and downs of this journey as the true gifts on the staircase of life.

~ I AM embracing the staircase of life with the REALIZATION that the peace within me becomes stronger with each step.

Blessings of Inner Wisdom are sent to you today. May you be surrounded in the REALIZATION that every moment is a precious gift.

Day 6

RECOGNIZE~ Today amidst all that surrounds us in the world, let us choose to RECOGNIZE the core of our being as love. As our list of added responsibilities and tasks begins to grow, let us RECOGNIZE that we always have the choice to say no to that which does not serve the highest good. We are the master of our unique destiny; masters of who we are and who we are becoming in each and every moment. Let us RECOGNIZE the core of who we are today, which is love. May we be aware of the possibilities of our tomorrows and all that we bring into the world.

~ I AM choosing that which is of the highest good, and I RECOGNIZE that it leads me to the expansion of my essence.

~~~~~~~

Blessings of Guidance are sent to you today. May you be aligned physically, mentally, and spiritually to RECOGNIZE your wisest choices in this journey.

~~~~~~~

Day 7

RISING~ Are we RISING to our destiny, or to that which speaks to our hearts? Do we take a moment of silence to hear the guidance of the Universe? It is easy to get wrapped up in the outer world and to live in a constant state of stress. You and I must take moments of solitude and do things that assist with detoxifying from the stress of each day. De-stressing may look different to each of us; it may be walking in nature, spending time in the garden, knitting or crocheting, or being in a meditative state. It is in RISING to be the best version of ourselves that we become conscious of our wisest choices. When we are present, we hear the inner guidance to assist us in our journey. The call from within for each of us to create, explore, experience, and expand our being, is waiting for the RISING of our essence.

~ I AM RISING to my inner call by becoming conscious of my choices in each moment.

~~~~~~~

Blessings of Universal Guidance are sent to you today. May your actions and words be consciously RISING to your highest essence.

~~~~~~~

Notes

Image captured by Susan Gossett.

Week 14
Dreams Aligned

~~~~~~~~

Blessings of Awareness are sent to you today. May your conscious choices be Aligned with the actions to fulfill your Dreams.

~~~~~~~~

When you and I are aligned with our essence, everything appears to fall into place with such grace. Our actions no longer take great effort, but come with ease when we move with guided action.

How do we align ourselves with that which is greater than pride or ego? How do we get out of our own way? How do we get past our fears, into the Universal flow of life?

It begins with intention and balancing our heart, mind, body, and soul. Each of these areas, when we awaken to their guidance, will communicate to us through thoughts, ailments, coincidences, insights, and inner or outer wisdom. These nudges from the Universe can assist us in knowing how to shift our areas of focus. We just need to pay attention.

It is not uncommon that when we do not tune into the guidance, we can eventually encounter physical ailments. These conditions are a roadmap, directing us to place our focus on the areas that are causing discomfort.

For instance, I had pain in my left shoulder. A physical injury had not occurred, but the discomfort persisted month after month. It became a part of my sleeping and waking world.

Through the guidance of meditation, I began to understand how I had manifested this pain through a deep need to bring more Light to the world through my words.

The left side of the body is the feminine and spiritual, and the shoulders are where we take on the weight of the world. My late nights of physical and mental work at the computer had left me exhausted and out of balance.

Even though my efforts were from my heart and soul, I was depleting my physical and mental resources.

Once I understood the source of the physical discomfort, I was able to heighten my awareness around the judgment of the physical pain. I no longer approached it as if it was bad or good but truly validated, honored, loved, and bonded with the experience and all it was here to teach me.

I then took it one step further. What if I could be aware of every single hair on my body, tens of thousands of them from my head to my toes? How would this change my Earthly experience physically, mentally, and spiritually? What if my awareness on every level was in alignment with my hopes and dreams? Would my thoughts, words, and actions be more powerful and have more impact on the world around me?

I knew that it would, and, through this conscious awareness, my perception around pain began to shift. It was not an overnight physical healing process, but it was an immediate mental and spiritual epiphany moment into a deeper understanding of the holistic alignment that needed to be a part of my journey.

Let us place our intentions on aligning every aspect of our being from that which we see, what intuitively feel, and all that we believe. When you and I are in spiritual, mental, and physical balance, our DREAMS become ALIGNED with the Universe.

Be thy Light.

Day 1
VITALITY~ Each of us desires a life of VITALITY; to live, grow, and develop into all that we know we can be. Everything that we need to accomplish our dreams was given to us when we came into the world. It is our responsibility to nurture our gifts and to reach inside of ourselves to pursue that which we came here to do. Our hearts are leading us. The Universe is guiding us toward this life of VITALITY that we envision. Whether it is a talent we are developing, or the ability to find the resources to make it happen, each of us needs to embrace that which we came here to be. Let us live the life of VITALITY that we know is ours.

~ I AM living a life of VITALITY through my choices, which are in alignment with my heart.

~~~~~~~~

Blessings of Abundance are sent to you today. May you align your thoughts and actions to create a life of VITALITY.

~~~~~~~~

Day 2
VOICE~ As infants, we were not able to speak to those who surrounded our tiny being. Each of us would cry out for others to hear our needs and we would be soothed by love, caresses, and all that a babe needs. Through time, we found our VOICE. We began to imitate sounds and words, placing sentences together. We started to have thoughts and opinions concerning our dreams and goals. We became passionate in our beliefs. Each of us has debated what we believe and possibly criticized those who thought differently. Our journeys are uniquely our own. It is not in our best interest to convince others what is right, for we each have our own path, our own journey to discover our own unique VOICE. Let us be true to who we are and all that we are becoming. Let us use our VOICE in love, supporting one another as we walk this journey and discover the things and places that resonate with us. Let us follow our hearts into conversations infused with love and compassion for all.

~ I AM using my unique VOICE to share love and compassion with all those I encounter.

~~~~~~~~

Blessings of Openness are sent to you today. May your heart be courageous to share your unique VOICE with the world. Shine brilliantly, my friend.

~~~~~~~~

Day 3

WHISPERS~ Let us be fully present at this moment; breathing in the goodness of all that was, is, and is yet to be. Let us not give our power to the pull of the world against our shoulders, demanding that we invest more of our time and energy in that which does not line up with our truth. Let us be aligned with our hearts and listen not to the demands that fail to serve the highest good, nor to the WHISPERS that we are not worthy to live from our essence; let us say 'no' to that which is not love. We are allowed moments to be present with all that is around us and to listen for the WHISPERS of guidance. Let us reach not only for the situations that strengthen and nourish our physical bodies but also for the highest good that enriches our spiritual being. The Universe WHISPERS a reminder to be connected with the grass beneath our feet and the ever-changing clouds in the sky, and to mirror the tree with a firm foundation that reaches for the heavens. Let us take these moments to be in tune with the guidance that is available for each of us.

~ I AM listening to the WHISPERS of the Universe that urge me to follow my heart and be led to my truth.

~~~~~~~~

Blessings of Guidance are sent to you today. May your heart be open to the WHISPERS of the Universe as they guide and support you in all ways.

~~~~~~~~

Day 4

WITHIN~ The many temptations that steal our time, lead to much of our decline in productivity. When you and I are not following our hearts, the dreams WITHIN us are not nurtured. The visions within our souls become misaligned with the activities that we are doing, and we lose sight of our purpose. Each of us has a journey of steps that we must take to bring forth our visions into reality. We know when we are in tune with that which we came here to do because the Universe adds magic to our efforts. Let us be present to the activities in which we partake, choosing that which nurtures our being with more love and Light. The spirit WITHIN each of us is always guiding us in the steps that we take toward our dreams. All that we seek is WITHIN our being; we need only to listen to the guidance and support throughout our journey.

~ I AM aligned to the spirit WITHIN me, listening to the guidance to fulfill my dreams.

~~~~~~~~~

Blessings of Faith are sent to you today. May you tune into the Universal guidance that is WITHIN your essence. You are forever supported in this journey.

~~~~~~~~~

Day 5

WORTHY~ You and I are more brilliant than any sunset, sweeter than honey, and more perfect than the reddest of roses. We possess every quality necessary to reach our dreams if only we reach out to claim them. Each of us is WORTHY of accomplishing that which we came here to achieve. Let us not live our lives with the regrets of that which we did not do. When the door opens, we must believe that we are WORTHY to walk through. Let us not live in fear of failure; for it is in the process of continuing to move forward that we follow through on the journey to our essence. Our dreams and goals were given to each of us to learn from, and rejoice in, as we take actions toward their fulfillment. We are the creators of our world, and all we envision can be realized; for we are WORTHY.

~ I AM WORTHY of accomplishing the dreams that I envision, and of being that which I came here to be.

Blessings of Assurance are sent to you today. May you follow your heart and step forth into all that you are WORTHY of creating and being in this lifetime.

~~~~~~~

Day 6

YIELD~ We are each free spirits, who continuously create our reality with our thoughts and belief systems. We can bring about the life of which we dream, or we can YIELD to fears and doubts that serve only to hinder our journey. Our life is a gift to be treasured and shared with others; one in which we are always expanding into our essence. Let us clear the things that encumber our experience, shift our perception of that which we cannot change into a more positive light, and not YIELD to that which fails to serve the highest good. When we follow our truth, we will become advocates for those who cannot speak, we will seek love in every situation, and we will not YIELD to that which is of darkness.

~ I AM in tune with that which is for the highest good. I will not YIELD to that which disregards my truth.

~~~~~~~

Blessings of Truth are sent to you today. May your choices be courageous and not YIELD to that which hinders your true essence.

~~~~~~~

Day 7

YOU~ YOU and I have all the things that we need to accomplish our destiny. There is nothing that we cannot do or be. It is when we believe that we have a purpose that the Universe will guide us toward bringing our dreams into reality. Our limiting thoughts and beliefs are the only things holding us back. YOU and I hold the power and the key to creating that which we seek. Let us begin today to shift our thoughts and buff the clouds of doubt, so that we may allow the Light within each of us to shine. YOU and I were conceived in perfection and our Light is so bright that everyone and everything can feel the rays of love.

~ I AM encompassing all that the Universe has given to YOU and me and creating a world of more Light.

~~~~~~~~~~

Blessings of Light are sent to you today. May YOU shine brilliantly upon the world and be all that you came to share with the world.

~~~~~~~~~~

Notes

Image captured by Steve McCall.

Week 15
Empowered Freedom

~~~~~~~

Blessings of Wisdom are sent to you today. May you choose the Empowered
Freedom that is available to you, always.

~~~~~~~

Peace on Earth is a concept we have been talking about for thousands of
years, and yet, in some ways, we seem further than ever from creating it.
Human beings fight over invisible lines, resources that we deem as valuable,
or the desire to hold power and control over others.

Is it possible to move closer towards a world of peace instead of further
away from it? Where does one begin and how can one person make a
difference in such a massive global population?

I believe it is possible. One person alone may not be able to save the world,
but imagine the possibilities of one plus one plus one, etc. Could this shift
our paradigm into what I call, BIG love?

It is not an easy process, but it begins with breaking down the old archaic ways of thinking and doing. Sometimes we find ourselves apologizing for things we didn't even know at the time were primordial words or actions.

It is in these moments that we learn, apologize and forgive one another. This is where we break the cycle, shifting the brain patterns into new and more empowered ways of thinking and being. When each of us takes responsibility, consciously choosing to love without conditions, we improve our human experience as well as others. This is a world we want to create together.

One moment, day, and year at a time, we have the ability to create peace within ourselves that ultimately creates peace within the world. We can empower our actions through BIG love, without conditions or reasons, loving because it is why we are here and what we came to share with others.

This way of living will create a world of love and Light, thus bringing our dreams of a peaceful world into reality through conscious choices, creating empowered freedom for all.

There is a concept that most of us have not witnessed, let alone taught. Yet, we all need it, think about it, and long for it; and that is to be loved for all that you were yesterday, that you are today, and all that you know you came here to be.

The only way we can love others this way is by loving ourselves first in the same unconditional way. EMPOWERED FREEDOM comes from healing your wounds of yesterday to then being able to assist others in healing theirs. The journey to BIG love begins within each of us.

Be thy Light.

Day 1
EMPOWERED~ Let us embrace our day by choosing the thoughts that will encourage us to take action. You and I can inspire one another to be bold and brave in living our truth and being the essence of who we are. Let us choose in every moment the EMPOWERED thought, the words of encouragement, and the actions that will inspire us to do more. We make hundreds of choices every day in our journey. Let us consciously choose the EMPOWERED

thought, creating positive actions in the world around us. Let us be EMPOWERED to be the essence of who we are.

~ I AM EMPOWERED to be the essence of my being and share that Light with the world.

~~~~~~~

Blessings of Consciousness are sent to you today. May you be EMPOWERED to take actions of love and compassion.

~~~~~~~

Day 2
FREEDOM~ We are wiser today because of yesterday's experiences. There is no need for the regrets of the things that have passed. Let us be grateful for all that was and focus on the FREEDOM of today with the wisdom that now surrounds us. The love and Light of today will bring blessings for our every tomorrow. You and I always have the FREEDOM to control our thoughts, words, and actions. May that FREEDOM empower each of us to choose wisely on this day.

~ I AM wiser because of yesterday's experiences. I have the FREEDOM to choose the highest thought and action in all my decisions.

~~~~~~~

Blessings of Wisdom are sent to you today. May your conscious FREEDOM create actions of love and Light.

~~~~~~~

Day 3
INITIATIVE~ Let us take the INITIATIVE to move closer to the Light, love, and all that we wish to be experiencing. You and I hold the key to open the doors of those things and experiences of which we want to see more. It is up to each of us to embody more of that Light and love. Do not wait for someone else to take the INITIATIVE, as this only delays that which we want to experience in our lifetime. Let us be the change that we long to see, the catalyst in forgiving that which we do not understand, the Light when all that is around us is dark, and the unconditional love to those that have

forgotten how to reciprocate. Let each of us take the INITIATIVE to live from our higher selves.

~ I AM taking the conscious INITIATIVE to live from my essence in every moment.

~~~~~~~

Blessings of Determination are sent to you today. May you take the INITIATIVE to create all that you want to see in the world.

~~~~~~~

Day 4
RESILIENCE~ It is through hope that each of us can find the RESILIENCE to move forward through a difficult time or experience. We are capable of finding peace no matter the situation. We can achieve this through our faith and the support of the Universe. It is through unconditional love for ourselves and our neighbor that compassion will encompass our journey. We are always guided. Let us embrace the RESILIENCE that resides in each cell of our being and at the core of who we are. Let us rise above the fear and the doubt. Let us be the Light when all is dark, for we are beings of RESILIENCE, spreading the love in all that we do.

~ I AM a being of RESILIENCE, supported and guided by the Universe.

~~~~~~~

Blessings of Faith are sent to you today. May you witness and celebrate the RESILIENCE of your personal journey. You are unconditionally loved and supported.

~~~~~~~

Day 5
RESPONSIBLE~ We are RESPONSIBLE for our personal journey and for creating the life that we are now living. If we look around us and do not like what we see, then it is our choice to change things in our life. No one else is going to do that for us, and it is not their responsibility; this is our life, with our unique calling and purpose. If we don't share that unique purpose with

112

the world, no one else will. It is why we are here. It is time to empower ourselves and answer the call within us. Let us take action today toward creating our heaven on Earth. Let us ask the Universe for guidance and make the smallest steps toward a change today. Those steps may involve changing our perception of the world, or perhaps, focusing on the aspects of our current situation for which we can express gratitude. Let us not wait until tomorrow or until the stars align. Let us begin now to take charge and create the life we want to be living. The world will continue to spin, but with each of us RESPONSIBLE for our happiness and fulfillment, and bringing more love to every situation. It is in this place, where each of us takes responsibility for our actions, that our planet will have a higher vibration, with more compassion. Let us respond to the call of being RESPONSIBLE for our amazing journey.

~ I AM RESPONSIBLE for my happiness and fulfillment. I AM creating my heaven on Earth.

~~~~~~~~

Blessings of Understanding are sent to you today. May your actions be consciously RESPONSIBLE as you create a life of love and compassion for all.

~~~~~~~~

Day 6

RISE~ Let us RISE and fill our lives with the experiences that will bring more joy into the world. Let us discard the TV show, news, or that article that leaves us feeling hopeless. Let us choose to bask in the glory of the sunset or gaze at the wonder of the stars above. When we reconnect with the world around us, we become in tune with where we are emotionally and spiritually. We can fill ourselves with more of the things that bring us joy. We must take the time to check in with ourselves to see how our choices are affecting our energy level. It is important to refuel our body and mind to align with our soul. Let us choose moments that will replenish our beings on all levels, to take the time to reconnect with the essence of who we are, and to RISE to a higher level of joy. Let us choose to RISE to the occasion that will bring more joy, love, and hope into our lives.

~ I AM choosing that which aligns my mind, body, and soul. I RISE to my highest level of joy.

~~~~~~~~

Blessings of Joy are sent to you today. May your energy level RISE as you begin to choose that which bring your body, mind, and soul into alignment.

~~~~~~~~

Day 7
THRIVE~ You and I came here to THRIVE as we walk this journey through life; to love unconditionally, witness generosity, listen to voices of compassion, and share our essence with the world. We came to this planet to THRIVE spiritually, mentally, and physically. Each of us is given the opportunity to expand through controversial situations to evolve into our highest self. Let us not waste another moment doubting our abilities and fearing the unknown. Today let us choose to take back our power and step forward into the life we should be living. Let us not wait for tomorrow, but embrace the decision to THRIVE at this moment, expanding into our true essence.

~ I AM choosing to THRIVE spiritually, mentally, and physically by empowering myself to live from my essence.

~~~~~~~~

Blessings of Consciousness are sent to you today. May you create a life of abundance and THRIVE in this journey you are creating in your essence.

~~~~~~~~

Notes

Image captured by Susan Gossett.

Week 16
Encouraging the Heart

~~~~~~~~

Blessings of Consciousness are sent to you today. May your thoughts and actions Encourage your Heart to blossom fully.

~~~~~~~~

There is a series on National Geographic called *One Strange Rock*. It is the story of the Earth, told through the unique perspective of astronauts that have spent anywhere from one-week up to two-years orbiting this planet we call home.

Each individual discusses a shift that took place in their consciousness as they viewed our blue sphere from the vast cosmos. They call this cognitive shift the Overview Effect.

It is when one no longer sees a particular building or city as their home but views the Earth as the residence for all things and beings. The astronauts no longer saw borders or walls as necessary. They no longer focused on the differences between inhabitants but on our similarities as Earthlings.

As each person discussed their experience, you could feel love exuding from their words for the experience, the planet, and the true connection of all things.

How can we shift our perspective without this physically altering experience? Is it possible to discover this feeling of Oneness with all that we encounter each day?

I believe it begins with our spiritual relationship with that which is greater than you and I. This connection evolves into a conscious understanding that your living experience, with all that is unfolding, is also happening to everything and everyone else on the Earth.

We begin to see that everything is intertwined and that it is always expanding and contrasting, just as we breathe in and out so does the planet and everything on it. It is through this awakening that our actions and words become encouraging to others and ourselves. We will begin not to compete, but to cheer each other forward to create more beauty and love.

If each of us could shift our perspective to see the importance of unity versus division and understand that together we are stronger; we could create abundance for all inhabitants on our planet.

When we place our intentions on consciously bringing hope and encouragement to all those we encounter, our conscious actions can empower others to truly create the life each of us came here to share with this world.

Let us encourage one another to align our hearts with our mind and soul by bringing hope to each other's unique dreams. Let us remember the Overview Effect and that we are all in this together, ENCOURAGING one another from THE HEART.

Be thy Light.

Day 1
APPRECIATED~ All beings love feeling APPRECIATED. It is an act that warms our hearts when someone recognizes the effort that was made to complete a task. When we receive encouragement in the beginning stages of a project, it gives energy to the creation. Let us send out a positive word to our spouse, daughter or son's efforts. Words of hope to those striving to be

117

more. Let us take a moment to appreciate our accomplishments. When you and I see that our efforts are recognized, we are motivated to keep moving toward our goals. Let us take action to assist someone in their journey today by showing or telling them how much they are APPRECIATED for their efforts on this path of life. Let each of us be the cheerleader in other's lives as well as our own so that each of us will be APPRECIATED in our personal journey.

~ I AM showing others that our efforts toward a world of more love are APPRECIATED.

~~~~~~~~

Blessings of Encouragement are sent to you today. May you recognize the APPRECIATED actions of others that are creating a more compassionate world.

~~~~~~~~

Day 2
ENCOURAGING~ Let us be the ENCOURAGING word to one another's journey; supportive and kind as we follow our hearts along these individual paths. Let us lend a hand when someone has fallen, ENCOURAGING them to keep striving to create their dreams. Let us cheer for each other, knowing that we both should have abundance. Let us change these limiting thoughts of lack and competition, ENCOURAGING our beliefs to evolve toward ones of an abundance of love and Light for all.

~ I AM ENCOURAGING others through my inspiring journey of love and Light.

~~~~~~~~

Blessings of Faith are sent to you today. May your words be kind and ENCOURAGING to all those you interact with in your journey.

~~~~~~~~

Day 3

FOREVER~ Each of our paths are guided and sprinkled with the stardust from the heavens. The Universe FOREVER supports you and me as we bring our Light into the world. We are one with everything around us. We have everything that we need to achieve our dreams. In each and every moment, even when we cease to function from our highest self, you and I are FOREVER loved. We may feel the discord through our experiences, but the Universe continues to support us in all that we do, to let us know from the deepest part of our being that we are always FOREVER loved and guided by the Universe.

~ I AM FOREVER guided and supported throughout every moment of my day.

~~~~~~~~

Blessings of Guidance are sent to you today. May you know that you are FOREVER loved and supported by the Universe.

~~~~~~~~

Day 4

MAGNIFICENT~ Each and every person, creature, tree, flower, fruit, vegetable, and grain of sand are MAGNIFICENT in their own unique and personal ways. We are creations filled with a combination of traits and characteristics that are individual to each of us. Let us not hide that which is uniquely who we are from the world. Let us not walk a path that is not our own. Follow the MAGNIFICENT heart in every moment that you and I are on this planet. Let us embrace those around us that are following their brilliance and inspire all to follow their path of Light. Let us not doubt that each and every one of us came here to do great things. Let us encourage and love one another as we follow our personal paths toward the MAGNIFICENT beings that we came here to be.

~ I AM following my heart to lead a MAGNIFICENT life in every moment.

~~~~~~~

Blessings of Uniqueness are sent to you today. May you embrace the
MAGNIFICENT path you are walking and creating in your life.

~~~~~~~

Day 5

NARRATOR~ We are each the NARRATOR of our lives; from the chitter-
chatter inside our head to that of which we speak to those around us. As the
NARRATOR, you and I choose to either speak with words and thoughts of
encouragement, or to be the naysayer of creative ideas or dreams. If each of
us chose words from a heart of love, how would the world around us
change? How many of our ideas would have been nurtured if the words
spoken to us would have been ones of encouragement? Let us each be a
NARRATOR with a heart of love. Let our words to others, as well as our
inner thoughts, be from this space in which all things are possible.

~ I AM the NARRATOR of my life. I interpret my experiences through an
open heart.

~~~~~~~

Blessings of Love are sent to you today. May you be a NARRATOR of love,
Light, and hope in all the words that you speak today.

~~~~~~~

Day 6

SMILE~ Let us take this moment to lift the corners of our mouths into a
radiant and shining SMILE. It is such a simple movement, and yet it is
powerful in changing our mood and increasing the joy within us. A SMILE
for a loved one or a stranger does wonders, and together we raise our
vibration with this simple gesture. Even when we do it in front of a mirror
and see our face transform into a happy expression, we can't help but feel
silly and laugh. Notice that the Light within our eyes begins to sparkle and
our noses crinkle in delight. We are amazing! Let us choose to use this
powerful and simple tool each day and SMILE with the beauty that we are
upon the world.

~ I AM embracing my SMILE and raising my vibration through this joyous act.

~~~~~~~

Blessings of Joy are sent to you today. May you SMILE upon the world, bringing your Light wherever you may journey too.

~~~~~~~

Day 7

SPARK~ As we journey through life, we never know what experience will provide the SPARK that ignites a new passion, or rekindles one that has been smoldering. A moment of crisis may seem painful, or even the worst thing that we have experienced, but it is often these difficulties that SPARK us to move out of our comfort zone. We as humans are often not willing to make a change or take a leap of faith until we are forced to jump. What may often seem like a fire out of control may be the SPARK that renews your true calling in life.

~ I AM open to the SPARK that rekindles the passion within me to share my gifts with the world.

~~~~~~~

Blessings of Faith are sent to you today. May you be the SPARK of encouragement and inspiration to others that enter your world.

~~~~~~~

Notes

Image captured by Susan Gossett.

Week 17
Nurturing thy Being

~~~~~~~~

Blessings of Insight are sent to you today. May you Nurture Thy Being with all that you need to align your heart, mind, and soul.

~~~~~~~~

It is not uncommon for us to become depleted in our journey. In these situations, you and I often forget to make the best choices or to take the time to nourish every aspect of our being.

You and I cannot bring the best version of ourselves to the world if our tank is running on empty. Sustaining our needs must take place on every level, from eating well and getting enough rest, to taking the time to pray and meditate, to spending time stimulating our minds by being creative.

Each one of us is a unique being, and the activities that fill me up emotionally and spiritually may or may not bring about the same results for you. Here are a few of my necessities that keep me sustained in this personal journey:

Sunshine- It is rare that I do not spend time outside taking in the rays of the sun and being in nature. I need this for my well-being.
Singing- It raises my vibration and allows me to become aligned with my true essence.
Animals- The creatures of the world bring me many lessons on how to love bigger, better, and without conditions.
Flowers- Every week I place several bouquets throughout my house. They are bright and cheery and bring joy to my home.
Essential Oils- I have a blend at my desk before I begin my day, a few drops in my tea, and oils diffusing throughout my home.

Above are just a few examples. I also incorporate meditation, writing, connecting with loved ones, and taking walks. I encourage you to find all that fills your moments with a bit more joy and incorporate more of that into your life.

Let us consciously nurture ourselves with our thoughts, words, and actions. Let us allow ourselves the time and space to fall in love with our journey and all that it has to teach us. You and I must take conscious action by NURTURING THY BEING, when we learn to listen to our needs; we evolve into the best version of ourselves.

It is when you and I feel nourished and shine brilliantly that we are assisting the whole world in raising its vibration. It is indeed our responsibility to share our essence and our unique gifts with the world.

Be thy Light.

Day 1
GIFT~ Let the words that leave our lips and enter into the world be from a place of love. Let the movements that you and I are taking upon our journey be in line with the essence of who we are. Let the thoughts that are crossing our minds be hopeful and empowering. Our hearts must be open as we say the words. Our actions must be taken in truth from a place of our highest being. Our thoughts need to encompass hope for the present moment as we enter into our tomorrow. This journey is a GIFT that each of us has been given. Let us treat each moment as if it is priceless by being present and embracing all that is around us. Every day let us give others the GIFT of who we are through our words and actions; our true essence and the highest version of who we are striving to be.

~ I AM embracing each moment that has been so graciously given. Time is an invaluable GIFT.

~~~~~~~~

Blessings of Gratitude are sent to you today. May your heart be open to the GIFT that your Light can be to the world.

~~~~~~~~

Day 2

INSIGHTFUL~ We can be in tune with a more INSIGHTFUL journey if we only take the moments of silence to reconnect with the essence of who we are. You and I have the wisdom to make decisions that can change the world around us if only we listen and follow our hearts. We may have an INSIGHTFUL thought, and yet we let fear stop the action from taking place. Let us step through the doubt with a belief that you and I are creating a world filled with more love. Let us not turn our backs on that INSIGHTFUL gift with which the Universe has blessed us. Let us embrace and nurture the gift that we have been given to share with the world.

~ I AM an INSIGHTFUL being who is guided and supported by the Universe in all ways.

~~~~~~~~

Blessings of Intuition are sent to you today. May you be INSIGHTFUL and open to the guidance that awaits you.

~~~~~~~~

Day 3

LOVED~ We are LOVED and supported by the Universe always. You and I are LOVED whether the sun is shining or the moon is glowing upon us. We are brought into this world with everything that we need and learn throughout our journey how to steadily become more of the Light that we came here to be. You and I need only to recognize the love in the highest of highs and lowest of lows that we experience. We are LOVED unconditionally and supported as we share our gifts with the world. Let us reflect the love and Light, knowing that we need only to shine our essence upon all that there is.

~ I AM LOVED unconditionally and supported by the Universe in all that I share with the world.

~~~~~~~~

Blessings of Wisdom are sent to you today. May you know that you are LOVED, supported and guided by the Universe always.

~~~~~~~~

Day 4
NURTURING~ We choose, in every moment, the perception of life that is NURTURING to the soul. As the rain falls, do we see the beauty that it brings to the Earth or do we groan that it will ruin our plans? The NURTURING of the soul takes place when we are present and in tune with that which is happening at the moment; true consciousness fills up our being, the heartbeat slows, and our breath becomes deeper. You and I are responsible for the energy that we bring into a room, relationship, and conversation. If we are in tune and balanced in our mind, body, and soul, then life is met with a perception of hope. Let us choose in every moment the NURTURING of our being and deliver more Light into the world.

~ I AM NURTURING the essence of my being in all that I do by being present in this moment.

~~~~~~~~

Blessings of Consciousness are sent to you today. May you be NURTURING to your heart, mind, and soul in all that you do.

~~~~~~~~

Day 5
PASSION~ Each of our paths should be a journey that is surrounded with PASSION. It is when we walk through life with an open heart that the PASSION for life is intertwined in all that we do. It assists us in making decisions about our future. It beckons us in choosing our careers. Let the rays of Light guide our PASSION today and every day.

~ I AM living my life with an open heart surrounded by PASSION.

Blessings of Awareness are sent to you today. May your heart be open to the
PASSION that is available to you in every moment.

~~~~~~~~

Day 6

PERFECT~ When you and I look around the world, what is it that we see?
Does it fail to measure up to our desires or do we see it as PERFECT in this
very moment? It is not uncommon for us to focus on the negativity of what
we lack in our life instead of on the positivity of what we have in this very
moment. Far too often we hear someone pining for the past and how they
didn't realize how PERFECT that moment was until it was gone forever. Let
us not live with the regrets of yesterday, or long for the future of our
tomorrows. Let us live with today's wisdom in this PERFECT moment of
now and embrace the essence of who we are.

~ I AM embracing the moment of now, living with the openness of a heart
that is PERFECT.

~~~~~~~~

Blessings of Gratitude are sent to you today. May you be open to the
PERFECT moments that surround you.

~~~~~~~~

Day 7

TRUE~ Our experience as we go through life should honor that which each
of us knows to be TRUE. The core of us knows when we are living and
speaking in line with our truth. It is in those moments when we walk away
from a conversation and say to ourselves "I wish I had not said that" or
"done that" when we realize and learn that those words and actions were not
from our TRUE self. Each of us came here to evolve into our essence
through the journey of life and to assist one another in the process. Let us
spread the love and joy that we came here to give the world. Let us live our
lives in the present, silencing the ego and expanding into our TRUE selves.

~ I AM expanding into my TRUE self and assisting others to do the same.

~~~~~~~~

Blessings of Trust are sent to you today. May your TRUE self, shine brilliantly in all that you do.

~~~~~~~~

Notes

Image captured by Susan Gossett.

Week 18
Expanding Growth

~~~~~~~~

Blessings of Openness are sent to you today. May your heart be open to the Expanding Growth that leads to your true essence.

~~~~~~~~

The Universe is not a stagnant place. It is filled with movement that expands and contracts just as you and I do. This journey of life brings us situations that assist in our personal expansion. It is when we choose to ignore the opportunities, due to our doubts or fears, that we find ourselves in discord with the flow of the Universe.

Change is constant, and it is not always the easiest path to take, but through it comes a deeper understanding of all we are here to create and share. When our journey is in tune with life's movements, we will find that our experiences bring inner wisdom and greater joy.

The one belief that always brings me comfort during transitional moments is the understanding that we are always supported and guided by the Universe. We need only take time to be in connection with the Divine through prayer and meditation. It is in these moments that we become more in tune to the ideas and gentle nudges, alerting us when we should take action.

You and I are here to share our unique gifts with the world. It is with an open heart that we will evolve and expand into the highest version of ourselves. Moment by moment and choice-by-choice will lead us to a deeper understanding of the world around us, EXPANDING our inner GROWTH.

Let us remember that we are supported, guided, and loved in all ways. Thank you for shining brilliantly in the world, my friend.

Be thy Light.

Day 1
EVOLVING~ The world around us is constantly changing. Even that which may appear not to change, such a mountain, evolves over time. You and I are not meant to be stagnant creatures. We should be EVOLVING individually, as should the entire human race that inhabits this planet. Let us expand spiritually, physically, mentally, and emotionally through life's experiences. Let us not become rigid and unmoving in the way in which we approach life. Let each of us have an open heart that is EVOLVING into a more loving, hopeful, and accepting state of being. It is through each of us EVOLVING that the human race will expand into a higher state of consciousness, and the world around us will move onto a more harmonious plane.

~ I AM expanding and EVOLVING through life's experiences into the essence of me.

~~~~~~~~

Blessings of Expansion are sent to you today. May your heart, mind, and soul be aligned and EVOLVING through life's experiences.

~~~~~~~~

Day 2
EXPERIENCE~ The journey that we EXPERIENCE is one of trust as we open our hearts to expand with more love, joy, and grace. In our lives, we have more tools, as a result of our EXPERIENCE, and we make our decisions for both today and tomorrow with a deeper wisdom. We do not

131

need to know the 'how' or 'when' of the unfolding surprises that will be gifted to us by the Universe, through manifestation. Let us walk our journey, learning from the lessons and sharing our gifts with the world around us. Let us live with a brave spirit, reaching for the stars and enjoying the EXPERIENCE of our unique and awe-inspiring journey.

~ I AM expanding and evolving into the is-ness of my being through each EXPERIENCE.

~~~~~~~

Blessings of Joy are sent to you today. May you move through each EXPERIENCE with grace and love.

~~~~~~~

Day 3

FLOW~ Our lives should FLOW like the water in a stream; effortlessly and with purpose. Living in the FLOW of life brings joy and peace throughout our day. It is when we fight against the current of the stream that we have inner turmoil and invite suffering into our hearts. Being in the FLOW allows the pain not to linger in our mind or body. As we witness the difficulties and feel the emotions of the experience, we must allow ourselves to expand and evolve. We do not linger in this space when life continues to move forward down the stream. Today let us visualize the stream of life and that we are a beautiful autumn leaf that is flowing effortlessly along the water. Enjoy the scenery, relish in the waterfalls, embrace the small whirlpools, and know that the stream of life is leading us to places of joy, happiness, laughter, grace, and peace. Let us be in the FLOW of life today.

~ I AM in the ebb and FLOW of life, always expanding in my consciousness.

~~~~~~~

Blessings of Insight are sent to you today. May your heart be open to the FLOW of the Universe that is with you always.

~~~~~~~

Day 4

GROWTH~ Our hearts will always heal from moments of sadness. These moments are to assist us with our GROWTH and expansion into our essence. We will have days where we may feel that we will never smile again; but this too shall pass, for these occasions are presented only as opportunities for GROWTH. This instance of contrast from all that we know and have experienced is giving us more insight and wisdom to carry into our future. Let us reach for the inspired thought, grasping for the wellspring of hope when all seems dark. The Light is here within you and me, supporting us on our journey. Let us genuinely open our eyes so that we may wholly sense the nurturing love of the Universe. This moment of GROWTH is providing the necessary tools that will assist us in becoming all that we came here to be.

~ I AM open to the ever-expanding GROWTH of my journey.

~~~~~~~~

Blessings of Openness are sent to you today. May you be open to the GROWTH that leads to your awakened consciousness.

~~~~~~~~

Day 5

EXPANDING~ Each of us are surrounded by a space of love. We only need to expand into that love that awaits us. Each of us is a being of hope, courage, and ever-EXPANDING possibilities. We only need to believe in our abilities and that we are capable of greatness. You and I are all that we need to accomplish our dreams, to reach the summit of possibility, to be all that we came here to be. We are ever-EXPANDING each and every day through the laughter and the tears of our experiences. Our brilliance is waiting to be buffed, shined, and revealed to the world in all the glory that we are. Let us avoid wasting a single moment not being the ever-EXPANDING being that we came here to be.

~ I AM ever-EXPANDING into the greatness of my being and sharing that beauty with the world.

Blessings of Possibilities are sent to you today. May you be open to EXPANDING into all that you came here to be and do.

~~~~~~~

Day 6

LIFE-GIVING~ You and I were brought here in a LIFE-GIVING moment. It was a moment when two people, despite all circumstances, came together and a miracle took place to bring each of us into the world. You and I are miracles, and we came here to share LIFE-GIVING moments with all those around us. We do this by loving one another unconditionally, creating that which we are here to share, assisting one another without expectation, and being true to ourselves by giving the essence of who we are to the world. Let us choose to live a life filled with miracles and to be a LIFE-GIVING source to all those who witness our amazing and unique journeys.

~ I AM sharing my LIFE-GIVING essence with the world by expanding into my highest self.

~~~~~~~

Blessings of Miracles are sent to you today. May you share your LIFE-GIVING moments with the world around you.

~~~~~~~

Day 7

OPEN~ Each day we make the choice to either live our lives with a heart that is OPEN to life's experiences, or to build a wall around our heart to protect us from the things in life that we fear. When we choose to build the wall, each brick is placed with special care. These bricks may represent experiences in our past that were so painful that we were unable to move beyond them; perhaps we didn't have the tools, knowledge, or even maturity to get to the other side of that pain. The bricks began to give us comfort and a sense of security, and even became a part of our identity. Let us take down the wall, for we are wiser now, and it is time to let that fear go. It is no longer serving us. Deep within our soul, we know that the fear is not allowing us to evolve into our greatness. We came here to express love through our experiences, in all ways. Our life cannot expand into the abundance of joy and Light if we don't walk the path with an OPEN heart. The bricks and mortar are no longer needed. They are holding back the destiny that we came here to fulfill. Let us walk through our wall of fear to the road that awaits us. Let us knock down the barriers that are holding us back. Let us turn our faces to the sun, lift our wings to the wind, and allow ourselves to fly with an OPEN heart filled with unconditional love.

~ I AM living each moment with an OPEN heart full of unconditional love.

~~~~~~~~

Blessings of Courage are sent to you today. May you be OPEN to the unconditional love you came here to experience and share.

~~~~~~~~

Notes

Image captured by Susan Gossett.

Week 19
Resilient Faith

~~~~~~~~~

Blessings of Resilient Faith are sent to you today. May you find comfort that you are always guided and supported in this journey through life.

~~~~~~~~~

One of the things that I love about growing older is my deep belief in that which is greater than myself. Each year I become more and more aware that life is not just random chaos and my faith strengthens through life's experiences.

Faith has accompanied my journey from the age of seven, when I had a deep desire to connect with the Divine through prayer and study. All of this changed when my cousin became a paraplegic in a car accident at the age of sixteen.

The anger that I felt was overwhelming and I couldn't get past the struggle of realizing bad things can happen to good people. It seemed unfair, and I no longer wanted to be a part of such illogical ideology that couldn't be proven.

137

I consciously chose to change that which I believed. I turned away from the Higher Power and anger followed my journey for the next ten years.

When one loses their faith, in my experience, it is because there is no hope and a cynicism penetrates all thoughts, words, and actions. This negativity only leads to the inner Light becoming dim, masked with such deep sadness and hopelessness.

It was curiosity that led me back to my faith. I became a self-appointed theologian of sorts with a desire to understand various religions and the belief systems of their followers. Though I approached the subjects with a logical mind, it ultimately led me back to my closed heart of over a decade.

How does one build a faith of resilience? Why do some individuals go through such devastating circumstances and become stronger while others lose their belief systems?

It appears that hope and faith go hand in hand. If one cannot find their hope, the foundation begins to crumble. My beliefs would be tested once again another decade later when my dear cousin, the same cousin that had been a paraplegic for twenty-three years, was diagnosed with cancer and died before his fortieth birthday.

This time I knew to look for the miracles when all seemed lost. I let hope lead me through the darkest hours of grief. I allowed faith to comfort me when all that was left was the vulnerability.

His life experiences were some of my greatest lessons, and through them, I found my connection with hope and faith. It is when we learn to hold onto hope and faith no matter the outcome, that we learn we are always guided, even in the darkest hours, if we can keep our hearts open through the experience. It is only through our open heart and mind that we can move through the pain and not experience suffering. It is in the surrender that we can find peace once again.

Let us renew our faith into a space of resilience, allowing hope to lead the way through all circumstances into our RESILIENT FAITH.

Be thy Light.

Day 1

FAITH~ Life is similar to planting a garden. The various efforts require FAITH that our labors will produce fruit. As you and I toil the Earth and plants seeds, we envision the growth of the garden and the abundant harvest of the future. One by one we place the seeds in their home where the dark, fertile soil covers them. We then sprinkle the ground with water to moisten the foundation for a new beginning. In life, we are always planting seeds. The act of preparing and nurturing the seeds provides for the possibility of a prosperous future. However, let us not underestimate the power of FAITH: It is within us as we bless and place our seeds out in the world, knowing that miracles will result. It is our FAITH in the seeds of possibilities that will bring hope into the world around us and that our dreams will come to fruition. May you and I find joy in the sharing of the seeds that we have planted in the garden of life and may they be prosperous for the world around us.

~ I AM filled with an unstoppable FAITH that all is unfolding perfectly.

~~~~~~~~

Blessings of Belief are sent to you today. May FAITH guide you passed all that no longer is serving your journey.

~~~~~~~~

Day 2

ACHIEVE~ When we look at the path before us, it may appear long. Our mind may grow weary with fear and self-doubt through time. It is in these moments that we can begin breaking down the goal into small steps that you and I can ACHIEVE. This simple act brings confidence to our movements, and our faith begins to rise within us as we complete the tasks one by one. Our enthusiasm cannot be contained, and the passion to ACHIEVE the dream pushes us forward and pulls us closer to the life we are envisioning. Let us move in the direction of the dream, the fulfillment of which we came here to do. Let us believe that it is possible with each step that we take. In this manner, we can ACHIEVE all that we came here to be!

~ I AM taking the steps that are leading me to ACHIEVE all that I came here to do and be.

Blessings of Faith are sent to you today. May you be aligned to ACHIEVE that which you came here to be and do.

Day 3

FEARS~ Let us live the life that is vibrantly the essence of you and I. Our world should be as expansive as all the array of colors on the canvas of this globe. We are each a being filled with limitless possibilities. We are here to assist with providing the world an abundance of love through all that we experience. Awaken from the FEARS and the darkness of doubts that hide our Light from others. Feel the breath of wisdom that enters the body as we exchange our inner wisdom back to the world through grace. Mature into a blossom of beauty and share the hope with those who have lost theirs. Let the FEARS melt away from our hearts, let the anger and bitterness subside from our memories, and swing open the gate to the essence of who we are. Our doubts are not worthy of stealing the love that we came here to share. You and I are beings of Light and love. Inhale the essence of wisdom, hope, and love; and let the FEARS fade into a distant memory, while we bask in the rays of light that we exchange with the world.

~ I AM walking through all FEARS to the Light of the Universal wisdom that is within me.

Blessings of Courage are sent to you today. May you step through the doubts and FEARS to shine your unique Light upon the world.

Day 4

GUIDED~ You and I are GUIDED with each and every moment, with each and every breath that we exchange. There is not a time where we are alone in life. In moments of both glory and sadness, we are surrounded by love, encouraging us to stretch and grow into the essence of who we know we came here to be. The opportunity is ours; we have the power to create each of our moments with clarity and purpose. We are forever GUIDED; the support is always there. Let us have faith and ask for the assistance we desire, and we shall receive. How glorious to know that each of us is GUIDED with genuine and everlasting love.

~ I AM GUIDED in every moment as I live my life in faith and a heart that is open to love.

~~~~~~~~

Blessings of Support are sent to you today. May you be in tune to all the GUIDED wisdom that surrounds your journey.

~~~~~~~~

Day 5

INNER VOICE~ Yesterday is no longer ours, for the past is now behind us. Were we aware at that moment, or did we let it slip away unconsciously? We cannot create an empowered future through worry and distress. These emotions, left unchecked, only serve to foster frustration and fear. Let us be cognizant of the whispers of our INNER VOICE, guiding us to more love, peace, and joy in the present moment. When you and I are centered and mindful of all that is happening, the INNER VOICE will lead us to places, people, and situations beyond what we have dreamed. Let us be in that state of love and present to all that is happening. May we be open to the flow of emotions; observing and honoring, and then allowing these feelings to move through our being. We are always supported and loved by the guidance of our INNER VOICE.

~ I AM conscious of the INNER VOICE, and I follow that guidance to more love, peace, and joy.

~~~~~~~~

Blessings of Guidance are sent to you today. May your heart, mind, and soul be open to the INNER VOICE of the Universe.

~~~~~~~~

141

Day 6

LEAN IN~ You and I are capable of all the things that we dream. Even in the moments when we do not see the path that will lead us to that reality, we need only to LEAN IN with our faith and believe that the Universe will provide all the necessary opportunities. When we hesitate and doubt our abilities, we are stifling the energy to make the impossible, possible. The dreamers of yesterday said that we would one day fly like birds, man would walk on the moon, and computers and cell phones would be accessible to all. Many in the world around them thought these dreams to be impossibilities, yet today we take those things for granted. Today as we walk our personal journey, LEAN IN to those dreams that may appear as impossible. LEAN IN with the faith that you and I can bring our dreams to reality.

~ I AM capable of all things that I dream. I LEAN IN to my dreams knowing with faith and trust that my dreams are becoming a reality.

~~~~~~~~~

Blessings of Faith are sent to you today. May you LEAN IN to that which you came here to be and share with the world, be uniquely you.

~~~~~~~~~

Day 7

RESILIENT~ Each of us has to be RESILIENT to overcome the obstacles in our life so that we can do what we came here to do. We have all read the stories of how others have turned their struggles into lives of prosperity and abundance. Each of us has our own obstacles in life. These hurdles are there to assist us in our journey to become stronger, more focused, and to find the inner strength to be RESILIENT. Let us nurture the essence of who we are and encourage ourselves to be brave in our actions; so that we may be RESILIENT to any self-doubt and have faith that our dreams are achievable.

~ I AM RESILIENT to all obstacles; overcoming them through my faith and inspired actions.

~~~~~~~

Blessings of Perseverance are sent to you today. May you be RESILIENT and overcome all of life's obstacles through your true essence.

~~~~~~~

Notes

Image captured by Susan Gossett.

Week 20
Beauty within Grace

~~~~~~~~

Blessings of Wisdom are sent to you today. May you see the Beauty and Grace that surround you in every moment.

~~~~~~~~

In the darkest or the brightest moments, you are unstoppable; for the Universe supports you graciously. It is in moments of disconnection that we often feel most alone. This is a sign that we must take intentional action to replenish our heart, mind, and soul.

Look for the moments of serenity during times of hopelessness or despair. It is in the witnessing of dawn or dusk that these can be found; and we can use this to reset our state of mind at the beginning or end of a day, by taking time to reconnect to that which is greater than ourselves. It is in this space that we can set our intentions on the beauty and grace of replenishing our soul.

All of our journeys bring us to crossroads, and we each have the opportunity to contract or expand within the situation. Moments of disappointment or heartbreak may penetrate our visions of the future, but we must maintain faith that these experiences are assisting us along our path to our highest essence. Even when all is not hopeful, there is grace that surrounds every circumstance.

It may be in a stranger's listening ear, or a loved one's selfless action, or the perfect dream that brings comfort and direction, or hope may bubble up when a butterfly flutters by and you witness the true beauty of the moment.

The signs are there when we approach life with an open heart. The guidance is given when we knock on the doors of what we envision. There is an ebb and flow to our journey, and when we listen to the universal guidance, we can ride life's rhythm. We need only to approach all things with grace to see the beauty that resides in the situation.

Let us place our intentions on consciously maintaining a state of grace and finding the beauty in the world around us. Each of us has the opportunity to share our essence with all those we meet along our path, sending our blessings of Light and love to all that which we both do and do not understand.

Let us remember that the Universe will always show us the path to BEAUTY WITHIN the GRACE. We only have to remain open to the guidance and bring the hope to each thought, every conversation, and in all of our conscious actions.

Be thy Light.

Day 1
BEAUTY~ As the hummingbird drinks the nectar from the flower, the BEAUTY that surrounds the flower and this creature of the Universe is an expression of grace. As the ducks glide across the water, our eyes witness complete perfection in the BEAUTY of the ripples that spread over the smooth surface. These moments of solitude surround us always; we need only open our hearts to the experience. Let us bask in the essence of what is and be a part of life's graceful movements. By allowing this opening, the inner turmoil and havoc of the mind can be minimized and used as lessons for that which brings us joy and that which does not. Let us be the BEAUTY that we came here to be, blessing all that you and I encounter today and always.

~ I AM the BEAUTY that was created by the Universe, and the joy of that BEAUTY surrounds me always.

146

Blessings of Unconditional Love are sent to you today. May you see the BEAUTY in all of life's creations.

~~~~~~~~~

Day 2

GRACE~ Sky of blue, clouds of white; your movement so fluid and true. Birds that sing in the cool summer breeze, a voice as sweet as the morning dew. Let us lift up our eyes, in love and GRACE, with gratitude for this moment. Let us embrace the beauty and the glory of everything we see as the amazing GRACE surrounds us. May the Light surround each of us today as we hold the blessings of life deep within our hearts, surrendering to the GRACE of the Universe.

~ I AM filled with the GRACE of the Universe. I share love and compassion with the world around me.

~~~~~~~~~

Blessings of Openness are sent to you today. May your heart and mind be open to the GRACE that surrounds every part of your journey.

~~~~~~~~~

Day 3

SERENELY~ Let us take a moment and breathe in the knowledge that we are being guided in this journey of life. Let us look up at the sky that is above us and find comfort that we are not alone. When we have moments of inner peace, then that which surrounds us will flow SERENELY. Let us reach for the space of tranquility to connect to that which we are…which is love. May we walk forward SERENELY and choose to follow our inner guidance through the chaos that we encounter. Each of us can bring more love and hope into the world with our presence every day. It is through this that the world around us will become SERENELY beautiful in all things that we experience.

~ I AM choosing to follow my inner guidance through the chaos and to walk forward SERENELY in the world.

Blessings of Grace are sent to you today. May your heart be filled with peace that you greet every moment of our journey SERENELY.

Day 4

TWILIGHT~ In the TWILIGHT of the day, the promise of hope lingers in the air; this moment between light and darkness, where there is a shift that opens our mind to the world of possibilities. There is beauty in the night as well as the day, but we often grow weary with the harshness that we see. TWILIGHT is but a time when we can catch our breath and steal away for a moment; to be present, to be conscious of all that we are here to be and do. Let us take this time to breathe in the essence of who we are. Each of us is a divine being with a beautiful soul. We are loved, cherished, and honored in the light, in the night, and in the TWILIGHT.

~ I AM present and partaking in a conscious moment of reflection. I step into the opening of the TWILIGHT, and I am guided to my essence.

Blessings of Hope are sent to you today. May you find peace in the moments of TWILIGHT and dusk to rest your heart, mind, and soul.

Day 5

EVERYTHING~ Our thoughts, words, and actions impact EVERYTHING around us. Let us be the Light that shines wherever we reside. Let us choose the higher thought over the one that is lacking in love and possibility. Let us be the person that others come to for insight and hope; not the one that speaks with a tone of fear and negativity. We are one with EVERYTHING that we see and do not see. The essence of you and I is pure unconditional love; let us be in tune with that inner wisdom where EVERYTHING is possible. It is here that we attract more moments of grace, compassion, love, and joy.

~ I AM one with EVERYTHING that I see and do not see. I send love to all
that is.

~~~~~~~~~

Blessings of Possibilities are sent to you today. May you be the hope and
Light in EVERYTHING that you do and say.

~~~~~~~~~

Day 6
GRACIOUSLY~ When we read the stories of the spiritual teachers who
have walked before us, we recognize a common theme. Each of them
demonstrated how to traverse GRACIOUSLY through life with their actions
and words. They treated those who were sick, poor or outcasts with love and
compassion. They GRACIOUSLY forgave those who treated them unkindly
or accused them of wrongful acts. Their hearts did not close in hatred or
anger for the injustice of that which they saw or experienced. They lived
with an inner, pure wisdom that all creatures and people should be loved
wholly; bearing witness to the fact that through unconditional love, the heart
may always be receptive to the miracles of life. May each of us live with a
heart that is open GRACIOUSLY to that which we do not understand but
knowing with godly wisdom that each of us needs to be loved
unconditionally. It is through this unconditional love and walking in grace,
that the miracles will unfold before us.

~ I AM walking GRACIOUSLY through every moment in life with
unconditional love.

~~~~~~~~~

Blessings of Truth are sent to you today. May you be GRACIOUSLY open
to all that lies before you.

~~~~~~~~~

Day 7
UNSTOPPABLE~ Together we can change the world and fill it with acts of
kindness and love. Let us create a home where songs are of joy and stories
are of hope. Let us come together and create the miracles that can heal this

149

planet. We can choose to be UNSTOPPABLE; a team sharing our love and Light with every creature and being that walks upon the Earth. Let us lay down our anger and extend a hand in peace. Let us surround hate with compassion and offer understanding for all of our misgivings. Together we could be united, embracing our differences with the wisdom of the Universe. Let us see each other as sisters and brothers, opening our hearts to the possibilities of hope, for we are a family that has the potential to be UNSTOPPABLE. Where there is poverty we can create abundance, where there is hatred we can be the love, where there is war, there can be peace, and where there is darkness, we can experience amazing Light. Let us come together and be UNSTOPPABLE in the hope and grace of all things today and always.

~ I AM taking actions that are filled with UNSTOPPABLE love for the world I call home.

~~~~~~~~

Blessings of Unity are sent to you today. May you be aligned to create UNSTOPPABLE actions of love and compassion.

~~~~~~~~

Notes

Image captured by Susan Gossett.

Week 21
Attention to Gratitude

~~~~~~~

Blessings of Unconditional Love are sent to you today. May you shift your Attention to Gratitude in each word that you speak and every action that you take.

~~~~~~~

When you and I focus our attention on consciously bringing love and compassion into every conversation and action, gratitude becomes abundant in our journey.

Our circumstances mirror what we believe is possible as we bring more of who we are to the world. Our generosity comes from a heart of intentional contribution, and our journey becomes abundant with vibrant colors, true depth, and richness that we realize we came here to experience.

Each of us may experience moments when we wake and know that we aren't ourselves. It may be caused by lack of sleep or a deadline that is looming. An excellent way to raise the vibrations within you is to create a thankful state of being.

As you place your feet on the floor, say, 'Thank you for the shelter that is above my head.' As you brush your teeth say, 'Thank you for the running water and that my basic needs are met.' As you drive your kids to school or head off to work say, 'Thank you for my loved ones and that I am able to provide for them.'

This simple tool of gratitude does wonders to shift one's perspective to the blessings that surround us. Let us choose to be the love in everything we do. Let us open our hearts, even where we may have resistance because of fear. Let us share the gifts that are uniquely ours to give to the world.

Let us focus our attention on gratitude this week, placing our intentions on being in a conscious state of thankfulness for our unique journey upon this planet.

You and I are responsible for the energy that we bring to each situation and what our spirit brings to the world around us. Let us consciously shift our attention into a state of true gratefulness. It is through our ATTENTION TO GRATITUDE that our world can shift into a place of abundance with love and joy for everyone.

Be thy Light.

Day 1
GRATITUDE~ In the early morning light as the rays of sun beam down upon the Earth let us take a moment in GRATITUDE for this new day that we have been given. As the birds soar in the wind and the fish swim in the depths of the ocean, let us be thankful for that which we are witnessing on our journey. Beauty and grace surround our lives so let us live in a state of GRATITUDE. It is in the remembering that we stay present. We appreciate that which is before us when we fully embrace the miracle of life. Each of our journeys is a unique blessing. Let us begin our day with complete and utter GRATITUDE for all that was, all that is and all that will be.

~ I AM living a life of GRATITUDE in each and every moment.

~~~~~~~~

Blessings of Awareness are sent to you today. May you live every moment in GRATITUDE for there is always something to be grateful for in your journey.

~~~~~~~~

153

Day 2

ATTENTION~ Let us begin our day by focusing within, taking this moment to connect with the power of the Universe and ourselves. Let us center our heart, mind, and soul; and place our ATTENTION on who we are and what our journeys represent in this world. By taking this moment and feeling the gratitude for all that we are experiencing, our journeys are enriched. Life is a blessing filled with unique experiences that have molded us into who we are at this moment. Our ATTENTION to the intention of our day and our life assists us in creating the life we know we should be living. As we embrace the day, let us aim our ATTENTION on the actions that will bring more love and Light into the world. Let us be grateful for all that is, was, and will be.

~ I AM focusing my ATTENTION on the intention of my day and the Light I am sharing with the world.

Blessings of Intention are sent to you today. May you place your ATTENTION on the love that you can bring to each situation.

Day 3

CIRCUMSTANCES~ The CIRCUMSTANCES of our past may have brought sorrow, but it is through these experiences of contrast that we evolve into our conscious selves. It is when we focus on the pain of yesterday or let the CIRCUMSTANCES of the past define who we are that we give our power away. We stifle the power of joy in the present moment when we live in the past. Let us embrace and accept our past for the lessons that result from the ebb and flow. Let us focus on the blessings and trust that all is unfolding according to the Universe's timing. Let us empower the present moment by lifting up today with hope to greet a bright tomorrow - the tomorrow that we envision and we know should be our reality. Let the CIRCUMSTANCES of yesterday guide us today so that you and I can embrace a hopeful future.

~ I AM holding my CIRCUMSTANCES with gratitude for all that I am learning from the ebb and flow.

Blessings of Trust are sent to you today. May you bring the Light to your CIRCUMSTANCES with love and compassion.

~~~~~~~~~

Day 4

COLORS~ Our lives are filled with the COLORS that bring dark and bright hues to our world. They always enrich our journey and experience. COLORS are magic in the air, just waiting for life to appear. They bring new images - dark, light, dull, or bright - but they are all part of life. COLORS are an element of life, no matter their shade or name. They each have the purpose of bringing new experiences to our world. Each hue is a gift to our eyes, enriching our planet with their constant presence and blessings. Let us be grateful for the COLORS that enhance the beauty of all that we see from the sun to the moon on each day to a world of many various shades.

~ I AM part of all the COLORS that make up the world, and I hold the various hues in my heart at all times.

~~~~~~~~~

Blessings of Gratefulness are sent to you today. May you see all the brilliant COLORS that your journey is bringing to you.

~~~~~~~~~

Day 5

CONTRIBUTION~ Today, as we prepare for our day, let us look into the mirror and appreciate our journey. Let us honor how you and I are striving to bring a CONTRIBUTION to the world around us. Let us see beyond our imperfections, and be thankful as we peer into ourselves to seek the clarity that has been disposed to us over time. Let us express gratitude for the moments when we have spoken with grace and compassion during our communication with others. Let us smile at our reflection in appreciation for all the moments of love. Let us acknowledge the responsibility that you and I are accepting by making a unique CONTRIBUTION to this planet. Now let us take on the day with more love and continue to give our daily CONTRIBUTION of the very best of ourselves.

~ I AM making my highest CONTRIBUTION to the world in all that I think, say and do.

~~~~~~~

Blessings of Gratitude are sent to you today. May your CONTRIBUTION to the world be from a state of higher consciousness.

~~~~~~~

Day 6

GENEROSITY~ Each of us desires a life of prosperity. The definition of prosperity may vary for each of us, but we all want to live a life of abundance in love, health, joy, and peace. The essence of who we are does not wish to suffer and struggle in this journey. If you and I speak to individuals who are at peace in the journey, we find that they all believe in GENEROSITY; they are generous with acceptance, love, gifts, money, and time. Again the definition of GENEROSITY may be different for each of us, but in our hearts, we know what it is that we should share with those around us. Let us find our truth in those moments when we feel that we are lacking and our perception focuses on scarcity, for every moment is meant to have abundance that is shared with others. The wisdom comes with the changing of our perception and living in gratitude. Let us renew our GENEROSITY today.

~ I AM taking actions of GENEROSITY today. I share that which I AM moved to give to the world.

~~~~~~~

Blessings of Abundance are sent to you today. May you truly see the gifts that you are here to share in GENEROSITY.

~~~~~~~

Day 7

REACH~ As we awaken and greet the day let us REACH out with gratefulness for the relationships in our lives; the ones that are effortless and supply laughter; and those that are challenging and bring tears, resulting in more clarity. Each relationship serves as a catalyst, prompting us to REACH for that which aids us in our expansion. The vast array of emotions that we experience through engagement in these relationships helps us to expand into the essence of who we are. The empathy and sympathy that we encounter through our interactions with each other brings new depth and fortitude to our beings. It is by questioning the life we lead, that we find the answers that assist us to reach higher. Let us REACH for the love in all things, the good in others, the light amongst the darkness, and always the inspired thought.

~ I AM greeting each day in gratitude as I REACH for the love in all things.

~~~~~~~~

Blessings of Insight are sent to you today. May you REACH for the highest thoughts and actions as you journey through your life.

~~~~~~~~

Notes

Image captured by Susan Gossett.

Week 22
Certainty of Guidance

~~~~~~~~

Blessings of Knowing are sent to you today. May your journey transpire in the space of Certainty within the Guidance.

~~~~~~~~

You and I can always find peace in the silence, but it is essential during the challenging times to uncover moments of serenity. It is when we take the time to sit and listen, that the inner guidance may come in a wave of thought, a commercial on TV, a song on the radio or a conversation with others.

In my younger days, I did not have the knowledge or understanding that I could ask for assistance. Instead, I would complain, whine, cry, and yet never request guidance of the Higher Power or listen for the answers of the current dilemma. My reality reflected my disconnection with Spirit, which highlighted my lack of faith that the Universe was supporting me.

My pessimistic attitude brought me the outcome that I focused on and that I spoke about to others. I attracted individuals into my life with the same perspective because we supported each other's point of view. We would spend hours complaining about the things that were going wrong instead of focusing on what was right.

One day something changed, it was not one epiphany moment, but many, that began to change my perspective on life. I remember having this thought; *I am exhausted from complaining and the more I criticize, the more depleted I am. These actions or lack of actions aren't working. Something, anything, has to change.*

I noticed that many relationships faded away, or I had to limit the amount of time I spent with particular individuals. I found that I couldn't pull myself out of the negativity when I was surrounded by it. I stepped back and began working on the inner me.

My alone time focused on creating, and it was in this space that I filled my life with more joy and peace. My soul soon possessed a deep comfort, and I found more reasons to smile. My perspective on life changed, and I began to understand the power of thoughts and words.

When we focus on finding peace within, we become aligned with that which is greater than you and I. Our relationship strengthens with the silence; the listening ear becomes in tune, and the interpretation identifies explicit action that should be taken. This is how we create a life of more joy and compassion.

Let us open our hearts into the knowing that awaits us and place our intentions on the certainty that the Universe always supports us. Let us be conscious of the thoughts that form as words are spoken for they have the power to awaken the guidance that is waiting for us. It is our responsibility to ask, listen, and to take action when the opportunities arise.

You and I are creating a masterpiece on this journey. May we create a path with beauty and love that focuses upon our CERTAINTY in the GUIDANCE within every moment.

Be thy Light.

Day 1
GUIDANCE~ As we awake each morning upon our journey, let us ask for GUIDANCE throughout the day, that our thoughts may be compassionate, and the words that we speak bring more love and Light to those around us. May we strive to awaken our minds from the noisy chatter each day, and

consciously endeavor to be more present and aware than we were yesterday. It is through conscious thoughts and actions that we can bring more grace into the world. The GUIDANCE comes in the stillness, when we are present and living in the now. It comes in various forms such as a fluttering butterfly, the smile of a stranger, the words that you read, and in an intuitive thought. The GUIDANCE is always there, even in the moments of contrast - we need only to follow our heart.

~ I AM eternally guided. The GUIDANCE of the Universe is always there.

~~~~~~~

Blessings of Stillness are sent to you today. May you be in tune to the inner GUIDANCE that is with you in every moment.

~~~~~~~

Day 2

ALWAYS~ You and I are ALWAYS loved and supported by the Universe. This support applies to everything that we do, including the decisions and actions that we make towards our dreams. You and I are ALWAYS connected to everything and everyone around us. All of the words that we speak and the actions that we place out in the world are woven together as one. Let us choose them with love and our inner wisdom, in order to spread more kindness into the world in which we live. You and I manifest and create the world that we live in through the past of our yesterdays, the present of today, and the future of our tomorrows. May we feel the love and kindness that ALWAYS surrounds us in each and every moment.

~ I AM ALWAYS supported and guided by the Universe.

~~~~~~~

Blessings of Connection are sent to you today. May you be in tune to the Universal guidance that surrounds you ALWAYS.

~~~~~~~

Day 3

ANSWERS~ You and I, from the moment that we could put words together, began asking questions. Questions regarding the whys and hows of the lives that had been placed in front of our eyes. The majority of us were never told

161

that the ANSWERS to our questions lie within our hearts; to follow the Light within us, that the ANSWERS are given to us in the silence when we tune into that which is all things. The world around us spends so much time seeking and not being in the present moment. Let us be in this moment as this poem gives us guidance:

> Star, star that I see. How you shine your light on me. Will you tell the secrets of this life to me? Child, child you silly being. The answers aren't hidden from you to see. It lies within each of you, pure and true, this is the key, but you're so busy the truth can't find you. So lie on the grass and breathe in the dew until the calmness finds you. The ANSWERS will appear this I promise my dear.

~ I AM one with the stillness that holds the ANSWERS and guidance to my journey.

~~~~~~~~

Blessings of Wisdom are sent to you today. May you be open to the Universal guidance that leads to all of the ANSWERS you seek.

~~~~~~~~

Day 4

ASK~ Let us not sit and worry about things or situations over which we have no control. Let us not stress when things don't go according to our plans. The Universe is always assisting in our journey; guiding and supporting us. Let us release the worry and ASK for clarification or answers we are seeking. Let us ASK and be guided as we go out into the world, remaining present for the answers and clarification. We must let go of the result or the 'how' that only the Universe can provide. If we believe the doors will open, the possibilities will arise, we only need to keep the hope that all is working out perfectly. Let us ASK with a heart of belief and gratitude for our unique journey that we are experiencing.

~ I AM the hope that believes that all things are possible as I ASK of the Universe.

Blessings of Clarification are sent to you today. May you be clear in the questions that you ASK and may you act upon the intuitive guidance that is given.

Day 5

CERTAINTY~ Life is always changing and evolving with each breath that we take. It is with CERTAINTY that when you and I work against the flow of change, it is followed by discord and inner turmoil. It is when we are open to change that we evolve and continue to expand our spiritual growth. It is with CERTAINTY that by living with an open heart and embracing moments of silence, our journey will be enhanced through the guidance of the Universe. Let us go into the world with the CERTAINTY that we are being supported in all ways to evolve into the highest state of our being.

~ I AM with CERTAINTY, guided and supported by the Universe in my journey.

~~~~~~~~

Blessings of Openness are sent to you today. May you live each moment in CERTAINTY that you are always guided in your journey.

~~~~~~~~

Day 6

CHALLENGE~ Let our dreams CHALLENGE us to be the best that we can be. Let you and I choose to be bold in our choices today, and to step through fear, conquering that which we came here to achieve. Let us close our eyes and take a deep breath into our bodies, the breath expands and contracts as we become aware of this present moment. The CHALLENGE that you and I encounter as we bring our dreams to fruition will bring our journey to a greater depth, enriching the essence of who we are. Let us not look at the CHALLENGE with doubt or fear, but know that we are guided by the Universe with every move that we make. Despite all the obstacles, let us believe that the answers will be shown to us in perfect timing.

~ I AM embracing the CHALLENGE for I am always supported by the
Universe.

~~~~~~~~

Blessings of Faith are sent to you today. May you greet each CHALLENGE
with an open heart and mind, knowing that you are always guided.

~~~~~~~~

Day 7

CONFIDENCE~ Today and every day we should walk forth in
CONFIDENCE for we are always guided by the Universe. Let us ask for
guidance in our journey and to be open to our inner wisdom when making
decisions throughout our day. Let us listen with CONFIDENCE that the
intuitive thoughts will lead us step by step, and bring us closer to our goals
and dreams. Each of us must walk forward in CONFIDENCE that our paths
are being guided and that our spiritual journeys will be filled with more joy,
happiness, peace, love, and grace in every situation. Today we walk forth
with CONFIDENCE.

~ I AM walking forth with CONFIDENCE that the Universe is always
guiding and supporting me.

~~~~~~~~

Blessings of Awareness are sent to you today. May your words and actions
be surrounded in CONFIDENCE because you are always supported and
guided.

~~~~~~~~

Notes

Image captured by Tim Chinn.

Week 23
Harmonious Moments

~~~~~~~~~

Blessings of Peace are sent to you today. May you be the creator of
Harmonious Moments wherever your journey may lead you.

~~~~~~~~~

Stress is that which causes emotional or mental tension in your
circumstances and may vary from person to person. It is those moments
when concern and uncertainty creep into every corner of the room, and the
more you attempt to corral or control the cause, the more profound the
feeling becomes. We begin to long for moments of harmony, but somehow
the stress is a heavy-laden blanket we cannot put down.

In these moments, you and I have to take the time to re-center, even if we
feel that it will cause more tension. When we are that frazzled, we only feed
the chaotic energy instead of assisting in diffusing it.

Once we have stepped away, it is essential to shift our focus to something in
nature and bring all of our senses to becoming one with it. It can be the

166

trickle of water, placing your feet on the ground, focusing on a tree, or one of my favorites, becoming one with the sun.

I begin becoming one with the sun by feeling its rays on my skin, the warmth that I can experience without even touching it. I can see its power by all that grows around me, including the food that I take into my body for nutrition. I can view its beauty as it rises in the morning or sets at the end of the day. It is when I become one with the sun that I am no longer focusing on the issue at hand. My heartbeat is no longer elevated, and I have found a moment of harmony.

It is here that we can consciously choose to see the hope and Light, and bring peace back into the current experience by finding it within ourselves.

Stress comes from the uncertainty of that which we cannot control and the unraveling of that which does not go as planned. We need only to remember that these are our teachable moments to assist us in our expansion.

There is no need to worry about tomorrow for it has not yet been determined. It does not serve us to think of days gone because we cannot change that which has already occurred. When you and I spend our time in the past or the future we are missing the present moment.

Instead of spending energy on all that we cannot control, let us focus on creating harmony in every situation we encounter today. Let us be conscious creators of love and compassion in our journey, choosing to share our Light with the world. We can create and become the HARMONIOUS MOMENTS in every situation.

Be thy Light.

Day 1
BELIEFS~ Each of us has core BELIEFS, and our decisions should be made around those every day. When you and I go against our BELIEFS. we are out of harmony with the soul of who we are. You and I came into the world as peaceful and loving beings. We came here to share our Light, and the grace of the Universe with all that inhabit this world. When we are not in tune to that which we believe, we feel at odds with all that is around us. Let us take a moment to reflect on our core BELIEFS, on the essence of who we truly are. Does the life we are living mirror that which we believe? You and I have been given this moment, this lifetime, to share Light and love. Let us not live in discord with the essence of our souls.

167

~ I AM living a life and making choices that reflect that of my core
BELIEFS.

~~~~~~~

Blessings of Faith are sent to you today. May you be in tune to your core
BELIEFS and live each moment in harmony with them.

~~~~~~~

Day 2

HARMONIOUS~ It may seem like a daunting task to live a
HARMONIOUS life with everything that makes up the planet; to be in
balance with the creatures, the atmosphere, the ecosystem, our fellow beings,
and even ourselves. How is it possible for all things and beings to live and
thrive in harmony? The answer to the dilemma is for each of us to live and
make decisions from the truth of who we are. We must make decisions from
our higher selves and a place of love for all of Creation. When we live our
lives from a place of Universal Light, our thoughts will be with the infinite
possibilities of a better world. Our words will be spoken through wisdom
and hope to one another, despite all that has taken place in the past. Our
actions of love will be the catalyst for raising the vibration of our planet
today. We have all had times in our lives where we have witnessed
HARMONIOUS moments; ones in which all things and beings came
together in love, and peace surrounded all those involved. These are
moments of grace that pass by quickly, but they are blessings for us to
witness. Let us envision these moments as the norm instead of the exception.
Let us do all things from a place of love. Let us be the catalyst for creating
more HARMONIOUS moments today in this amazing world that surrounds
us.

~ I AM HARMONIOUS with the Universal Light and everything that makes
up our planet as I walk my personal path.

~~~~~~~

Blessings of Peace are sent to you today. May you be open to every
possibility of living a HARMONIOUS and peaceful life.

~~~~~~~

Day 3

UNCERTAINTY~ You and I may experience many moments of UNCERTAINTY in our lives. It is easy in those moments, to fight against that which we do not want or desire in our world. We do not know what will cross our path during our journey, but we can choose our perception of, and reaction to, our experiences. When we are open to all things in life and allow them to pass over, and through us, we continue to grow and expand into our essence. It is through negative thoughts, words, and actions that the experience lingers and surrounds our being, transforming the moment into one filled with anger, sadness, or hopelessness. In the moment of UNCERTAINTY, let us begin to focus on the positive and the Light that is within us; instead of fighting against the current, let us flow with the moment. Let us give gratitude for the simplest things and hope will begin to stream into our world once more. Anger and sadness prosper in darkness and negativity; let us choose to thrive in a state of love in our mind, body, heart, and soul. It is through the UNCERTAINTY of life that we can expand, grow, and have more clarity as we reach a peaceful state of being. Let us choose to shine our inner Light today and bring more love and peace into the world.

~ I AM shining my Light on the moments of UNCERTAINTY and expanding into my essence with each experience.

~~~~~~~~

Blessings of Knowing are sent to you today. May you greet the moments of UNCERTAINTY with a remembrance that you are here to expand into your true essence.

~~~~~~~~

Day 4

UNDOING~ Each of our lives flows through ups and downs, and moments of UNDOING that shake the foundation of what we think we know. Let us learn from the spider in its determination and perseverance. Each morning the intricate web of the spider appears on sunny paths, and as individuals walk by, they mindlessly wipe away the creative masterpiece. Without fail the spider's home appears the following morning to greet the sun again. This eight-legged creature is diligent and resolute in its purpose, unwavering in its duty to create a space it calls home. Though the forces around destroy his work and livelihood, he moves forward creating his haven. What constitutes our UNDOING, and how can we find peace in the process? Are we as persistent and determined as the spider or do we falter when things do not go as planned? Let us be the essence of our truth, living and moving through each moment of the UNDOING of that over which we have no control, seeking joy and following our hearts in the process.

~ I AM moving through the UNDOING of that which I cannot control and embrace the joy of following my heart to my essence.

~~~~~~~~

Blessings of Perseverance are sent to you today. May you greet the moments of UNDOING with an open heart of acceptance and compassion.

~~~~~~~~

Day 5
UNION~ When we are not in UNION with our heart, mind, body, and soul, there is discord within. Each of us finds happiness and peace within this UNION, which allows us to follow our truth for the highest good. When decisions are made from this peaceful place, we are in harmony with everything that surrounds us. When we choose to live our lives from the perspective of the ego, we will only long for more; thereby creating a void which cannot be filled. It is when we live in UNION with our truth that the heart, mind, body, and soul fluently align and nurture peace within our beings.

~ I AM in UNION with my essence, living each moment in truth and striving for the highest good.

Blessings of Alignment are sent to you today. May you be in tune to the inner wisdom that brings UNION to every aspect of your life.

~~~~~~~~~

Day 6
HARMONY~ May our lives be filled with HARMONY, and all aspects of our lives produce a unity with one another as a whole. The HARMONY of the Universe is our teacher. The more we are present and conscious of our choices, and how they affect the world around us, the wiser we become. Let us witness the miracles of life that take place in every moment and live in HARMONY with one another.

~ I AM living a life of HARMONY with the world around me.

~~~~~~~~~

Blessings of Understanding are sent to you today. May you be open to the wisdom that guides you to live each moment in HARMONY.

~~~~~~~~~

Day 7
UNIQUE~ Each of us is a UNIQUE being who came here to experience life within the vessel of our individual bodies. Our perceptions of what we see and experience, write the story from where we gain our inner wisdom. The creatures and plants in this world are also UNIQUE; they, too, came here to fulfill their purpose. Although we are each UNIQUE, the one thing that we have in common is that we are each striving to fulfill our soul's purpose. Let us not step on one another in competition, or dominate those who are unable to protect themselves. Let us choose to walk through the world with love and compassion. Let us embrace our essence with the intention that each footprint we leave bears the mark of a united truth.

~ I AM a UNIQUE being who shares my love and compassion with the world around me.

~~~~~~~~

Blessings of Unity are sent to you today. May you consciously embrace that every sentient being is here to shine their UNIQUE Light upon the world.

~~~~~~~~

Notes

Image captured by Susan Gossett.

Week 24
Embracing Intention

~~~~~~~~

Blessings of Consciousness are sent to you today. May your heart be clear as your actions Embrace your Intentions.

~~~~~~~~

Our desire for harmony and peace for those that we know, or those we do not know, embodies our human compassion for the world. We all have basic physical, emotional, and spiritual needs. Each of us desires to share our love and to be loved for the uniqueness we came here to be.

Love without conditions begins in our hearts, by choosing to forgive ourselves for the shortfalls of our yesterdays, and expands to include the actions of others. We do this as a gift to ourselves, because a connection to one another is key to raising the Universal Consciousness.

When we embrace the power of intentions, the seeds of our heart are being planted out into the world. Our desires bring clarity to that which we know we came here to be and do in the world. You and I came here in love, to be loved, and to share the love.

174

My life began to change when I came to understand the difference between intentions as opposed to goals and dreams. One's goals and dreams are in the future and are what we are working towards, but our intentions are in the present moment, the now. Intention places conscious energy into your thoughts, words, and actions more powerful.

It was one of those epiphany moments when I leaned back into my chair, and it all became clear. *If I do the same thing, but with intention, my dreams will come into fruition faster and with more ease.*

I began creating a word for each day to assist me in remembering my daily intention. Placing the word within an, 'I am' affirmation encouraged my actions to become clear and focused.

Even during a stressful event, I would center myself with the repetition of my affirmation. It grounded me, and through time I began to see that my actions were bringing the corresponding dreams and goals into reality.

Let us use the power of intention to create our heaven upon Earth, to have the basic needs met for all that inhabit the planet. Together we can focus our intentions on creating a world of peace and harmony. You and I can create a world of compassion for all. Let us consciously contribute to this miracle by EMBRACING our INTENTIONS.

Be thy Light.

Day 1
EMBRACE~ When a family member is in pain, you and I EMBRACE them with our hearts in a loving and supporting way. When we hear someone crying in grief, sorrow or loss, we EMBRACE their journey with empathy and reach out to help with a gentle hand. We have listened to the woes of another and, when called upon, assisted those in need. Do we give the same empathy and love to ourselves when our personal journey has brought us sorrow or pain? You and I must also EMBRACE our own unique path with kindness, love, and gentleness – acknowledging all that we are striving to be. Each of us are of Light and love, longing only to reflect hearts filled with love. Let us EMBRACE all that we are, the essence of our uniqueness, in each and every moment.

~ I AM able to EMBRACE all with unconditional love. The Light of the Universe shines through me.

Blessings of Compassion are sent to you today. May your heart EMBRACE forgiveness for all those moments in life when you and I falter.

Day 2

ARISING~ Are we ARISING to what the Universe brings to you and I; or are we stifled by our limiting thoughts of frustration and doubt? You and I must embrace the challenges in life to evolve into the essence of who we are. It is through the diversity of life that we find clarity and focus. If you and I are ARISING to that which is around us, then we are ARISING to our highest self. If we keep peace within our hearts, then we will bring this peace to each and every situation that we encounter. Let each of us keep ARISING to all that we are.

~ I AM ARISING to the essence of my truth. My heart is ever-expanding with possibility.

Blessings of Clarity are sent to you today. May you be aligned with the Universe for you are always ARISING into the greatest version of you. Be the peace and wisdom in every situation.

Day 3

BEGINNING~ The sun flashes a goodbye upon the horizon and, at that moment between sun and moon, there is the prelude that we call dusk. It comes and goes in an instant as one says goodbye and the other hello. Our lives are in constant motion with endings that may abound, but it is important to remember that each goodbye can be that of a BEGINNING. When we awake in the morning, it is a gift, a new BEGINNING to achieve that which we are striving to share with the world and a chance to raise our vibrations a bit higher than yesterday. You and I make choices each day of what our priorities are going to be. Let us not wait for the perfect moment, for we may never see that perceived time. Today is the moment for a new BEGINNING, in which to renew the heartfelt choices, to dust off the vessel brimming with passion, and to be more of whom we came here to be.

~ I AM BEGINNING that which I came here to do and be. I choose that which my heart knows is true.

~~~~~~~~

Blessings of Awakened Perception are sent to you today. May each ending bring you comfort, in knowing, that a new BEGINNING is awaiting your journey.

~~~~~~~~

Day 4

CLARITY~ When we communicate with others, often the differences are more apparent than the similarities. The situations and relationships that bring you and I contrast are also the ones that bring us more CLARITY. Let us seek the truth by being open to the CLARITY of the situation. Let us embrace each person we meet with a heart that is open to what they may have to teach us. Let us seek the CLARITY in each experience.

~ I AM open to the CLARITY of each situation that I encounter in my life.

~~~~~~~~

Blessings of Inner Wisdom are sent to you today. May you tune into the CLARITY that awaits you with each experience.

~~~~~~~~

Day 5

DESIRE~ The DESIRE that whispers to us in the middle of the night and urges us to strive towards our dreams is the reminder of why we are here. The photograph, saying, or the moment of reminiscing about our passion is not an accident but a sign that we should move forward along our path. The DESIRE that is within our heart will not disappear with time. It will only be surrounded by regret for those steps that you and I did not take; for the dream that we did not follow and bring into the world. Let us embrace the DESIRE that is running through us and create that which brings joy to the world. Let us take action today.

~ I AM acting and bringing to fruition the DESIRE that is within my heart.

Blessings of Guidance are sent to you today. May the DESIRE within you bring action and movement to your life's purpose.

Day 6

HEART~ Let us take a moment to listen to the rhythm of our HEART. Our HEART is a miracle that lives inside each of us that leads us in our journey to our passion. It guides us at all times; to hear the guidance of the HEART, we need only to sit and listen and tune into its messages. Let us trust this inner wisdom to assist us in living our truth. Let us listen to the whispers of our HEART, for it will not lead us astray.

~ I AM listening to the guidance of my HEART in this present moment.

Blessings of Self-Love are sent to you today. May you be open to the wisdom of your HEART and all that you came here to experience.

Day 7

INTENTIONS~ Our INTENTIONS for today and tomorrow, no matter how big or small, are supported by the Universe. When we focus on our desires and the passion that is within our hearts, synchronicities manifest, doors begin to open, and the love that surrounds us becomes more apparent. The purpose of this very moment – the destiny that you and I are fulfilling each and every day – is a reflection of our highest INTENTIONS. The fulfillment of our destiny is supported by the love within our hearts and that we send out into the world and now is our opportunity; to be the driver, the sailor, the rider, and the creator of that destiny. Today let us set our INTENTIONS high and ride upon the wave of love that awaits us.

~ I AM setting my INTENTIONS to share all things from the heart of my being.

~~~~~~~

Blessings of Clarity are sent to you today. May your INTENTIONS be clear as you speak words and take actions throughout your day.

~~~~~~~

Notes

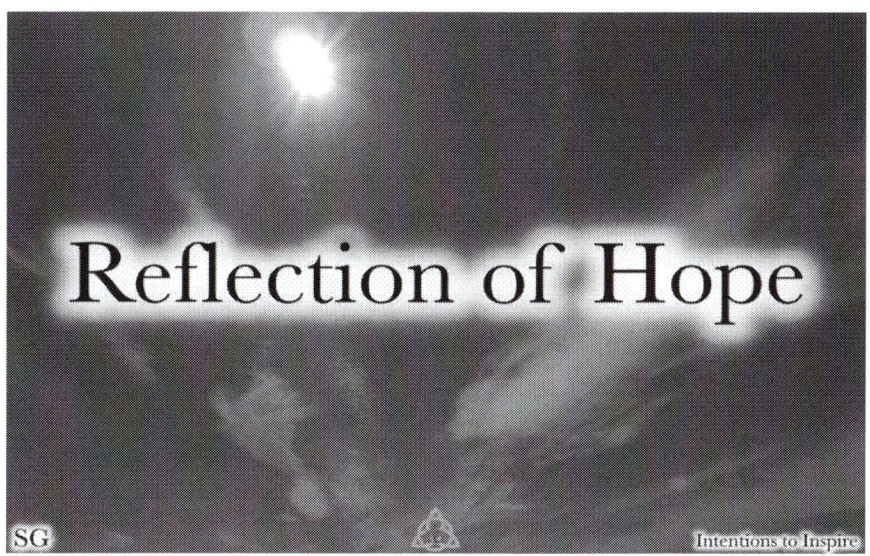

Image captured by Susan Gossett.

Week 25
Reflection of Hope

~~~~~~~~~

Blessings of Faith are sent to you today. May you be present in your Reflections of Hope that you share with the world.

~~~~~~~~~

When you and I live life with faith, it brings hope to every moment, a knowing that we are supported and guided, always and in all ways. When life does not go as planned, when it appears unfair and cruel, and when we find ourselves in our darkest and most difficult moments, our faith leads us to the Light, where hope lives.

We have the ability to witness faith in others, and we can hear them speak of hope, but our personal faith and level of trust comes from our connection with the Higher Power. No one can feed our soul or give us hope. It is ours to nurture and to bring into every aspect of our life.

It is through moments of reflection that the perfect opportunities arise to give us a time to clarify and to assess the feelings that dominate our world. Do we live our days in fear and worry, or do we focus on love by envisioning a world with more forgiveness and compassion? Are we waking with aspirations to bring the best version of ourselves to the day? Are we giving our soul the necessary quiet moments that bring peace, clarity, and fulfillment into our lives?

Our faith is a direct reflection of the hope that we have in our life. The trust that we have is mirrored in the words that we say and in our perspective of others. It is the love that we give to ourselves and to all those in our lives. This is how we create peace and harmony within our inner and outer world.

Together we can create a planet filled with more love by shining our Light wherever we journey. Let us consciously contribute by living a life full of faith and hope. Let our lives be a REFLECTION OF HOPE.

Be thy Light.

Day 1
HOPE~ When we lose HOPE, all seems lost and impossible. It is important that we take the time to keep our HOPE alive and that we nurture the Light within us to keep this energy strong. How you and I nurture our faith may vary immensely, so let us tune into what renews our sense of HOPE at this moment. A poem follows to inspire us as we reflect:

> There is a feeling within me, and it won't disappear. It is the essence of me and why I care. No matter the words that I hear of doubt or despair; I will embrace this feeling and not live in fear. It bubbles and rises flowing over the rim until the Light shines from deep within. So please, take a moment to reflect and embrace the feelings of HOPE and renew the possibilities of Universal Grace.

~ I AM the reflection of HOPE and possibility in my thoughts, words, and actions.

~~~~~~~~

Blessings of Inner Light are sent to you today. May you know the Universal love and HOPE that surrounds each moment of your journey.

~~~~~~~~

Day 2
CLARIFY~ When we CLARIFY the negative thoughts that cloud our judgment, we find the clarity that each of us needs. It is when we filter

through our self-doubt to a place of self-love that our personal journey becomes an opportunity to live for the highest good. Let us take each moment and reach for the hope when all seems dark. It is in this space where clarity will come, and all will appear as a miracle which we can assist to create. Let us CLARIFY our thoughts, our hearts, and our minds through a filter of love today. The outcome will be a place of hope and clarity for all of our tomorrows.

~ I AM open to the guidance of the Universe to CLARIFY all that I need to assist my journey.

~~~~~~~~

Blessings of clarity are sent to you today. May you CLARIFY your thoughts, words, and actions as you bring your unique Light to every situation.

~~~~~~~~

Day 3
ENVISION~ Let us ENVISION all of those whom we love. They may be faces of the past or those we see every day, but they all hold a special place in our heart. Let us visualize the gathering of all of these loved ones coming together to support each other's journeys, smiling and holding hands. The joy is beaming from each of us because there is abundant and unconditional love in this space in which we have gathered. Let us ENVISION that this magnitude of love surrounds us in every moment as we walk in this world, sharing the gifts that only we can give to brighten the world with more love and Light. You and I can ENVISION that which we want to see and bring to fruition.

~ I AM all that I ENVISION. The unconditional love and support guides me always.

~~~~~~~~

Blessings of Guidance are sent to you today. May you be clear as you ENVISION all that you are capable of sharing with others.

~~~~~~~~

183

Day 4

FEELINGS~ Our lives are filled with an array of emotional FEELINGS. You and I know that the more positive vibrations that we experience, the better we feel. The experiences that make us joyful can leave us with an emotional high and a feeling of being fully present to the world around us. Whereas moments of darkness and loss can deplete us, resulting in feelings of hopelessness. The negative thoughts begin to creep in making our bodies feel heavy and lifeless. You and I have the choice to see life from the light or the darkness. We choose the FEELINGS that permeate our lives. We either choose to look at the positive in the darkest of times, or we choose to see the negative in the brightest. Today, as we walk out into the world, let us choose to shine our Light of love even if others may see only the clouds of the storm. Let us choose the possibilities, and embrace the FEELINGS of hope, as we view the world around us.

~ I AM choosing the FEELINGS of possibility and hope in every situation.

~~~~~~~~~

Blessings of Light are sent to you today. May you choose thoughts, words, and actions that bring FEELINGS of love, forgiveness, and compassion.

~~~~~~~~~

Day 5

FOCUS~ Let us FOCUS on the Light as the difficulties enter our world. Let us FOCUS on each step as we move forward in our journey, knowing that we must walk in love. Thoughts, words, and actions that make us feel good will lead us closer to the Light as we make the journey. Our task is to FOCUS on that which brings us to a higher level of consciousness. This is the beacon that keeps our path filled with hope. FOCUS on the hope, and this will lead us closer to the Light and love of all things.

~ I AM placing my FOCUS on the highest level of consciousness in every moment.

184

Blessings of Hope are sent to you today. May you FOCUS on that which brings more joy and Light to the world.

Day 6

FULFILLMENT~ We wake up each morning to a new day, and with that comes the opportunity to take a few more steps towards our dreams. Let us grasp the opportunity to live each moment from our passion; raising our vibrations higher, and allowing our smiles to become wider. It is when we live our truth that FULFILLMENT seeps into all aspects of our world. We become clearer and more joyful; our eyes sparkle as bright as the stars in a darkened sky. Let us place our intentions to be filled with grace in all that we do surrounding our every movement with FULFILLMENT. Let our lives be surrounded in hope for a life full of more joy and love, allowing ourselves to experience the FULFILLMENT of knowing that we are placing the highest intentions of love out into the world.

~ I AM placing my intentions of unconditional love out into the world, bringing FULFILLMENT to all aspects of my being.

Blessings of Truth are sent to you today. May your choices create a life that brings you deep, inner FULFILLMENT.

Day 7

ASPIRATION~ When you and I have the feelings of ASPIRATION within us, possibilities appear endless. The essence of each of us desires to live in and be surrounded by a world of compassion. When we are not in tune with our truth, our compassion is diminished, and all seems lost. You and I must raise our vibrations through activities that feed our soul. Rejuvenation may be found through such activities as walking in nature, meditation, prayer, writing, singing, being with animals, or many other avenues. It is with a foundation of faith that we walk through feelings of doubt, despair, and fear; yet at the same time, allow the ASPIRATION to bubble and rise, flowing over the rim into our lives, causing our Light to shine upon the world.

185

~ I AM living my life on a foundation of faith that gives me ASPIRATION and hope for a compassionate world.

~~~~~~~~

Blessings of Faith are sent to you today. May you be filled with the ASPIRATION to shine your Light brightly in the world.

~~~~~~~~

Notes

Image captured by Susan Gossett.

Week 26
Renewing the Song

~~~~~~~~

Blessings of Unconditional Love are sent to you today. May your actions lead you to Renewing the Song within you.

~~~~~~~~

Each of us has a unique and beautiful song we came here to share with the world. It is through our experiences that our lives become enriched with a deeper understanding of the importance of all we witness. Let us renew our faith in the possibility that you and I are here to share our unique song with all who cross our path and that together we can create beautiful music.

Life's sagas will include moments of expansion and contraction. We are here to embrace each of those by continuing to plant the seeds of love and compassion. To this we bring insight through our connection with the Higher Power, acting upon our inspired spontaneity to bring more Light into the world.

Let us establish through our renewed faith that we are capable of creating an environment of peace and harmony. It is only by coming together that we can build true collaborations with one another. It is in the space of our Oneness that our unique song can be joined with others to create a symphony of music for all.

Let us focus our attention on the music that we are creating, the seeds we are planting, and the energy we must keep renewing, to create a life of love and compassion. We are here to expand fully into our essence, to shine our Light brightly in the world, and to live our truth from a conscious state of being.

You and I must come together with openness to hear and see the beauty of our unique music. May our actions lead to RENEWING THE SONG of that which brings unity and hope to one another and the highest good for all.

Be thy Light.

Day 1
ENRICHED~ At some point in our personal journey, each of us will come to a crossroad; a moment when a decision has to be made, and we weigh all of the options. The status quo may seem tempting, but it is when we follow our heart that we find an ENRICHED life. It is when we share our talents with the world that we experience miracles and the Light within us shines brightly. Let us choose the options in life that are compassionate, giving and loving to each other and ourselves. Let us travel an ENRICHED journey that encourages others to do the same. Let this be the new status quo and the new norm for the world in which we live. Let us be inspired to reach for the ENRICHED life that we know we should be experiencing.

~ I AM living a life that is ENRICHED by the highest choices of my essence.

~~~~~~~~

Blessings of Renewal are sent to you today. May you take actions that bring your journey ENRICHED experiences of love and compassion.

~~~~~~~~

Day 2
INSIGHT~ The Universe is always guiding us in our personal journey and spiritual quest toward a state of being which is overflowing with abundant

189

peace, love, and hope. INSIGHT may come in various forms, such as the words from a stranger or the action of a friend. These may be the ways of the Universe that assist us to keep moving forward in our journey with hope. Let us not ignore the INSIGHT that bubbles up inside of our hearts as a result of these interactions, for it is a gift that provides us with more clarity. Let us not lose our hope when we are surrounded by that which we are unable to comprehend. Choose to trust, and allow the INSIGHT to come. Let us open our heart to receive the guidance; embracing the new step that moves our journey forward.

~ I AM open to the INSIGHT and guidance of the Universe in every moment.

~~~~~~~~

Blessings of Guidance are sent to you today. May your heart be open to the INSIGHT that bubbles up within you. Shine your Light brilliantly.

~~~~~~~~

Day 3
INSPIRE~ Let us reach for the encouraging thoughts to INSPIRE the world around us. If each of us were to reach for the highest thoughts of love, words of encouragement, and actions to create a better world, the barriers would come crumbling down. We each create the mountains within our mind through thoughts of negativity, hatred, anger, and bitterness. Let us choose to let go of that which does not serve the world in hope and love. Let us be the Light of every situation, even if it is only by sending silent blessings to the person who is speaking through a whirlwind of darkness. Let us INSPIRE others through our actions of love, Light, and compassion; serving as the Light that brightens the room with just a smile, and offers hope for the possibility of a better world.

~ I AM the thoughts, words, and actions that INSPIRE others to live from a place of unconditional love.

Blessings of Encouragement are sent to you today. May you INSPIRE yourself and others through your words and actions.

~~~~~~

Day 4

RENEWED~ We all know the feeling of being RENEWED. This sense of restoration occurs when we awake after a good night's rest, when a nutritious meal has nurtured our body, and when time in nature has centered our being. It is essential for our health to allow ourselves time and space to be RENEWED. The replenishing of our spiritual, physical, and mental states allows us to function from our higher consciousness. When we are depleted at any level, our creativity wanes, and our mood can be irritable. Let us take the time for ourselves to sit in silence, feed our body the nutrition that it needs, and walk in nature, grounding ourselves with the Earth. Through this process, we will be RENEWED, and our radiance will shine, our hearts will expand, and our compassion for the world will be abundant.

~ I AM RENEWED as I embrace the moments that replenish my well-being.

~~~~~~

Blessings of Balance are sent to you today. May you be RENEWED through the words that you speak and the actions that you take.

~~~~~~

Day 5

SEEDS~ Let us plant our dreams, preparing them with the foundation of a strong beginning. Let us bless the SEEDS with love and hope, and with the faith that they have the potential to become all that we envision. Let us tend to the seedlings, nurturing them with the water and Light of encouragement. As they mature and the buds begin to bloom, let us take a moment to sing the joy of our hearts for the entire world to hear. The blossom will fade, and the SEEDS will once again need to be sprinkled into the Earth, for this is the circle of life. It is all a process that begins with the sowing of our dreams; nurturing that which we cannot see until opportunities begin to form; having gratitude for fulfilling a vision, and beginning once again with a new dream -

the new SEEDS of our tomorrow. Let us take the time to tend to the garden of our soul in every way.

~ I AM planting and nurturing the SEEDS of my soul to share with the world.

~~~~~~~

Blessings of Faith are sent to you today. May you plant the seeds of love and Light, nurturing them with hope and joy into the life you came here to create and live.

~~~~~~~

Day 6

SONG~ Each of us has a SONG, a unique melody, that brings us joy throughout each day. It has crescendos that bring goosebumps to our skin and decrescendos that bring tears to our eyes. It is a SONG that is familiar as we walk through the day and that whispers to us as we sleep at night. We are not here to compare our melodies to one another but to share our one of a kind music with the world. Let us embrace the tune and not be ashamed of the symphony that we have been given. Each of us came here to share our SONG with the world around us. May we dance to the beat, sing the lyrics, hum the melody, and embrace the symphony within us.

~ I AM singing my one of a kind SONG for the world to hear.

~~~~~~~

Blessings of Joy are sent to you today. May you sing and play your unique SONG, sharing its beauty with the world.

~~~~~~~

Day 7

SPONTANEITY~ It is when we do things with SPONTANEITY that the magical moments become more frequent in our lives. The butterfly does not plan his journey. He goes to the flower to which he is drawn and rides the breeze that beckons him. The bud of a leaf does not fear that one day he will fall to the ground and become one with the Earth. He embraces each season from spring, to fall, and lastly, winter. When we have a moment of thought, a flash of SPONTANEITY to act upon something, and we choose to do nothing with that energy, we are not following our hearts--nor are we in tune with the moments in which to expand our consciousness. Let us be open to the inner calling to witness a flower's beauty and bask in its glorious fragrance, vibrant color, and velvety sheen. Let us always embrace the SPONTANEITY that bubbles up within us.

~ I AM open to the moments of SPONTANEITY that beckon me to experience life.

~~~~~~~~

Blessings of Inner Guidance are sent to you today. May you fill your life with joyful moments of SPONTANEITY, living in the present moment.

~~~~~~~~

Notes

Image captured by Tim Chinn.

Week 27
Positive Perspective

~~~~~~~~

Blessings of Expansion are sent to you today. May your heart, mind, and soul be aligned with a Positive Perspective in all that you do.

~~~~~~~~

Perspective evolves through life's experiences. It may be positive, negative or somewhere in between, but often it is difficult for individuals to change the way they view the world. It is not impossible, but it takes conscious effort or a life-changing event to shift one's perspective.

We are here to be open to life and all that it brings before us. Through life's difficult moments, one may become bitter and shut oneself off from the world, not wanting to be disappointed or hurt.

These actions only close our mind and heart to all that we came here to experience. When you and I build walls between one another, we lessen the love and hope we can receive and give to the world. The walls that we created to protect us eventually bring us more pain because we are closed off from meaningful connection with others.

195

It is when we are in sync to the guidance of the Universe that our passion flourishes and we are able to be ourselves entirely and to blossom into the most brilliant Light. Our heart will have more openness to the possibilities, and our perspective will shift to become more positive with all that unfolds, seeing the love, always.

Let us take responsibility for our perception and choose to bring more love, Light, and compassion into every moment. Let us focus on how we can influence each scenario with all that we bring to our experience. When you and I feed our conversations with hope instead of despair and with Light instead of gloom, we create solutions instead of problems.

It is in our conscious awareness that we witness life's miracles and act upon the guidance that leads to spontaneous moments of more hope. It is in our POSITIVE PERSPECTIVE that we are able to lead by example through a heart of love and compassion for the world.

Be thy Light.

Day 1

BREATH~ In this moment, let us breathe a deep and present BREATH into the miraculous bodies with which we have been gifted. Let us breathe into our lungs the love of all that we are, filling each of our cells with all the possibilities of our day, and then breathe out into the world all the love and Light that we want to share with those around us. The first thing that one does when entering our world is to inhale the BREATH of life. We take in all that the world is, was and yet striving to be; wailing our cry for all to hear. You and I breathe without even a conscious thought. It is a miracle and one that is the foundation of our existence. Let us be thankful as we speak, sing, laugh, sleep - all while breathing the BREATH of life. Let us take one more moment and fill our amazing being with a conscious BREATH, and be thankful for all that we have been given and are experiencing at this time.

~ I AM the BREATH of life, and I honor this miraculous representation of the give and take of my existence.

~~~~~~~~

Blessings of Miracles are sent to you today. May you live every BREATH with a conscious state of love and compassion.

~~~~~~~~

Day 2

PASSION~ Many of us are living our lives with a PASSION that lies dormant within our souls, and others are embracing the fire that burns within and sharing their gifts with the world. We all know the signs of living a life from a place of PASSION, for we have seen and felt them, and hopefully will renew them once again. If we do not awaken to greet our day with an attitude of gratitude, for the sun that shines above us and the song of the glorious creature outside our window, then let us get in touch with that PASSION within our souls today. Let us begin the task, or play the melody of a song, or read the words that may have inspired the core of who we are. Let us breathe renewed life into each cell within our beings, taking movements with PASSION for awakening the aligning of stars, bringing more joy into the world. May rays of Light guide the PASSION within each of us today and every day.

~ I AM living a life filled with PASSION for all that I am a part of, witness and create.

Blessings of Clarity are sent to you today. May the PASSION within you rise to motivate your actions of creativity.

Day 3

IN SYNC~ As we rise to meet the day, let us take a moment to become IN SYNC with our heart, mind, and soul. Let us ask the Universe for guidance, love, and wisdom as we go out into the world to share our gifts. You and I are supported and loved in all that we do. It is only in those moments when we fail to take the time to be IN SYNC, that we perceive an absence of support and guidance. Let us be conscious of the rhythm of our breath, becoming IN SYNC with the essence of our being.

~ I AM IN SYNC at this moment while being conscious of my breath as it enters and leaves my body.

Blessings of Harmony are sent to you today. May your heart, mind, and soul be IN SYNC as you complete your daily tasks.

Day 4

OPENNESS~ Let us whisper to the Universe, "How can I be of service today? What can I do to assist the world?" It is in our OPENNESS to all that is, and all that will be, that facilitates the flow of life. When you and I battle against that which is around us, it only brings more conflict into the world. Let us bring the energy of OPENNESS to each conversation in which we partake, forgoing judgment and offering compassion instead. When others witness our lives of OPENNESS to love and hope they expand their view of the world. Let us live our lives with an open heart of love.

~ I AM living my life with the OPENNESS that all things are possible through love.

~~~~~~~

Blessings of Compassion are sent to you today. May you bring the energy of OPENNESS to each and every situation.

~~~~~~~

Day 5

PERSPECTIVE~ The PERSPECTIVE of how we perceive situations, others, and ourselves determines if we see the world with a positive or negative outlook. Depending on whether our veil of perception is colored with compassion or with judgment, we experience feelings of either hope or hopelessness. In the moments when our energy begins to wane and we feel the Light within us dim, let us choose to do something to shift our PERSPECTIVE; such as climb, drive, or walk to a place of elevation, high above the normal view. Take some time to look out across a landscape where the homes appear tiny, and the city is at a distance; the sky is nearer and the air clearer in this place. This change in vantage point will assist in putting life back into PERSPECTIVE, and renew our faith that we are each part of a beautiful world that is all connected. Let us take a deep breath in acknowledgment that the Universe with support and abounding love surrounds us.

~ I AM in control of my PERSPECTIVE, and I take responsibility for the energy that I bring to the world.

Blessings of Hope are sent to you today. May your PERSPECTIVE be seen through a veil of compassion and unconditional love.

Day 6

POSITIVE~ Today as we step out into the world, let us focus our attention on those things and situations of which we want more in our lives. It is with a POSITIVE perspective that we will have more joy throughout our days. If traffic is heavy, let us take a deep breath and enjoy the moment of solitude before we begin our day at work. If our plans are canceled, let us be grateful for the change and do something spontaneous with the unexpected moment. If you and I choose to focus on the POSITIVE, this will bring more POSITIVE situations into our world. Today let us be the Light when the situation appears grim. We can surround ourselves with positivity and bring more joy to the world.

~ I AM living my life with a POSITIVE perspective and sharing my joy with the world.

Blessings of Universal Light are sent to you today. May you bring a POSITIVE perspective in every word that is spoken and action that is taken.

Day 7

SPONTANEOUS~ Let us take a moment to be SPONTANEOUS. Let us dance in the rain like children and sing our favorite song at the top of our lungs. Let us call the old friend that crosses our mind or smile at a stranger as we hold open the door. How about we skip down the hall with a carefree attitude, smiling at everyone we see? And now, let us take the time to reflect upon our SPONTANEOUS moment and how it has lifted our vibrations. We are a creative spirit that desires to be present and enlivened by what we experience. It is through SPONTANEOUS moments that we feel in tune with the Universe and our hearts open to the possibilities of life.

~ I AM open to the SPONTANEOUS moments of my life that raise my vibrations to the possibilities of life.

~~~~~~~~

Blessings of Awareness are sent to you today. May you be in tune to the guidance of the Universe to be SPONTANEOUS in your daily steps.

~~~~~~~~

Notes

Image captured by Tim Chinn.

Week 28
Receptive Change

~~~~~~~

Blessings of Acceptance are sent to you today. May you be Receptive to Change as you move forward in your path.

~~~~~~~

Let us be receptive to change, open to the lessons, and responsive to the guidance that dwells within every experience. It is in this space of allowing that synchronicities take place, Universal magic unfolds, and effortless miracles inspire us to be in tune to all that blossoms before us.

Let us take the time to observe our reactions to what we do not always understand and to the resistance of all we do not plan. Let our actions follow with true conscious awareness as we live and create in the Light.

You and I have dreams and ideas. We desire to manifest the life we came here to live, but often we forget to focus upon the present moment, finding ourselves living in the mindset of tomorrow instead of now.

The Universe is unfolding in ways that we do not always comprehend, but often it is in these confusing moments that we uncover new spiritual tools. These are our gifts. It is in these events that we need to strengthen or shift our perceptions as we move forward.

Over the years, I have built a relationship with change. It reminds me of a muscle, the more you use it, the stronger it becomes. There are certain things I now look forward to as I adapt to new surroundings.

For example, if I am moving physical locations, I enjoy the purging cycle and letting go of that extra stuff that is no longer serving my life. Removing items is not only a physical task, but there is a release that happens mentally and spiritually as well. It can be an empowering act when it is approached with the intention of cleansing areas of your life.

I am still working on my perception of flexibility when things don't go as planned but I have even improved this process through my trust in the Universe; *All is unfolding as it should.*

I perceive this as a benefit of growing older. Time brings us more opportunities to learn what works best in the journey we are creating. It assists us in adapting and not becoming stagnant or complacent in our lives. We are here to expand, and it is through change that we are motivated to step out of our comfort zone and realize the areas in which we need to improve.

Let us be RECEPTIVE to CHANGE, focusing on our attitude towards change and being receptive to the universal guidance that is there for each of us. Let us open our heart, mind, and soul in alignment with the highest version of ourselves that we came here to be.

Be thy Light.

Day 1
RECEPTIVE~ In each of our lives we witness and experience difficult moments, we tend to resist the contrast as it rolls in, fighting against the current or the storm that has entered our world. Let us witness the tree that effortlessly sways in rhythm, RECEPTIVE to that which it cannot control. The tree does not resist as the rain begins to fall upon it; it takes in the moisture through the leaves of its branches and through the roots that give it stability. Let us witness the object in a creek; it does not fight the current but flows freely in the water, not knowing where it will go, but trusting in the journey. Let us be an observer in life and learn from one of our greatest

203

teachers; nature. There is never resistance, only a RECEPTIVE energy to what the external forces bring. Even in the heaviest of storms, new growth will appear with the warmth of the sun. You and I will experience more beauty and power, more giving and taking, of all that is available from life, when we greet the storms with a RECEPTIVE and trusting heart.

~ I AM RECEPTIVE to all that the Universe brings to me, ever-expanding into the essence of me.

Blessings of Flow are sent to you today. May you be RECEPTIVE to the inner guidance as you walk in faith that all is unfolding as it should.

Day 2
BLOSSOMS~ The vision of the tree through the window, laden with heavy BLOSSOMS, brings continuous joy to butterflies, bees, and you and me. The silver-grey of the tree's trunk has a look of strength and longevity, while the mahogany-rose branches glisten in the sun, swaying in the warm breeze. The seasons in life and the relationships encountered, provide lessons for us to witness, as does each season in nature. These are the BLOSSOMS in life from which, with our efforts and energy, the potential fruit will come. By centering with the essence of who we are, life's more challenging moments become tolerable. We learn to have flexibility in the dance of life. Let us allow for the seasons of the journey to lead and assist us by being in tune to the Universal guidance, allowing for the lessons of the BLOSSOMS to bring more joy into our world.

~ I AM the seeds, the BLOSSOMS and the fruit of my journey. I AM embracing all that the Universe is teaching me.

Blessings of Joy are sent to you today. May you witness the beauty of life from the planting of the seeds to smelling the BLOSSOMS of the flowers.

Day 3
ALLOWING~ Let go of the thoughts of yesterday and our judgment of what has taken place. Let us have faith in tomorrow that it will unfold as it should. Let us embrace the present moment, ALLOWING for inner peace to flow through our mind, body, and soul; and make a promise that we will be more

present today. Let us notice the leaves that rustle upon the tree beyond the window, the distant wind chime that sends a unique melody for our ears to hear, and the rays of sun that touch our face as we greet our day. Let us take this moment, ALLOWING ourselves to be in tune to the things around us by breathing these gifts into our body and then exhaling the breath out into the world. Let the mind chatter fade into nothingness and let us be in the now. By ALLOWING ourselves to live in the now, we are one with the wind and all the melodies it brings to the soul.

~ I AM ALLOWING myself to live in the now and be fully present in my life.

~~~~~~~

Blessings of Inner Peace are sent to you today. May you be in a state of ALLOWING the Universe for life's endless possibilities.

~~~~~~~

Day 4

CHANGE~ We each have dreams and goals for our future. For this desire in each of us to be met there has to be a CHANGE in our lives. Perhaps the change may be physical, mental, spiritual or financial, providing us the opportunity to grow and obtain the tools needed to make our dreams a reality. Let us embrace the CHANGE that will lead to the life we know we should be living. Let us perceive changes as opportunities that will guide us closer to accomplishing the tasks at hand. Let us be open, confident, and willing to let go of the old and embrace the new. It is through CHANGE that the magic begins to happen, and we can create the miracles of our tomorrows.

~ I AM in tune with the Universal guidance to flow with the CHANGE that may be needed in my life.

~~~~~~~

Blessings of Miracles are sent to you today. May you be open to the CHANGE that brings your journey into a higher state of consciousness.

~~~~~~~

Day 5

CONTEMPLATE~ Let us CONTEMPLATE the things that we would like to leave behind and that which we want more of in our lives. Let us begin by releasing that which does not serve us, that which has brought feelings of sadness, anger, or despair. Let us embrace that which brings joy, happiness, and more love to the world. Let us CONTEMPLATE that which we have witnessed, heard, touched, and been a part of, and come to terms with the disappointments and lessons, which are no longer needed. Let us choose to cleanse our mind, body, and soul; renewing our hearts with hope so that we can experience life's highest vibrations. As you and I CONTEMPLATE our yesterdays, let us bring the Light of all that we have learned and release that which no longer serves our journey, allowing more love to fill our lives, our hearts, our essence.

~ I AM releasing that which no longer serves me. I CONTEMPLATE all that I witness and place out into the world.

~~~~~~~~~

Blessings of Clarity are sent to you today. Let us CONTEMPLATE the love and Light we came here to share with the world.

~~~~~~~~~

Day 6

EFFORTLESS~ When you and I greet our day with enthusiasm for all of the endless possibilities, the joy flows through us and out into the world. It is here in the stream of life that all seems EFFORTLESS. The synchronicities come into play to bring more smiles into our world. We hear the song of the bird because we are consciously listening. We are in tune with our day because we are aware of the warmth and light of the rays of sunshine. You and I begin to feel that the Universe is indeed guiding us with an EFFORTLESS wisdom. Let us rise, with the joy in our heart, taking steps toward the life that we know is ours to share with the world. Let us be open, feeling the EFFORTLESS guidance by the Universe to live a life of abundance.

~ I AM in tune with the Universe, feeling the EFFORTLESS guidance throughout my day.

~~~~~~~~

Blessings of Peace are sent to you today. May you be in the Universal flow that allows your actions to be EFFORTLESS.

~~~~~~~~

Day 7

IN TUNE~ When we are IN TUNE to the wisdom of the Universe the synchronicities are abundant and the doors that were invisible suddenly appear. For our continued support, you and I consciously need to take moments to receive the inner guidance from the Universe. Only in the silence do we hear the whispers of the guidance that empowers us to take actions, to step forward into the darkness in complete faith, and to heed the inner knowing that the light is just ahead of us. When life becomes stagnant, or the feelings of doubt come into our world, it is time to check back in with the Universe and become IN TUNE to that which we came here to do. May you and I find a moment of silence to hear the whispers that guide us to be IN TUNE once more.

~ I AM consciously taking the time to be IN TUNE to my heart, mind, and soul.

~~~~~~~~

Blessings of Alignment are sent to you today. May you be IN TUNE to the Universal guidance that resides within you in all that you do.

~~~~~~~~

Notes

208

Image captured by Susan Gossett.

Week 29
Journey of Joy

~~~~~~

Blessings of Consciousness are sent to you today. May you choose a Journey of Joy as you move forward along your path.

~~~~~~

Joy is something that we can encourage in our world by changing past beliefs and finding abundant gratitude in our daily lives. There is always something to be grateful for, from the air that we breathe to the bodies we experience life through.

Let our choices and actions be conscious, rising into our essence and surrounding each moment with compassion. We are the creators of when, where and how much joy we have in our lives. Even in the most challenging moments, one can choose to not sink into hopelessness or despair. We always have a choice to rise higher in our perception through love and compassion.

Our society doesn't teach us that we hold the power to create our happiness. Parents may not have learned this themselves to pass on to their children.

The media suggests, through advertising, that we can buy things that will bring us enjoyment, but we can see over time that 'stuff' does not bring inner peace and joy.

It is in the acceptance of what is before us that we ease our difficulty and keep the suffering at bay. Each of our journeys will have moments of disappointment, and even times of sorrow or loss. It is when we fight against these feelings in the moment that we stop the natural flow of life. There is a saying, 'What you resist, will persist.'

You and I can move through these feelings, acknowledging them but choosing not to let them become part of our identity. This is how we continue to grow, expand, flow into the highest essence of ourselves.

When we feel curiosity move within us, we must rise to meet it. This is the space where enthusiasm grows into excitement; excitement grows into exhilaration, and, wrapped up in between the experience, we discover the joy and hopefully some giggles too.

Let us choose to create a JOURNEY of JOY by rising above that which we may not understand, becoming consciously aware of that which we are grateful for in every moment.

Be thy Light.

Day 1
ACCEPTANCE~ As the storm rolls in and the wind begins to blow, let us take a moment to be present and watch the flowers, bushes, and trees move effortlessly in a beautiful dance with mother nature. The flora all move as one, not resisting one another, for they know that soon the rain will begin to fall and the moisture will be greeted with ACCEPTANCE - the gift that is brought by the storm. Let us learn from the storms of life and dance with the wind as it howls out our name. Let us not cry and ask, "why is it so?"; but instead, may we open our hearts in ACCEPTANCE of the lessons to be learned. Nature is one of our greatest teachers; the beauty, the power, the giving, and taking of all that comes in moments of drought or flood. Whatever life brings, may you greet it with ACCEPTANCE and not resistance, for your heart will know more joy in this way.

~ I AM joyfully sharing ACCEPTANCE of all that life brings to me.

Blessings of Understanding are sent to you today. May you be open with ACCEPTANCE to each situation and all the lessons it brings to your journey.

Day 2

JOY~ You and I have the opportunity to bring JOY into the world and to walk a path of truth that is surrounded in love. Not one of our paths is a duplicate to another's path. All are a unique blessing to be shared with the world. What is it that you and I should be giving to this amazing miracle of life? How are we sharing the JOY with those around us? Let us be present within the moments of our day and make a concerted effort to share our gifts with others. Let us choose to hear the beautiful melody of the bird's song with a heart of love. Let us observe the branches of a tree, knowing that the root system below is even wider than that which we see. Let us allow JOY into our hearts and watch it runneth over to all those who witness our unique and amazing journeys upon this planet. Let us accompany our day with a song from the soul and allow our hearts to expand with the JOY of this precious moment.

~ I AM the JOY that brings a song from my heart to share with the world.

Blessings of Bliss are sent to you today. May you find and bring JOY into every moment. You are the Light.

Day 3

ENTHUSIASM~ The essence of our being is waiting for us to embrace life with the ENTHUSIASM of a child. Laughing until the tears form in our eyes, lifting our voices in song for the angels to hear and dancing with the joy with the knowing that we are always guided by the Universe. Let us embrace life with ENTHUSIASM and a heart filled with joy. Let us play as the little ones do with dance, song, and laughter, trusting entirely in the ever-present moment of now. Let us embrace this moment with ENTHUSIASM.

~ I AM living my life filled with ENTHUSIASM and joy.

Blessings of Joy are sent to you today. May ENTHUSIASM surround every your step as you create a beautiful and loving life.

Day 4

EXCITEMENT~ Let us greet our day with EXCITEMENT and unbridled enthusiasm. Let us see the vivid colors of the world around us in the brilliant blue skies, the sapphire lakes, the emerald seas, the shimmery greens of grass, and the multi-hued leaves on the trees. Let us hear the angelic melodies of the birds, the joyful purr of the cat and the spirited conversations of the coyote. It is with EXCITEMENT that we should embrace the opportunities of the precious time that we are given in this life. Let us bring forth the joy that bubbles up inside of us, sharing that energy with everyone we meet. Let it be contagious and ripple over land and sea that we may all live a life of joy and EXCITEMENT in each of the moments with which we are gifted.

~ I AM greeting each moment on this journey with EXCITEMENT and joy.

Blessings of Bliss are sent to you today. May you create moments of EXCITEMENT that bring your life inner joy.

Day 5

EXHILARATION~ Let us visualize the breeze touching our skin as we sit on a swing under the old oak tree. We tighten our hands around the ropes and begin to rise into the air. Higher and higher we climb as the EXHILARATION of the moment washes over our being. You and I are connected to the tree by the rope, tied to the branch, that supports us; the tree is connected to the Earth as the roots spread throughout the dirt and provide stability. Our ties connect us all to humanity, and we enrich our experiences through creating memories that are filled with love. These moments of EXHILARATION are priceless occasions when every cell of our being is alive and present. Find that moment today where the smile cannot be hidden, when the giggle bubbles up inside, and we look to the sky and shout 'thank you.' Let us allow the EXHILARATION to wash over us in the moment that presents itself, for it will not come again.

~ I AM bringing to light the EXHILARATION within my being and infusing this energy into my experiences.

~~~~~~~~

Blessings of Connection are sent to you today. May your day be filled with moments of EXHILARATION and inner joy.

~~~~~~~~

Day 6

ENJOY~ Let us be present in this day that we have been graciously given and ENJOY the process of life as it unfolds. Let us choose the silliness that brings a giggle to our lips and ENJOY the sound in our ears. Let us experience this journey with gratitude, for even the longest paths are rather short in comparison to the Universal timing. Today we choose to ENJOY that which enters our world, encompassing all with a joyful heart.

~ I AM present in this moment as I ENJOY the opportunity to be the essence of me.

~~~~~~~~

Blessings of Gratitude are sent to you today. May your journey be filled with openness to ENJOY the ever-present moment of now.

~~~~~~~~

Day 7

GIGGLES~ Life is full of serious moments, meaningful conversations, and responsibilities that must be completed. It is easy to get caught up in the heaviness of all you, and I have to do. Let us not forget to find the joy in each day; to smile when humor seeps into the moment, to be curious and astonished by life's wonders, and to engage in silliness with unrestrained GIGGLES. Life passes by quickly, so let us embrace the laughter, dance wildly, and play 'tag you're it' or hopscotch on the sidewalk. Let us bring the innocent joy back into our day, as when blowing bubbles were a part of every summer, lemonade stands were on the neighborhood corner, and Saturday morning cartoons were always accompanied by a favorite bowl of cereal. Let us fill our life with more GIGGLES, much joy, and embrace the child-like part of who we are today.

~ I AM embracing the moment with more GIGGLES in my life.

~~~~~~~~~

Blessings of Joy are sent to you today. May you embrace the moments where GIGGLES seep into your day, bringing moments of joy to your life.

~~~~~~~~~

Notes

Image captured by Susan Gossett.

Week 30
Mantra of Kindness

~~~~~~~~

Blessings of Grace are sent to you today. May you choose a Mantra of Kindness in your thoughts, words, and actions.

~~~~~~~~

The old saying is true; you must, 'Love yourself before you can love others.' If we are limiting our thoughts of kindness, love, and compassion for ourselves, then we are not able to love others without conditions.

We also find ourselves unable to reflect our true essence from within our hearts out into the world. It is our responsibility to ensure that we bring compassion into every conversation that we have, with ourselves as well as with others.

We all seek to be loved, accepted and understood for the uniqueness that we offer to the world and all that we came here to be. Let us stop trying to be like everyone else and step fully into our authenticity.

We should not be expending energy on wanting to be or to look like someone else. Your beauty is uniquely yours, and you are here to share that authentic self throughout every moment of your life.

In this journey, all that we do is unfolding into manifestation experiences. Let us consciously choose to honor the preciousness of each moment with love and compassion.

Let us bring conscious awareness to acts of kindness in all that we say and do, not only to the actions that we place out into the world but into the inner conversations that we have with ourselves.

Are we thinking and speaking from a state of kindness? Let our mantra be to come forth from this loving state in order to triumph over our fears and doubts and move into the Light of unconditional love. Let us create a world with more moments of grace.

This week we begin listening to our inner thoughts and shifting them to a MANTRA OF KINDNESS. It is in this space that we will manifest a world of peace and compassion. Let our thoughts and words become conscious actions of kindness.

Be thy Light.

Day 1
KINDNESS~ The language that we speak can bring tears of joy or pain. They are mere words, brought together by our thoughts and feelings, yet they have the power to tell someone if they are our friend or foe. No matter the language we speak, the sentences that form from our lips today and every day should be spoken in KINDNESS to one another. If a negative thought comes to the mind, let us bless it as we think a higher thought of KINDNESS. Let us not speak these negative thoughts nor send them out into the world. Let us not write the words that are not from a loving heart. Let us instead embrace one another with the KINDNESS of grace and understanding.

~ I AM reflecting the KINDNESS that I wish to see in the world.

Blessings of Understanding are sent to you today. May your words and actions reflect KINDNESS in all that you say and do.

Day 2

MANIFESTATION~ It is through MANIFESTATION that we achieve our goals. We create our dreams through our thoughts, and then it is through our actions that we accomplish that which we envision. You and I hold the key to overcoming all that we fear and to walk through that which appears as impossible. The world that we see around us, that we are physically touching and experiencing, is the MANIFESTATION of yesterday, and all the days before. Let us choose to live a life filled with abundance in love, joy, relationships, and experiences. Let us dream of a better life; one that is of a more loving world and that begins with you and I being the best version of ourselves. Let each of our actions be with an open heart and a kind soul. Together we can create the MANIFESTATION of a better world.

~ I AM, and all that I create is the MANIFESTATION of a life filled with love and kindness.

~~~~~~~~

Blessings of Wisdom are sent to you today. May the MANIFESTATION of all you create be from a state of love, compassion, and true grace.

~~~~~~~~

Day 3

MANTRA~ The Universe loves us unconditionally. Can you and I say the same thing of self-love? Are the words that we speak in silence coming from a place of unconditional love? Each of us has a MANTRA, yet some of us may not even be consciously aware of what that MANTRA is. Today as we accomplish the tasks on our 'to do list,' let us listen to the words that we are speaking. Are they positive, encouraging, and loving as we gaze into the mirror? Can we see the perfection in which we came to this world and how we are to share our Light? Let us begin today by having our MANTRA be one of love and kindness.

~ I AM speaking a MANTRA of love and kindness to myself in all that I do today.

~~~~~~~

Blessings of Self Love are sent to you today. May your inner MANTRA be of kindness, love, and forgiveness for all you have and have not done.

~~~~~~~

Day 4

PRECIOUSNESS~ You and I are worthy of all of that which we dream. We are a part of the PRECIOUSNESS of life that is represented by all that we are striving to be on this planet. Let us realize the magnificence that we are and know that our life is like none other that has gone before us, or that will ever come after us. It is a gift, at this very moment, to breathe the air into our miracle bodies and to go out into the world to experience life through all of our senses. It is a blessing to be here on this planet. Let us shine our Light; let us wrap ourselves with the PRECIOUSNESS that we are and share it abundantly. You and I are more brilliant than all the stars above and have more possibilities than all the grains of sand. Let us embrace this moment with the knowing that we exude PRECIOUSNESS in our unique brilliance.

~ I AM embracing the PRECIOUSNESS of my being and sharing it with the world.

~~~~~~~

Blessings of Possibilities are sent to you today. May you embrace the PRECIOUSNESS of this journey for you are unconditionally loved.

~~~~~~~

Day 5

TRIUMPH~ Today we can TRIUMPH over the darkness around us with the Light that we hold within ourselves. We can send more love to those who act out of hatred. We do this by loving that and those whom we do not understand. We can bring the best version of ourselves to each and every moment and make a difference by living a life of tolerance, acceptance, and compassion. Let us TRIUMPH over that which does not serve us or our planet. Let us make the best choices and bring more love into each and every situation. Let us TRIUMPH over the troubles of today so that we may usher in a better tomorrow.

~ I AM taking the actions of tolerance and compassion to TRIUMPH over the hatred and judgment that I witness.

Blessings of Kindness are sent to you today. May we TRIUMPH over that which is not of love and compassion, creating a world of true acceptance and understanding.

Day 6

LOVINGKINDNESS~ As we walk through our day, may each thought that crosses the mind be from a space of LOVINGKINDNESS. As you and I accomplish the tasks on our lists and as new items are added, may the actions to complete those tasks be from the intention of LOVINGKINDNESS. Our journey is enriched and our heart more fulfilled when each thought and action comes from this state of being. You and I were created in love, and the Universe shows us kindness each and every day. The birds sing their songs, the grass reaches for the sky, the sun shines, and the moon glows for us to witness the beauty of life. Let us see the kindness, feel the love and share all things with a state of LOVINGKINDNESS.

~ I AM in a state of LOVINGKINDNESS and sharing it with the world.

Blessings of Openness are sent to you today. May each thought, every word and all of your actions be from a state of LOVINGKINDNESS.

Day 7

TRULY~ Let us take this moment and listen to our soul speak to us in the silence. It is when we TRULY align our mind, body, and soul in the present that the guidance comes to us. It may be the simplest of things that will bring a bit more joy into our day, but to receive that joy, we need to connect to our essence. It is important that we do not allow ourselves to become depleted. We cannot TRULY be functioning from a conscious state when we are empty and feeling hopeless. It is challenging to be the best version of ourselves if we are not TRULY loving and nurturing our mind, body, and soul. Let us take the time today to TRULY give ourselves that tender loving care that each of us needs.

~ I AM TRULY connecting to the present moment to assist in replenishing my mind, body, and soul.

~~~~~~~~

Blessings of Self-care are sent to you today. May you be TRULY aligned to expand into the best version of yourself.

~~~~~~~~

Notes

Image captured by Susan Gossett.

Week 31
Essence of Bliss

~~~~~~~

Blessings of Wisdom are sent to you today. May you choose to create life from your Essence of Bliss in all that you say and do.

~~~~~~~

We shine our Light brighter when we allow our authenticity to shine through in all that we do. It is in when we are aware of the universal inner guidance that we awaken into our essence, the spirit of who we genuinely are.

When you and I live from this state of truth, we find our bliss, and there is a comfort in knowing that we are always being guided and supported. There is an understanding, even in the painful experiences, that things will not be difficult forever. This too shall pass, and the clouds of grey will disappear, and the sun will shine once more.

Theologians define bliss as the joy of heaven. I embrace this concept and the idea that each of us can create our heaven on Earth through moments, days, weeks, and decades of bliss.

223

We may not stay in this state 100% of the time, but the more time that we spend there, the easier it is to return there.

It is a bit like muscle memory, the more you make the movement, the easier it is for the body to perfect the action. The more we experience bliss, the more we can raise our vibrations to this state once again.

Let us be in tune with our true selves, the essence of who we are. What is your essence you might ask? It is the spirit of what makes you uniquely you and what you came to share with the world.

You and I are irreplaceable beings with various talents and gifts. Our Light is pure brilliance that comes from the heavenly stars. We are one with the Divine, and all that was and has been created.

Let us tune in to the highest version of ourselves, consciously awakening into our ESSENCE OF BLISS and sharing our unique Light with the world around us.

Let our thoughts, words, and actions be aligned, learning to shine our Light brilliantly with unconditional love in all that we encounter.

Be thy Light.

Day 1
ESSENCE~ The journey of life is not meant to be stagnant. Even on our unique paths, there will always be changes that happen in and around us. There may be days during which joy bubbles up and brings laughter to our ears. There may be waves of sadness that touch the core of our ESSENCE far more than we thought possible. In each of the moments, we will encounter lessons. If we embrace these experiences, we allow for growth. Our hearts will love more deeply, the tears will flow more freely, and joy will be more abundant than ever before. In everyone that we meet and every situation that we encounter, you and I choose to be the ESSENCE of our being, moving through the good and bad, the positive and negative - these judgments are only that of one's perception. Be the sparkle on the water. Be the ray of light that shimmers on the window. Let us be the ESSENCE of who we are in every moment.

~ I AM the ESSENCE of unconditional love and endless possibilities, and I am one with the Universe.

~~~~~~~~

Blessings of Remembrance are sent to you today. May you be in tune to your true ESSENCE in all the words that you speak and actions that you take.

~~~~~~~~

Day 2

AUTHENTICITY~ When you and I are true to ourselves, everything else will follow, including our visions of the future. One must stay true to themselves and live from a place of AUTHENTICITY; for when we follow our hearts, the lives that we experience are filled with joy and love. You and I are unique individuals, and our journey is not to follow another's dream, but to follow our own. The AUTHENTICITY of who each of us wants to be shines upon the world. Let us not hide the essence of who we are. Each of us is needed to bring our unique gifts to the world. Let us honor the journey and embrace the AUTHENTICITY of each of us today.

~ I AM shining the AUTHENTICITY of my being in the world.

~~~~~~~~

Blessings of Courage are sent to you today. May your journey reflect the AUTHENTICITY of the life you came here to create and live fully.

~~~~~~~~

Day 3

AWAKENED~ Let us be AWAKENED in our heart, mind, and soul to a new day with the possibilities of hope and grace. The shadows that may cross our paths assist us in clarity with our views of the world. It is our lesson to learn from the shadows and the light. Let us focus on the Light - heralding the AWAKENED moments that lead us to ours. Let us bless the shadows for the lessons and send them on their way. Do not let them linger and fester. Let us shine our Light upon the shadows; opening our hearts to the AWAKENED moments of truth and compassion within each of us.

~ I AM open to the AWAKENED moments that lead me to find the Light within me.

Blessings of Remembrance are sent to you today. May your heart, mind, and soul be AWAKENED to the brilliance of your true Light.

Day 4

AWARE~ The Universe is always surrounding us with unconditional love and support in every moment. You and I have been given unique gifts to share with the world just by bringing our Light to each and every situation. Let us not cloud our destiny with doubts and fears that we are not worthy of creating our visions. Let the fears disappear, for they are hindering our mental, physical, and spiritual well-being. We are here to live a life of meaning, a life filled with grace and love. Be AWARE of the negative thoughts and shift them to a more positive outlook. If stress creeps in through an experience, breathe through it, reaching for the wiser outcome. If you hear or read words that bring sadness or anger, take a moment to send blessings of love to that situation. Let us not add to the negativity, but always strive to bring more Light by being AWARE of the power of our thoughts and actions. Let each of us be AWARE of the contribution that we can make to the world around us.

~ I AM AWARE that my loving thoughts and actions are bringing more Light to the world.

~~~~~~~~~

Blessings of Light are sent to you today. May you be AWARE of your words and actions that you place out into the world.

~~~~~~~~~

Day 5

BLISS~ Our lives are intended to have moments that you and I experience in a state of BLISS. These moments are when we have reached the top of the mountain after a long climb or when a dream has been brought to fruition after the completion of many small steps. Each of us has moments when we want to give up on the journey, for it seems too long and difficult, but you and I cannot abandon our heart's desire. We need to share our Light with the world, for the moment of BLISS fulfills all that depletes the journey. May this poem inspire you today.

> We may see things in life that seem cruel and unfair; that bring us feelings of deep despair. Our hearts may be broken by a plan that went awry, and in these moments we ask ourselves why? In these times, it seems easier to become callous and bitter, but before you do that, please reconsider. A closed heart can only hinder the feelings of BLISS that we do not want to miss.

~ I AM made of the same dust as the stars above; and as they share their light, so must I, for we must all experience moments of Eternal BLISS.

~~~~~~~~~

Blessings of Joy are sent to you today. May you create a life that is abundant in moments of BLISS.

~~~~~~~~~

Day 6

BRILLIANCE~ Each of us is a unique being with thoughts and experiences that vary widely. Our physical appearance is our outer reflection even though we live with billions of people on this planet. You and I also interpret that which we see, hear and feel differently. We then take those experiences and create a life that is all our own. The BRILLIANCE of our journey, and who we are, should be shown to all courageously. Let us find the compassion to see the BRILLIANCE in that which is not similar to one another. Let us see that the differences bring more Light and if we choose, more love to our world. Embrace the BRILLIANCE of an empathetic Light upon all that you see.

~ I AM the Light that shines for all to see. The BRILLIANCE of who I AM cannot be darkened in my journey.

~~~~~~~~~

Blessings of Courage are sent to you today. May you create a life of BRILLIANCE to shine your Light upon the world.

~~~~~~~~~

227

Day 7

LIGHT~ Even on the blackest of nights a single candle can bring the warmth of LIGHT into a place of darkness. It is through a single ray of hope that we bring the inner Light into the heaviest of shadows. You and I can be the LIGHT when all around us seems dark. We can create hope when all seems lost. The essence of who we are is brighter than the darkest hour. Let us share our LIGHT and be the hope wherever we are, for it is through our journey that we are an example to the world.

~ I AM a LIGHT of hope for all who witness my journey.

~~~~~~~~~

Blessings of Wisdom are sent to you today. May your LIGHT shine brilliantly in each and every moment.

~~~~~~~~~

Notes

Image captured by Susan Gossett.

Week 32
Mirror of Love

~~~~~~~

Blessings of Reflection are sent to you today. May you choose to create moments in which you can be a Mirror of Love in all that you say and do.

~~~~~~~

In each situation that we encounter, we can choose to be a compassionate interpreter and ask, 'What miracle is needed to bring peace, harmony, and unity to this experience?'

We can then consciously choose to reflect the energy and love that is needed for the event. This is how each of us can assist in shifting conversations and actions into a space filled with more love. We are already witnessing these interactions. Why not collectively use these opportunities to bring the essence of who you are to each and every witnessed moment?

The majority of humankind is not asking themselves the questions of 'how' or 'what' they can do to improve a situation. Instead, they react with emotions on their sleeve, often feeding into the negativity of doubt and fear.

I was recently leading a group discussion with individuals that had unresolved issues between them. It appeared cordial to all who were witnessing with their eyes, but the energy felt otherwise.

There was lingering anger and resentment about spoken words and actions from the past. It reminded me of the resting coals of a fire that is no longer burning; the emotions were simply waiting for fuel to flare them into existence once more.

Though it wasn't a situation where I was able to bring closure to the ongoing issues, I could hold space for shifts to begin happening between them. Before each meeting, I would chant and sing my mantra *Nam-myoho-renge-kyo.*

One of my favorite mantras, *Nam-myo-ho-renge-kyo (pronounced Nam Myōhō Renge Kyō)*, is a Sanskrit principle indicating that all who are on this journey and make consistent efforts will triumph over their personal obstacles. The following are the meanings of each word:

> *Nam* is to devote or dedicate oneself.
> *Myo* means mystic or wonderful.
> *Ho* is the law that humans are able to solve their problems.
> *Renge* means lotus blossom, which represents that all can blossom as pure and fragrant, amidst the muddy water in which it grows. Therefore, our humanity can be brought forth to beauty even in the pain and sufferings of our journey.
> *Kyo* represents the eternal truth.

As I would sing my mantra on the way to my meeting, I would visualize the two individuals at peace and that the highest version of themselves would be representing their presence in the meeting.

In the end, there were conscious discussions. All was not resolved or forgiven, but there was movement and communication towards further shifts in the future.

You and I always have the option to bring more love into our experiences. It begins by becoming aware and tuning in to that which is happening around us. When we are consciously choosing higher vibrations of energy, we assist in raising the overall Universal Consciousness.

You and I can activate more moments with vibrant and deliberate love through our intentional words and actions. Let us place our intentions on being a reflection of the love and Light that we want to see more of in the world, becoming a MIRROR of LOVE in all that we send out into the world.

Let our thoughts, words, and actions be infused with the intention of unconditional love, knowing we are bringing the hope and Light into every moment of true connection.

Be thy Light.

Day 1

LOVE~ May only LOVE enter into the essence of you and me today, and may that same unconditional LOVE emerge from the spirit of who we are, as we share it with the world. Each of us is the radiating Light of LOVE to all whom we encounter today. Just as a candle lights the darkest of rooms, let us choose to be the hope today when another has a heavy burden. Let us choose to function from the highest vibrations and share that with the words that we speak, the thoughts that we think and the actions that we take. May we feel the unconditional LOVE and support of the Universe in every moment of this day.

~ I AM the brightest of Lights, and my unconditional LOVE flows freely.

Blessings of Openness are sent to you today. May you remember that you are guided and supported in unconditional LOVE always.

Day 2

ACTIVATE~ If we want more love in our lives, we must give love to those around us and feel love within our hearts to ACTIVATE that emotion. If we want our days to be filled with joy and happiness, we must see the joy and happiness in our current circumstances to ACTIVATE those feelings. You and I must feel the emotions of positivity to bring more positivity into our lives. We do not bring more love by focusing on that which is negative. We bring more love by accepting that which is around us as a continual blessing, even without the understanding of the whys in the world. Let us ACTIVATE

232

the love, joy, and happiness within each of our hearts and share it with all those around us.

~ I AM willing to ACTIVATE the emotions of love, joy, and happiness in all that I do today.

~~~~~~~~

Blessings of Wisdom are sent to you today. May your actions ACTIVATE the feelings of joy and love that you share with the world.

~~~~~~~~

Day 3

ETERNITY~ It is through the contrast that our clarity will come, and through the moments of darkness that we will see the light. Let us feel all that rises within us as a passing breeze, for everything we see is but a moment, not ETERNITY. Let us believe that the sun will shimmer once more when all around us is a raging storm. Our faith and trust will carry us through to a world of more love, Light, and grace for ETERNITY. It is only love that stands the test of time. It is only unconditional love that lives for ETERNITY.

~ I AM trusting in the unconditional love that lives for ETERNITY.

~~~~~~~~

Blessings of Clarity are sent to you today. May you awaken into the knowing that we are one for all of ETERNITY.

~~~~~~~~

Day 4

INTERPRETER~ Today, as we witness the actions of others, let us see them through a filter of love and compassion. Let us not be the judge that gives criticism through our thoughts or our words. Let us see the behavior, not through the ego, but as a moment in time that quickly passes. It is only a fleeting moment that appears as a reflection upon the water. Let us not absorb, nor take the moment into our beings, pondering the whys or hows. Let us instead be an INTERPRETER, who sees things as the water does - a

233

mere reflection - realizing that this moment is not ours to judge or control. We are the INTERPRETER of the life we are living, reflecting the Light of who we are out into the world. As an INTERPRETER, let us choose to see things with love and compassion always

~ I AM the INTERPRETER of my story and all that flows in and out my world. I choose to interpret my life through love and compassion.

~~~~~~~~

Blessings of Wisdom are sent to you today. May you be an INTERPRETER of love and compassion in all that you see.

~~~~~~~~

Day 5
LOVING~ Love surrounds us in all that we do, in the places that we go and with the people that we meet. The mountains or walls that separate us do not limit love; love penetrates through all barriers in life. The act of LOVING is a gift that we can feel in our hearts and then pass on to one another in good times or bad. It is the doorway to experience the good in all that we witness, dream and create. You and I are supported in our journey in a LOVING and empowering way when we allow our hearts to be open to the possibilities. Love is a cherished gift that we receive and give in this precious life. Let us act in a LOVING manner in all situations that we encounter to be open to how it enriches our lives.

~ I AM open to the possibilities that the act of LOVING brings into my life.

~~~~~~~~

Blessings of Connection are sent to you today. May you open your heart fully into the LOVING being that you came here to share with others.

~~~~~~~~

Day 6
MIRROR~ Let us be a MIRROR of the unconditional love that resides within our essence, reflecting this love out into the world. Let us MIRROR love, grace, peace, joy, faith, and compassion. We are a reflection of how we

234

feel inside and that energy permeates to everyone and everything around us. May we be conscious of who we are - our highest self - and MIRROR that essence to all that we see. Through this awareness, we can create a world of unconditional love.

~ I AM a MIRROR of the unconditional love that resides within my spirit, and I reflect this love out into the world.

~~~~~~~~~

Blessings of Reflection are sent to you today. May your actions and words MIRROR love and compassion in your life's journey.

~~~~~~~~~

Day 7
VIBRANT~ Each of us is a VIBRANT Light that came to share our gifts with the world. Let us embrace the fullness of who we are and live each moment embodying the perfection of the gifts that have been so graciously bestowed upon us. Let us reach for the VIBRANT part of us that is full of love, laughter, and joy. Let us tap into the energy that brings a smile to our face and reunites us with our unique dance. The seriousness of life is easier to comprehend with the sweetness of our VIBRANT being.

~ I AM a VIBRANT being that brings my Light to every situation.

~~~~~~~~~

Blessings of Light are sent to you today. May you consciously choose to be the VIBRANT being that you came here to be.

~~~~~~~~~

Notes

Image captured by Susan Gossett.

Week 33
Manifesting Prosperity

~~~~~~~~~

Blessings of Endless Possibilities are sent to you today. May you choose to create moments where you are Manifesting Prosperity in all that you say and do.

~~~~~~~~~

Prosperity includes abundance in all aspects of our lives, such as health, relationships, finances, spirituality, passions and the myriad of experiences that we came here to embrace as a conscious part of our lifetime.

Each of us came here to share our essence through our intentional thoughts, words, and actions. It is in this space of awareness that we encounter our human need to experience a connection with the world around us, and that we enhance that relationship with love and compassion for all that exists.

We have more impact when we rise together to create unity for all; but, as individuals, we can always bring more hope to all we are experiencing. Let us consciously manifest moments of abundant connection.

237

We are master creators of this life, and when we are in tune with the Divine, the possibilities are limitless.

You and I are capable of manifesting more moments of prosperity when we consciously change our beliefs from 'there is not enough' to 'there is enough for everyone when we work as One.'

Prosperity is not just fulfilling one need; it is finding a balance in all aspects of our lives. If we are only abundant in finances or spirituality, we are not fulfilling all that we came here to do. We are not here simply to accumulate. We are here to experience our lives fully, and if we are lacking or depleted in any area, it is a sign that we have more work to do and further actions to take.

It is through being consciously and intentionally proactive that our words and actions can change the world around us. Together we can dissolve the lines of limitations into limitless possibilities. We can become the manifesting masters that we came here to be.

Let us consciously create that which we want to see in the world. Our beliefs, aligned with our actions incorporating prosperity for one and all, allow us to begin MANIFESTING PROSPERITY in the world.

Be thy Light.

Day 1

CREATOR~ The melody of a nightingale's song is so loud and strong as he sings, sharing his truth with the world from the heart. The summer night beckons with the moon lighting up the sky; her beauty cascades down upon you and I as we rise to see her glorious shimmer. We are the CREATOR of the world we live in, and all moments can be surrounded by beauty and truth. It is in our perception and view that we choose to see the CREATOR in all things, such as the choices of our highest self and the solutions to the problems that we see. The Universe created a world of beauty and truth; with every moment, you and I choose to act in love and to be a CREATOR of a world of compassion and hope.

~ I AM the CREATOR of a world filled with compassion and hope.

Blessings of Consciousness are sent to you today. May you consciously choose to be a CREATOR of love and compassion in all that you do.

~~~~~~~~

Day 2

DIVINE~ Within each of us is the DIVINE power to make our goals and dreams come true. The Light within us is brighter than the sun. We need only to sit in silence, allowing ourselves to become in tune with the DIVINE within us. Let us be clear in what we are seeking through our journey, for clarity is the key to making our visions a reality. Let us manifest the life that we know we should be living, with the belief that we have the power to make our dreams come true. May we feel empowered by the DIVINE within each of us.

~ I AM one with the DIVINE that resides within my being. I bring the Light to all that I encounter.

~~~~~~~~

Blessings of Grace are sent to you today. May you be in tune to the DIVINE that is guiding and supporting you always.

~~~~~~~~

Day 3

LIMITLESS~ Let us visualize the LIMITLESS places in which we can reach past the boundaries that we have created for ourselves. Let us walk through our feelings of doubt and fear to the other side, where LIMITLESS possibilities await; to the door that will lead us to the life we know should be ours. We are beings who have the capacity to create and bring into our reality that which may appear impossible. You and I can manifest a world without the boundaries of negativity and live in a world of LIMITLESS positivity.

~ I AM manifesting the world in which I wish to live and embracing a life of LIMITLESS possibilities.

Blessings of Faith are sent to you today. May your heart, mind, and soul be aligned with your LIMITLESS possibilities in this journey.

Day 4

MANIFEST~ You and I have the power to MANIFEST that which we desire in our lives. It is through our thought process that dreams start to unfold, and the feelings begin to bubble up inside of us. It is through our actions that the dreams begin to evolve and shift, further clarifying the details in our mind, until one day they MANIFEST into our reality. Today is the day; the perfect time to dust off those dreams, clear the cobwebs from the thought processes, and choose to bring the joy and excitement into our lives. We are the creator of our lives. It is through our thoughts, feelings, and actions that our dreams will MANIFEST into our reality.

~ I AM choosing to MANIFEST a life of love which I share with the world around me.

Blessings of Insight are sent to you today. May you be aligned with the Universal wisdom and MANIFEST a life of abundance.

Day 5

MASTER~ We choose the direction of our life and have the ability to change that which does not serve us. We have the power to create abundance through our thoughts. Our talents are the tools that the Universe has given us to share with the world. Our words can move mountains, and our actions of love serve as the catalyst for miracles to occur. Let us not give our power away or believe that we are not worthy of greatness. We are the MASTER of the world that we are creating. Let us be in tune with the wisdom of the Universe that will guide us in living the life of which we dream. Let us choose the steps that will lead us closer to where we want to be. Let us not wait for the perfect moment, for it is our perception of perfection that is holding us back. Let us move in the direction of faith, choosing to walk in

240

trust and to believe in the possibilities of all things. Each of us has this precious moment to share the uniqueness of who we are with the world around us. Let us not waste this moment. Let us be the MASTER of our thoughts, our inspired actions, our words of empowerment, and a life of greatness.

~ I AM the MASTER of my life, and I choose to create a world of abundance.

~~~~~~~~~

Blessings of Wisdom are sent to you today. May you be aligned with your inner guidance for you are the MASTER creator of your life.

~~~~~~~~~

Day 6

PROACTIVE~ Often in life we are reacting unconsciously to that which is happening around us because we are not in tune with our highest self. Let us choose to be PROACTIVE in our journey, addressing those items that have long been on our list of things to do. Let us not wait for the deadline to provide the needed motivation. Let us take PROACTIVE steps to complete the tasks that will bring us closer to achieving our dreams. It is in this space that stress may creep in, threatening to change our moment of joy into one of self-criticism. Each unique journey being created and experienced should be filled with joy during the process. It is through our PROACTIVE intentions that we can minimize the negativity and self-doubts within ourselves.

~ I AM placing my intentions out into the world and being PROACTIVE by taking steps toward my dreams.

~~~~~~~~~

Blessings of Inspiration are sent to you today. May your words and actions be PROACTIVE in the life you are creating.

~~~~~~~~~

Day 7

PROSPERITY~ Each of us came here to discover the journey of PROSPERITY. Now often, when we hear this word, we think of physical and tangible things, or of money and financial wealth. PROSPERITY can be all of those things, but it is so much more. You and I have witnessed the monetary wealth of others, yet have also observed that their lives may appear void of spiritual substance. Each of us came here to be prosperous in love and joy; to be spiritually rich within our souls, knowing that we are guided and cared for beyond what we see with our eyes. We came here for the journey of discovery; to see the beauty of all that is around us and of that which we can create and share with the world. Each of us may define PROSPERITY a bit differently, because our journeys are unique, but the commonalities encompass an abundance of love, joy, peace, grace, sharing, compassion, and kindness. Let us open our hearts to the belief that our path is meant to be one of PROSPERITY in all things.

~ I AM living a life of PROSPERITY in every aspect of my journey.

~~~~~~~~~

Blessings of Clarity are sent to you today. May you manifest a life of PROSPERITY, creating abundance mentally, spiritually, and physically.

~~~~~~~~~

Notes

Image captured by Tim Chinn.

Week 34
Mysterious Miracles

~~~~~~~

Blessings of Sacred Wisdom are sent to you today. May you choose to embrace openness when the Mysterious Miracles take place in your life.

~~~~~~~

You and I are living miracles that are capable of creating and bringing magic to each and every moment. Let us shift our perception and live our lives with a conviction that every experience should be honored in its sacredness, embracing the mysterious wonder of this life we are witnessing.

You and I can choose to create, witness, and bring the sacred into the world we are manifesting. Let us choose to honor the mystery space where miracles unfold and where we can decide to observe the magic in our lives.

The Divine always surrounds us with guidance, if we only take a moment to listen, see, and feel the mysterious wonder of the many signs, visions, and guides that show us the way to more love, joy, and compassion for everyone and everything.

As a child, I always thought of miracles as significant events, and indeed it is these that are mostly spoken about. However, miracles need not be newsworthy, for they show up in many ways throughout each and every day.

Sometimes you hit every red light and what should have taken 20 minutes takes 35 minutes. Yet, when you arrive, you are the first to the meeting because of other small miracles that took place. You realize at that moment that there was no need to worry or fret, for all was unfolding as it should.

Miracles can take place when it appears something terrible has occurred, only to discover later that the adverse outcome was a good thing. One of my favorite stories of this type of miracle was on a freeway drive. I was singing my affirmations, and feeling grateful and blessed.

Suddenly, a shiny object came towards this vehicle that I had only owned for ten days. I had an immediate flat tire going 70 miles an hour. Fortunately, I was able to get on to the side of the road without incident. Shortly after, the Freeway Service Patrol changed my tire, and I was back on the road.

I felt disgruntled though. How had I manifested this incident when my energy level was high? The answer to the question would be revealed when I went to have my tire replaced. The serviceman brought me a piece of angle metal that was 6 inches long, 2 inches wide and thick, and weighed over a pound.

If I had hit this with my older vehicle ten days earlier, it could have been a very different outcome. It could also have been a far worse scenario if it had missed my tire and instead gone through somebody's windshield. My vibration was precisely where it needed to be. I had been at service to the world at that moment. I had been a part of a miracle.

Together we encompass Oneness for all, sometimes we witness the miracle, and sometimes we are part of it. You and I are connected to all things.

The magic of the Universe surrounds you and me, and it feeds our souls until we know that all things are possible. We are the catalyst for creating the MYSTERIOUS MIRACLES of our world.

Be thy Light.

Day 1

MIRACLE~ In this very moment, as we sit and are present, let us listen to the MIRACLE of the body that we are so blessed to reside within. Our hearts beat steadily while the blood rushes through the veins, flowing like a stream to the ocean. We do not will it to be; it just is. This MIRACLE, a capsule that holds the spirit of you and me, allows us to touch and experience the textures of all that we see. It allows us to smell the freshness after a rain shower when all seems anew. It allows us to hear the music of nature, instruments, and the voices of others. It allows us to see the various colors, the flora and fauna that surround us, and the beauty of our amazing planet in this blessed life. Let us take this moment to be in the presence of the MIRACLE of our bodies - true wonders, to be loved unconditionally – and radiate gratitude for all they provide us to experience in our journey.

~ I AM embracing the MIRACLE that I AM in heart, mind, and soul.

~~~~~~~~

Blessings of Faith are sent to you today. May you be present in the moment to witness the MIRACLE of all that is taking place.

~~~~~~~~

Day 2

CAPABLE~ You and I are a unified divine soul that has come to experience life as beings through the senses of sight, sound, hearing, touch, and smell. We are CAPABLE of great things by being the catalyst to change the world around us as a shining light through our thoughts and words. Our actions are the pebble that is tossed into the lake, and the ripples that move in all directions are the results of those actions touching those around us. Let our actions be from a place of love and hope; may they inspire others to create their own and to send them out into the world. Together our thoughts, words, and actions of love are CAPABLE of creating miracles of change. By shining our Light, and infusing our actions with love and hope, we are CAPABLE of being the pebble which spreads the ripples of possibility that create a better world.

~ I AM CAPABLE of creating the miracles that can create a better world.

246

Blessings of Hope are sent to you today. May you see all that your unique Light is CAPABLE of sharing with the world.

Day 3

CONVICTION~ You and I are living in a miracle Universe, on a miracle planet, in a miracle body. Let us have the faith and CONVICTION that we can create the miracles that we long to see in our world. Let us go forth every day making conscious choices to improve this world in which we live; giving to our world, not just taking. Let us have the CONVICTION that each of us can make a difference and together we can enhance our world with more love and compassion. Let us embrace the power within our beings, choosing the highest version of who we are and sharing our Light with everyone we see. Let us know that our CONVICTION and faith are the foundation of forever hope, which leads to more and more joy in all that we see.

~ I AM taking actions in the world with a deep, abiding CONVICTION that I can make a difference.

Blessings of Perseverance are sent to you today. May your Light guide your personal CONVICTION to create a life of unconditional love.

Day 4

MAGIC~ When the sun shines its rays upon the wings of a butterfly you can see through them, and if the dust is damaged in any way they can no longer fly. One could say that this dust is a bit like MAGIC. If we open our hearts to MAGIC, the possibilities become endless. May the MAGIC dust of the butterflies be sprinkled over the struggles and difficulties of our lives. May clarity come to us when the questions are difficult to answer. May the solutions we seek be abundant in all that we do. Let our lives be filled with MAGIC as we open our hearts to all of its possibilities.

~ I AM surrounded by the guidance of the Universe in all aspects of my life as I open my heart to MAGIC.

Blessings of Wonder are sent to you today. May the veil fall away, that you may see the MAGIC that unfolds before you every day.

Day 5

MYSTERIOUS~ It is not up to you or I to know the hows or whys of life. We don't need to worry our minds to figure out the answers of yesterday. The Universe will continue to conspire to bring the synchronicities into play for each of our lives, and to create the MYSTERIOUS miracles that we witness as our dreams come to fruition. It is our job to keep creating, sharing, and taking inspired steps into the MYSTERIOUS unknown, to keep believing that we are always being supported in our journey. Let us find joy in the experience. May we smile at the moments that come together perfectly and bless the moments that may appear to be flawed. Let us embrace the MYSTERIOUS ways of life.

~ I AM embracing the MYSTERIOUS aspects of life and enjoying its little surprises as I journey through this world.

Blessings of Openness are sent to you today. May you embrace the MYSTERIOUS moments that you witness with a heart of wonder.

Day 6

PERCEPTION~ Our PERCEPTION of life is shown to the world and ourselves through the thoughts in which we engage, the words that we speak, and in our daily actions. It is through our PERCEPTION of the world that we believe that either "miracles never happen" or "everything is a miracle." Both mantras are correct for the believer because each of us brings about our reality through our belief system. Let us choose to believe that we are miracles and that we can create more miracles in the world in which we live. Let us embrace the PERCEPTION that we are from unconditional love and came here to gift the world with a life filled with abundant joy.

~ I AM a miracle that is creating miracles in every moment. My PERCEPTION of the world is a place of love and joy.

~~~~~~~~~

Blessings of Guidance are sent to you today. May you be aligned with your wisdom as you view the world through a PERCEPTION of love.

~~~~~~~~~

Day 7
SACREDNESS~ You and I were brought into the world from a place of SACREDNESS; a place in time where the stars aligned and a miracle came into the world; the unique creation of you and me, to be shared with the world. We were brought from a place of love, and we can choose to live in that space of love in every moment. It is when our journey is over that we will go back to the SACREDNESS of Universal love. Let us choose to honor our journey with unconditional love and to function from that space. Let us remember that we are a beautiful miracle experiencing the world, and we can choose to honor the SACREDNESS that we are in every moment of our journey.

~ I AM from the place of SACREDNESS, and I choose to live every moment in this space of unconditional love.

~~~~~~~~~

Blessings of Divine Wisdom are sent to you today. May you be in tune with the SACREDNESS that supports and guides you always.

~~~~~~~~~

Notes

Image captured by Susan Gossett.

Week 35
Rejuvenating Laughter

~~~~~~~~

Blessings of Abundant Joy are sent to you today. May you choose to bring Rejuvenating Laughter into your life.

~~~~~~~~

Let us focus on all that brings more joy into our lives. It is through these joyful moments that we bring more laughter into our day, which leads to a rejuvenation of our spirit.

You and I are the narrators of our journey by being the interpreter of all that we see and hear. We can choose to nurture our spirit through an outlook of positivity and hope, or allow doubt and negativity into our world. We do this with the thoughts we hold, the words we speak, and the actions we take.

Laughter is a powerful tool we can use to raise our vibrations. When our energy is elevated, we feel joyful. It is that simple. There is nothing like getting the giggles with your loved ones, and you can barely catch your breath. It is exhilarating, timeless and feels amazing whether you are five or eighty-five year old.

251

My mother and I had one of these moments just the other day. My young dog had made a colossal mess of my house, and I was not happy with him. As I was relating the story to my mom, it morphed into a hilarious moment. We were both gasping for air and tears were falling down my face.

In the scheme of life, the incident with my dog mattered very little; yet I was letting it taint my mood for the day, even though what was done was done. I couldn't change the situation and now one moment was affecting an entire morning.

In the end, my mother validated my frustration over the things the mess had destroyed, but it was a moot point once I had raised my vibration through the laughter.

You and I can align our mind, body and, spirit when bringing laughter into our life through a veil of fascination, curiosity, bewilderment, and even complete surrender into all that we have no control over.

We have the ability to choose the moments that rejuvenate our journey. We can cradle our dreams with love, faith, and the perseverance to share our unique gifts with others.

It is through the simple acts of REJUVENATING LAUGHTER that we bring more creative energy into manifesting the life we came here to live.

Be thy Light.

Day 1

CRADLE~ The essence of each of us is as big and strong as the tallest mountain. The essence of you and I is as loving and gentle as the butterfly dancing in the breeze. Let us each CRADLE our soul with gentleness and share our gifts with the world around us. Each of us can tap into the wisdom of the Universe when we listen to our inner guidance. Let us embrace that which appears as a weakness and let our perceptions evolve to see that imperfections are also our pathway to wisdom. Let us CRADLE and nurture all that we are, bestowing love without judgment and changing misguided perceptions into the beauty of acceptance. Let us CRADLE our heart, mind, and soul for all that we understand and that which we do not, opening ourselves to all possibilities.

~ I AM open to that which I understand and that which I do not. I CRADLE the essence of who I am, knowing that all is possible in love.

~~~~~~~~

Blessings of Possibilities are sent to you today. May you CRADLE your dreams into the reality of your life.

~~~~~~~~

Day 2

IN THE BEGINNING~ IN THE BEGINNING, you and I were each a perfect bundle of joy and hope. IN THE BEGINNING, each of us was given all the talents and gifts necessary to accomplish that which we came to give to the world. We knew our destiny and that all things would be possible if only we believed and placed our intention behind our actions. Nothing has changed, except that fear has taken over our hope, that doubts have covered our beliefs, and that our hearts have forgotten the purpose of unconditional love and compassion for all things. Let us embrace the possibilities, release the fears and doubts, and open our hearts to remembering the essence of who we came here to be IN THE BEGINNING.

~ I AM embracing the possibilities with a heart that is open, remembering who I came here to be IN THE BEGINNING.

~~~~~~~~

Blessings of Remembrance are sent to you today. IN THE BEGINNING and in every moment you are guided and supported.

~~~~~~~~

Day 3

FASCINATION~ The FASCINATION with this life we are living is filled with love, beauty, people, creatures, sound, touch, sight, and all the things that we choose to experience in the world. Let us view our experiences without judgment or critique, embracing all things in the essence of love. Let us see all things with a FASCINATION and acceptance for our differences. We are one with everything. Let us give the love, joy, and compassion to all that we are and embrace the FASCINATION of our world today.

~ I AM in tune with the flow of emotions that results from a FASCINATION with the world in which I live.

~~~~~~~

Blessings of Wonder are sent to you today. May you view the world through eyes of FASCINATION and curiosity.

~~~~~~~

Day 4

LAUGHTER~ As the sun rises in the sky and we awaken to experience this amazing world, let us remember the power of LAUGHTER. When you and I laugh, it awakens our body and refreshes our soul. Our energy level rises, and all that we do seems achievable. It is also fun and enjoyable to laugh until our sides ache and the tears run down our face. Let us release the seriousness that sits heavy on our souls, allowing the joy to enter into our hearts. May we embrace the giggles that bubble up inside of us and choose LAUGHTER in this very moment.

~ I AM choosing to fill my day with LAUGHTER and joy.

~~~~~~~

Blessings of Joy are sent to you today. May the moments of LAUGHTER be abundant in your journey.

~~~~~~~

Day 5

NARRATOR~ We are each the NARRATOR of our lives; from the chitter-chatter inside our head, to that of which we speak to those around us. As the NARRATOR, you and I choose to either speak with words and thoughts of encouragement or to be the naysayer of creative ideas or dreams. If each of us chose words from a heart of love, how would the world around us change? How many of our ideas would have been nurtured if the words spoken to us would have been ones of encouragement? Let us each be a NARRATOR with a heart of love. Let our words to others, as well as our inner thoughts, be from this space in which all things are possible.

~ I AM the NARRATOR of my life. I interpret my experiences through an open heart.

~~~~~~~

Blessings of Inner Peace are sent to you today. May you be a NARRATOR of Light as you observe and participate in the world.

~~~~~~~

Day 6

NURTURE~ As we walk through days that turn into the weeks, months and years of yesterday, let us remember to NURTURE our soul. Through the breath of a quiet moment, may we hear the melody of a song and take in the love of all that surrounds us. It is through the tending of the garden that it comes into its full beauty and harvest. We take care of that which we love and encourage, that in which we believe. Let us take care of the essence that makes us unique. Let us encourage our heart to be open to the guidance the Universe is giving to each of us. We can choose to NURTURE our body today by giving it a moment with no stress, and deep breaths to expand our lungs and calm the mind. Let us surround ourselves with loving energy and nourish the soul today with thoughts of kindness and joy. This moment is ours to cherish, honor and NURTURE all that we are today and every day.

~ I AM choosing to NURTURE the essence of my being in the thoughts, words, and actions that I take today.

~~~~~~~

Blessings of Restoration are sent to you today. May you embrace the moments to NURTURE yourself on this beautiful journey you are creating.

~~~~~~~

Day 7

REJUVENATE~ You and I REJUVENATE the spirit of who we are with our decisions every day. By taking care of the needs of our mind and body, we will REJUVENATE our soul's mission to fulfill our dreams. Let us remember to breathe in the love as stress knocks upon the door. Let us drink water to hydrate our body to function at its best. Let us sit in silence and be

255

present and grateful for the moment that we have been given. Let us choose to REJUVENATE our mind and body, and to stay in tune with our soul, taking in this moment of being fully present.

~ I AM making the choices that REJUVENATE my mind and body.

~~~~~~~~

Blessings of Well-being are sent to you today. May you REJUVENATE your mind, body, and spirit with the choices that you make in every moment.

~~~~~~~~

Notes

Image captured by Susan Gossett.

Week 36
Union of Peace

~~~~~~~~~

Blessings of Heart to Heart Connection are sent to you today. May you create a life that is surrounded by the Union of Peace.

~~~~~~~~~

Let us consciously choose to bring unity and peace into our lives. When you and I begin to experience true connection with our essence, it leads us to moments of inner peace with all that we are witnessing in life's experiences.

You and I have the potential to create all that we dream of in this lifetime. It begins with our ability to see the similarities within the stories that each of us creates. We need to focus on all that enhances our togetherness versus the things that divide us.

A book that has assisted me in my journey for inner peace is The Four Agreements by Don Miguel Ruiz. If you haven't read it, I encourage all my friends and family to do so. The four agreements that the book is based upon are:

- Be impeccable with your word.
- Don't take anything personally.
- Don't make assumptions.
- Always do your best.

Usually, if I find myself at odds with someone, or find that a situation is bringing me inner turmoil, it is because I am assuming something or I have taken something personally.

An assumption is the acceptance of something based on partial facts and our own imaginations of the remaining details. When you and I assume, we are no longer living in the reality of the here and now, which allows turmoil to rise within us. It is by living in the present moment, without assumptions, that we avoid this pitfall.

As humans, we tend to think that everything is about us, that others are speaking of us or actions are being taken with us in mind. The reality is that most people are just thinking about the best decision for their own journey.

They may not even know that it has caused you and I pain. This is precisely why a connection with others is vitally important to understanding how our actions affect the world. Many individuals are not living consciously and are not thinking about how their choices can change the world around them. This is a wonderful illustration of why we should not take things personally.

We can only find unity with one another through communication, not assumption, and through realizing that living presently will lead to less stress and misunderstanding.

Let us embrace that which brings our lives more peace and calmness. It is in this space that we tune in to the vibration of happiness. We realize that it was always our responsibility to align ourselves with the highest vibration. It was never a situation, a person or an accumulation of things that brought us everlasting joy. We held the power all along to create our balance, no matter what was happening around us.

Our UNION OF PEACE lies within the unconditional love we have for ourselves, this Earthly experience and those we meet along the way. It is all about connection with that which was created by the Divine.

Be thy Light.

Day 1

PEACE~ Let the sun shine down on us as we engage with the Light of the world. Let the light breeze caress our hair as we embrace those around us with compassion and grace. Let the scent of the honeysuckle fill the air with a lingering feeling of PEACE that abounds in all that you and I can perceive. May our hearts be filled with love, flowing abundantly to everyone we meet. May the joy of who we are, guide the words that we release out into the world. Through this unconditional love and abundant joy that resides within our souls and surrounds us in the grace of the Universe, let us embrace the possibility of PEACE between, and within, all the sentient beings who inhabit this Earthly space.

~ I AM the PEACE that I wish to see in the world. I reflect the essence of who I AM.

~~~~~~~~

Blessings of Compassion are sent to you today. May your thoughts, words, and actions be from a space of inner PEACE in all that you bring the world.

~~~~~~~~

Day 2

CALMNESS~ Let us envision a path of trees with fragrant white blossoms that fall in the breeze beneath our feet. The sun shines brightly upon the path of petals as we walk in CALMNESS and peace. You and I interpret all that is happening around us, creating either a feeling of hope or one of hopelessness. When we create hope, our heart, mind, and soul are aligned, and CALMNESS surrounds us. You and I have the power to raise the vibrations of the world by being responsible for our being, and that which we place in the world. Let us promise to choose the CALMNESS in all that we do and see, for our souls can lift the darkness into the Light.

~ I AM the CALMNESS within each cell of my being, bringing Light and love wherever I AM.

~~~~~~~~

Blessings of Balance are sent to you today. May you be the CALMNESS in each situation where life's changes are endless.

~~~~~~~~

260

Day 3

HAPPINESS~ HAPPINESS does not come from the things that surround us - it comes from our Light within. The balance that we are seeking comes from a place of acceptance of that which we cannot change or control. We may not agree with the way that others behave or feel, but theirs is not our journey. We can only control our thoughts, reactions, and the words that we speak in regards to these differences. When you and I reach for the hopeful thought, react in compassion, and speak to others in love, we will find the meaning of HAPPINESS and a life of balance. This feeling of HAPPINESS will well up inside of us, surrounding all that we are, spilling over, and serving as a beacon of light to those who are seeking and in need of love.

~ I AM at peace with my being and the feeling of HAPPINESS surrounds me fully.

~~~~~~~~~

Blessings of Joy are sent to you today. May you be the HAPPINESS that you wish to see in the world around you, creating abundant moments of love and Light.

~~~~~~~~~

Day 4

POTENTIAL~ Every one of us has the POTENTIAL to live a life filled with love and Light. Too often, you and I look for fulfillment elsewhere, but the eternal peace that we seek comes only from the Universal truth that resides within each of us. It is through loving ourselves that we learn to forgive that which is not perfect. It is through acceptance of all that we are that you and I edge ever closer to our highest truth. It is through love that we see the POTENTIAL for greatness in others and encourage them to keep striving. It is through hope that the POTENTIAL within us grows into that which we know we are capable of being.

~ I AM living each moment in the POTENTIAL of my being and sharing the joy with the world.

Blessings of Courage are sent to you today. May you act upon your POTENTIAL with love and compassion, creating all that you came here to share.

~~~~~~

Day 5

SIMILARITIES~ Clouds of gray bring rain that sustains the life of all living things on this planet. It is the raindrops of yesterday that filled our lakes and the rivers that flow into the sea. Each of these bodies of water, from the raindrops to the oceans, has SIMILARITIES in that they fulfill a need to sustain life in our world. They work with one another in unity, as all of nature does. What if you and I were like the raindrop, joining as one to create a new world of love and harmony? What if we put aside our egos and pride, focusing on the SIMILARITIES of what is best for our planet? What if we allowed our indifference to fade; and we embraced our collective need for compassion; not just for humanity, but for all life that inhabits the world. Let us focus on that which we have in common; the SIMILARITIES that will bring us together.

~ I AM focusing on the SIMILARITIES and the unity in the world.

~~~~~~

Blessings of Compassion are sent to you today. May you see the world through the eyes of love, focusing on all the SIMILARITIES that we have on this planet.

~~~~~~

Day 6

STORY~ We write our STORY each day through the words that we speak to ourselves and others. We can create an adventure, drama, or comedy. It is our choice through our actions and our perspective of that which happens around us. We cannot control the things that take place in the world, or the reactions of others, but we *can* control our thoughts and words. Let us choose a STORY of hope, love, and peace intertwined. Let us share our STORY of compassion with the world and be an example by our Light shining upon those around us. Let us be the STORY of love and follow our individual hearts to a universal truth.

~ I AM living a love STORY filled with hope and compassion for the world.

~~~~~~~~

Blessings of Hope are sent to you today. May your life's STORY be of love and Light for all the world to see.

~~~~~~~~

Day 7

TOGETHER~ When our lives are aligned with that which we believe in, our words and actions are in tune with our truth. We attract opportunities and individuals that enhance our experiences. We feel the guidance during our journey, and the support of the Universe during moments of controversy and expansion. Each of us becomes unified with like-minded souls, and TOGETHER we grow into a community. Our moments of joy, laughter, and sorrow are filled with abundant love and compassion for one another. TOGETHER, the positive energy is multiplied, and our love expands and grows with no barriers. You and I can make miracles happen; we can create a world of community that is filled with love. Let us align our hearts and come TOGETHER in community with one another.

~ I AM attracting like-minded individuals to my community, and TOGETHER we will create a world filled with love and compassion.

~~~~~~~~

Blessings of Alignment are sent to you today. May you be in tune to that which brings us TOGETHER in every moment.

~~~~~~~~

Notes

Image captured by Susan Gossett.

Week 37
Actions of Perseverance

~~~~~~~

Blessings of Determination are sent to you today. May your Actions be with Perseverance in all that you do.

~~~~~~~

Let us place our attention on the actions of intention that we send out into the world. Let us not just make meaningless movements to complete the task before us, but ensure each motion is born from consciousness with love for the moment.

As a writer, I have a relationship with words. Sometimes it is expressed in how they roll across my tongue, or the way they sound to my ear, or the interplay between the syllables, but often it is a combination of these things. Perseverance is one of these words. I think of it as a partnership and dance, together we inhabit my vision and bring it into reality.

When my dreams are accomplished, and my persevering actions come from the heart, it is empowering and rejuvenates my effort to keep striving to create more Light and love in the world.

My Grandfather wrote me a card many years ago when I graduated from college. It had been a long seven-year road, but I had accomplished what I set out to do. He congratulated me on my actions of 'perseverance' and 'determination', knowing that these traits would take me wherever I desired to travel in my future journeys.

He was an avid Scrabble player, a theologian, a writer, and a minister. He could tell a story like no other, and I know that he influenced my life greatly. I will always be thankful for those intentionally chosen words that he imparted long ago. I have carried them with me, and they have helped me overcome many challenges.

You and I are capable of great things, and when we step through the veil of fear and doubt, we can achieve all that we envision. It is through our determination and perseverance that we overcome our obstacles. Our diligence leads us to our accountability, and our insistence will create that which we came here to be and to share in the world.

Individually each of us can share our Light brightly wherever we may be, and together we can Light up the whole world with love and compassion for all. Let us forgive that which needs to heal, open our hearts with bravery, and release that which no longer serves us. Let our ACTIONS come from a place OF PERSEVERANCE and determination.

Be thy Light.

Day 1
ACHIEVING~ In our individual journeys we often go through phases where we think that our dreams are unachievable. It is not uncommon to even allow a dream to die because of the fearful thoughts that take the joy of dreaming away from us. When our dreams die and do not come to fruition, they do not find a new home; they live as lingering ghosts within us. So today, let us water and fertilize the dreams that reside within. Let us give ourselves a pep talk with loving words to encourage the creativity to flow. Let us think about the joy of ACHIEVING those dreams once again. Through our thoughts, our actions, and the desire that lives within us, each of our dreams will evolve with the energy that we place in them. We do not have to know the how of ACHIEVING our dreams for that is completed perfectly by the Universe.

266

Let us renew our passion today, for we are capable of ACHIEVING all that we envision.

~ I AM giving time and energy to ACHIEVING my dreams.

~~~~~~~~

Blessings of Knowing are sent to you today. May your actions be set into an ACHIEVING motion of Light, love, and compassion for all.

~~~~~~~~

Day 2

ACCOUNTABILITY~ As we walk along this path of life, the moments tend to become lost in time. Each of us has thoughts and visions of what we want to accomplish in our lifetime. Often these notions just pass us by with the busyness that life brings. It is with ACCOUNTABILITY that our thoughts become actions, and our visions are brought to fruition. How each of us obtains ACCOUNTABILITY may be different and vary considerably. It does not matter 'how' you and I complete the steps, only that they bring us closer to the life that we know we are capable of living. May each of us find the ACCOUNTABILITY within ourselves to grow closer to where and who we want to be.

~ I AM completing the tasks that assist me in the ACCOUNTABILITY of bringing my dreams to fruition.

~~~~~~~~

Blessings of Determination are sent to you today. May your ACCOUNTABILITY hold you in alignment to share your gifts of unconditional love with the world.

~~~~~~~~

Day 3

ACTION~ How often do you see something and say "I wish…"? It is part of each of our journeys to recognize the things that we want or don't want. This recognition serves as a catalyst for clarifying the direction in which we want to proceed to fulfill our dreams. The realization of our dreams only begins to form through ACTION. It is through our steps that we can usher a dream into a reality. No one else can take the ACTION for us, nor can we

267

take the steps for another person's path. Each of us came here to share our talents and gifts with the world. Let us live our lives with purpose, completing that which we came here to do. Let us take steps of ACTION toward our dreams today.

~ I AM taking ACTION to bring my dreams into reality.

<center>~~~~~~~~</center>

Blessings of Courage are sent to you today. May you take ACTION that leads to fulfilling all that you dream of in this lifetime.

<center>~~~~~~~~</center>

Day 4
BRAVERY~ The BRAVERY is within each of us as we step through fear and doubt toward our promising future. The path before us is ours to create and fill with enriched moments of joy and grace. The road that appears long today is one to be taken with a single step of BRAVERY. When we grow weary, know that this is a sign to rest and replenish the soul. We must take care of our mind, body, and soul, gifting ourselves moments to renew our hope. Then let us step forth again with renewed BRAVERY that all things are possible and that the Universe is working with and through us to create a magnificent journey.

~ I AM stepping forward in BRAVERY, trusting that the Universe is working with, and through me, every day.

<center>~~~~~~~~</center>

Blessings of Courage are sent to you today. May your actions be surrounded in BRAVERY, that you are supported and guided always.

<center>~~~~~~~~</center>

Day 5
EMPOWERING~ Let you and I choose the EMPOWERING thought that brings energy to our being; the one that encourages you and I to be kinder and more loving to all those around us. Let us choose the EMPOWERING words that lift others up from where they stand, encouraging each other to follow our hearts in finding our truth. Let us choose the EMPOWERING action that brings each of us closer to our highest self, to that which gives us encouragement and, to be the essence of who we are.

268

~ I AM EMPOWERING myself through my thoughts, words, and actions in every moment.

~~~~~~~~

Blessings of Encouragement are sent to you today. May your thoughts, words, and actions be EMPOWERING to your journey.

~~~~~~~~

Day 6

INTEGRITY~ Each of us have a personal truth by which we intuitively know we should live. We choose each day to honor that truth and to live our lives with INTEGRITY. Life may bring us experiences where someone else's decisions or words conflict with our truth. It is in these moments of contrast that we will be given the gift of clarity, if we remain open to guidance. Let us never compromise our personal truth, always being true to ourselves and choosing to live a life of INTEGRITY. Let us also be respectful to one another when contrast arises, for it is in these moments that INTEGRITY and love are most needed.

~ I AM living a life of INTEGRITY and unconditional love in all that I do.

~~~~~~~~

Blessings of Authenticity are sent to you today. May your INTEGRITY shine through in all of your words and actions.

~~~~~~~~

Day 7

PERSEVERANCE~ You and I are capable of great things. May we know and believe this with every cell of our being. Let me say that again… you and I are capable of great things! It is through PERSEVERANCE and determination that mighty things have been achieved. When naysayers said to the dreamers of yesterday that their dreams were not possible, the dreamers kept moving forward, following the guidance of the Universe. Even if they may have wondered how they would accomplish their dreams, they did not give up faith that somehow it would be achieved. Each of us has the capacity for PERSEVERANCE; we need only to call upon it and act. You and I each have moments during which the Universe inspires us to move forward, to take an action, or to stop the procrastination. It is in these moments that we receive the encouragement to continue in the direction in which we are being guided. Even if that movement seems minuscule or gigantic, let us not hesitate in our PERSEVERANCE to achieve our dreams.

~ I AM living a life filled with PERSEVERANCE and determination.

~~~~~~~~~

Blessings of Determination are sent to you today. May your heart be aligned with your soul's PERSEVERANCE to create joy throughout your lifetime.

~~~~~~~~~

Notes

Image captured by Susan Gossett.

Week 38
Intuitive Presence

~~~~~~~

Blessings of Inner Wisdom are sent to you today. May you be in tune with your Intuitive Presence.

~~~~~~~

When we are in the present moment, we have the ability to be in tune with our body, mind, and spirit. It is in this space that we are able to hear the intuitive guidance that is with us always.

When you and I begin to live in the present moment our consciousness awakens, creating a journey with more thankfulness in all that we are witnessing. We start to understand how everything is connected and become more compassionate to the journeys of others.

Our connection with all things begins to shift our conversations and choices toward the highest good. The intuitive spirit within you will rise and align your priorities differently, delivering you from the need to chase anything. That which no longer serves you will simply begin to fade and subside from your desires.

When my consciousness began to awaken, I no longer only saw a bumblebee on a flower. My heart opened to the understanding that this sentient being was pollinating a flower in order to assist in feeding his hive and to ensure the plant would thrive.

The smallest events were no longer separate or insignificant; they were part of a Universal design to assist in a healthy planet for all.

The presence of that which is greater than you and I is in all that we see, smell, touch, hear, and taste. Our intuition is the GPS that leads us to a real connection with the world and encourages us to share our gifts in this journey.

When you and I go through life with blinders on, ignoring our gut feelings or intuitive nudges, our journey becomes easily sidetracked. We may wonder about the meaning of life, or attempt to fill our lives up with stuff or unhealthy habits.

You and I have everything within us to create all that we came here to share with the world. We feel connected when we tune in to the guidance and support that is always there to assist us.

Let us appreciate every moment and connect with the INTUITIVE PRESENCE that waits to guide us in our journey.

Be thy Light.

Day 1
APPRECIATE~ We spend so much of our days in the momentum of getting all the things done that are on the 'to do' list, that too often we are not taking the moments to APPRECIATE the miracle of our journey. Cars rush by with speeds that no creature that God has made can attain. Airplanes fly overhead, transporting us to a different time zone and over oceans to another continent within hours. Ringing cell phones can instantly connect us to a loved one who could be hundreds, or possibly thousands, of miles away. All of this technology can be a true blessing in life, but we must stay grounded to who we are at the deepest core of ourselves. Let us APPRECIATE the advancements for how they connect us to others all over the world with more ease; but let us not forget that we also have the power of prayer, blessings, and love that we can send out into the world at each and every moment. What you and I release into the world is more powerful than we often realize. Let us not discount how each of us is contributing to our

surroundings. Let us be awake in this journey of life and not let a week, a year, a lifetime pass before our eyes without a conscious moment. May each of us APPRECIATE the time, the moments, and the love today.

~ I AM aware of the blessings in my life, and I APPRECIATE this moment of consciousness.

~~~~~~~~~

Blessings of Gratitude are sent to you today. May you APPRECIATE the present moment not looking ahead or behind, but embracing all that presence has to teach you.

~~~~~~~~~

Day 2
WITNESS~ Let us WITNESS the moon that shines in the night as it gently touches the Earth with a tender glow. This can be our blessing if we choose to WITNESS that which is already waiting for us. Have you gazed at the trees swaying in the breeze, listened to the coyotes crying out to one another underneath the sky of stars, and rejoiced with the music of the crickets chirping in the fields of grass? If we are not present, we may be missing these beautiful moments that encompass us. Let our hearts open to hear, see, and be with the multiple gifts that surround us. This present moment, we have the opportunity to contribute by sending our blessing of love, gratitude, compassion, and joy to all that inhabit this amazing world. Let us choose to be a WITNESS in this life - to take notice of all that is happening around us - and let us choose to see the continued blessings that fill our world.

~ I AM present as I greet the day, a WITNESS to all that I see, hear, touch, and feel.

~~~~~~~~~

Blessings of Insight are sent to you today. May you WITNESS all that is happening with a deep inner wisdom that all is unfolding with grace.

~~~~~~~~~

Day 3
PRESENT~ When we live in the PRESENT, there are no regrets about the past regarding how life could, or should, have unfolded differently. When we live in the PRESENT, the thoughts of tomorrow do not bring worry or anxiety over things that may or may not come to pass. Grounding ourselves in the now brings more peace to our minds. Our lives tend to fall into place

effortlessly, and the grace of the Universe becomes apparent in all that we see. The perfection of life's timing was always there, waiting for us to become PRESENT enough to see the blessings of the journey. We are the best version of ourselves when we live in the moment of now.

~ I AM PRESENT as I walk through this glorious day.

Blessings of Awakening are sent to you today. May you be PRESENT as you form your thoughts and as you send your words out into the world.

Day 4

COMPLETE~ The essence of you and I is COMPLETE in every way. It is through our journey that we strive to tap into the depths of our soul and into the essence that holds the Universal wisdom to guide our every step. It is the unconscious part of us that brings discomfort into our everyday experiences. When you and I let go of that which we cannot change or predict, we become more present. It is in the current moment that we are COMPLETE and witness this peace within ourselves. We are no longer searching for anything outside of us. It is through trust that we begin to understand that life is unfolding with perfect timing and that we are one with all that is visible and invisible. You and I only need to embrace our unique experiences to bring more COMPLETE love and Light from our conscious being to everything that we witness.

~ I AM COMPLETE and at peace with my heart, mind, and body.

Blessings of Peace are sent to you today. May your heart, mind, and soul be at COMPLETE peace in this journey of life.

Day 5

DELIVERANCE~ The mind that ceases to have thoughts within, silently asks for the DELIVERANCE of solitude. The stress that tightens the muscles within our body begs for the DELIVERANCE of peace within each cell. The solitude and peace come from being present at the very moment in which we are residing. Let us release yesterday's regrets and tomorrow's anxiety. The DELIVERANCE comes from being present and experiencing life as it is, rather than how we want it to be according to our expectations and judgments. Let us take every moment and surround it with love, embracing the hope and choosing to see the beauty of life with all the possibilities.

~ I AM embracing the beauty of life's endless possibilities. The DELIVERANCE comes to me in the present moment.

Blessings of Openness are sent to you today. May you be open to the DELIVERANCE that awaits you in the Universal guidance.

Day 6
INTUITIVE~ Let us be present in this moment, listening for our INTUITIVE voice to emerge in the silence. The whispers of love and the images of hope appear with the steady beat of each of our hearts. You and I are INTUITIVE beings, and the answers to our questions are available to us in every moment. We only need to ask, and they will appear in a song that plays on the radio, in the words that someone speaks, or through a thought that crosses our mind. It will come when we least expect it but are ready to hear the answers. Let us be open to the INTUITIVE being of who you and I are in every moment.

~ I AM an INTUITIVE being, open to the guidance of the Universe.

Blessings of Wisdom are sent to you today. May you be open to the INTUITIVE guidance that supports your journey.

Day 7
THANKFULNESS~ It is when we adopt the practice of THANKFULNESS that we become present and appreciate the blessings of our journey. Each of us is experiencing life in our own unique way and the more THANKFULNESS we feel and express, the more we will have moments of joy. If we want more love and Light in our life, then we must give more love

and Light to the world. It is here that our heart will be filled with more joy, and the feelings will multiply. Let us bring our love and Light to every situation and approach all things with THANKFULNESS.

~ I AM living a life of THANKFULNESS as I share my love and Light with the world.

~~~~~~~~

Blessings of Gratitude are sent to you today. May you witness and express THANKFULNESS in the life you are creating.

~~~~~~~~

Notes

Image captured by Susan Gossett.

Week 39
Legacy of Relationships

~~~~~~~~~

Blessings of Harmony are sent to you today. May you value the Legacy of Relationships in your journey.

~~~~~~~~~

Our relationships with the world bring depth and richness into our journey, the friends that we choose, the family we are given, and the connection we have with ourselves. The truth is, if we are not kind and loving to ourselves it limits how deeply we can connect with others in our lives.

Indeed, our connections are inseparable, and it is for the highest good that we must begin to live together harmoniously. Let us choose to interpret our conversations with one another from a place of unconditional love in each and every gathering. May our actions toward one another be filled with empathy and compassion.

When our relationship with others is failing, we need to first look within ourselves to see if we are living in the present moment and whether or not we have peace within ourselves.

279

Healing and peace begin within each of us. It is not always easy to take down our walls and observe the status of our well-being; yet having the problematic inner dialogues of what is going well and what may need to change is essential to bringing us back into balance.

We did not come here to just move along with no direction or purpose. We are here to expand and contract, to fail and succeed, to give and receive love, and in doing so, to get just a bit closer with each experience to the highest version of ourselves.

Our relationships with others assist us in our process of self-discovery. We learn and grow through the individuals that 'get us' and those that don't. We often learn more in our failures than in our successes. We frequently become more focused on what we want in life when there is heartbreak.

It is not easy, but when we understand that our struggles guide us to our legacy, we can see the blessings, and even find gratitude, in that which we do not understand.

Let us create a LEGACY OF RELATIONSHIPS throughout our journey upon this planet. In the end, our connection with others, our world, and ourselves will carry on long after we have left this plane.

Be thy Light.

Day 1
FAMILY~ Each of us individually defines the meaning of FAMILY in our unique circumstances. Of course, there are the various roles that each of us play, such as parents, children, siblings, cousins, in-laws, and spouses, but we may have bonded with others outside of those traditional lines. We have all likely had the experience where we meet someone and forge an instant connection that lasts a lifetime. These are the relationships in our lives that bring joy and compassion, assisting us to expand into our highest self through love for where we are and where we are striving to be. These individuals are our tribe, community, and FAMILY in this journey of life. These are the relationships that bring light in the darkest of times that assist us in the moments where the hope seems lost. The relationships between one another and the bonding between our spirits are what define our FAMILY.

May each of us have a community of joy, love, grace, and peace that surround our world.

~ I AM surrounded by relationships that I call FAMILY, which are supportive and loving in my journey.

~~~~~~~~~

Blessings of Gratitude are sent to you today. May you live a life of thankfulness in the words that you speak and the actions that you take with those that you call FAMILY.

~~~~~~~~~

Day 2

GATHERING~ The human race has been GATHERING together since the beginning of time. We come together to celebrate special dates and our accomplishments, to mourn that which we have lost, to reminisce about days gone by, and to say goodbye and wish each other the best in life's endeavors. We delight in GATHERING with those we love; to converse, to eat and drink, to hug one another, and to just be in each other's presence, heart to heart. As we gather together with the ones that we love, let us be present in love, grace, and joy; taking in the significance of all those who fill the room. Let us be the Light in the words that are spoken in the blessed GATHERING at that moment.

~ I AM supporting and loving those that are GATHERING in this conscious moment.

~~~~~~~~~

Blessings of Connection are sent to you. May you be the Light and bring the hope to every GATHERING, making heart to heart connections with all those you meet.

~~~~~~~~~

Day 3

HARMONIOUSLY~ You and I are one with the world. Let us choose to live HARMONIOUSLY with all things that we encounter as we walk

281

through life. Everything that we see, touch, hear, and smell is connected with the Universe. Let us consciously be at peace with those that bring us joy, as well as those who bring contrast to our lives, and live HARMONIOUSLY with the expansion of our consciousness. You and I are one with all things that we have seen and that which we cannot see. Let the highest version of who we are offer kindness and compassion to the Earth, sky and everything in between. May we live each moment HARMONIOUSLY with all that is. Even when our wisdom is not deep enough to see, may we still choose to believe that we are one.

~ I AM living HARMONIOUSLY in my mind, body, and soul.

~~~~~~~~

Blessings of Peace are sent you. May you find the wisdom to live HARMONIOUSLY in all that you do.

~~~~~~~~

Day 4
INSEPARABLE~ You and I are not separate from the Universe. We are connected with each wave that forms in the ocean and every grain of sand upon which we walk. We are INSEPARABLE from one another; each action that we take has a reaction, just as the pebble dropped in a pool of water ripples to the shoreline. Just as the process of photosynthesis that occurs within the tree produces the oxygen which sustains our breath; the decay of all living things enriches the soil with nutrients, allowing the tree to grow and flourish. Let us look within ourselves today and connect with the truth of who we are. Let us see the connectedness that is evident within each cell of our bodies and choose to shine our Light upon the world by creating ripples of love. The Universe, the stars, our planet, you, and I in this present moment; we *all* are INSEPARABLE.

~ I AM INSEPARABLE from all that I can and cannot see. I AM one with the world.

Blessings of Universal Wisdom are sent to you. May you be aware that everything that you see and do not see is INSEPARABLE.

Day 5

INTERPRET~ This is the life that we are creating, and we are the main ingredient of that which we INTERPRET. You and I make choices in every moment through our relationships with others and the physical things that we bring into this life. They are the source of many lessons that provide the seasoning, which adds flavor to our lives. We bring the meaning to our relationships and all that we encounter. You and I INTERPRET that which happens around us. We decide if the words of another have the power to bring in the clouds to cover our brilliant Light. Let us INTERPRET all things through love, the joy that we are and the shining Light that guides us.

~ I AM love in all situations. I INTERPRET the world around me through love and compassion.

Blessings of Inner Wisdom are sent to you. May you INTERPRET all communications with a heart of love and a mind that is open.

Day 6

LEGACY~ You and I came here to experience life to its fullest, to expand our consciousness, and to grow through our journey. Each of us has a LEGACY to leave to those who will continue when our journey has ended. Let us consciously choose to leave a LEGACY that will linger with the ones who knew and loved us during our time upon this planet. How are the goals and dreams in harmony with that which we want to be remembered? As we live in the moment of today and make decisions at every turn, may we be aware of how the present moment shapes and molds our LEGACY for tomorrow.

~ I AM creating my LEGACY with each moment that I share love with the world around me.

~~~~~~~~

Blessings of Intuitive Guidance are sent to you today. May you consciously choose your actions to be in alignment with your LEGACY.

~~~~~~~~

Day 7
RELATIONSHIPS~ The RELATIONSHIPS in our lives are a direct reflection of where we are in our personal journey. As if you are looking into a mirror and seeing your face; but instead, you are peering into who you are and where you have been. Those whom you and I have attracted into our world in the past may be very different from the individuals we would attract today. The behaviors that we dislike in someone else are the behaviors we avoid in ourselves. The same holds true for the characteristics that we admire. Let us view our RELATIONSHIPS as a looking glass into who we are striving to become. It can be an enlightening reflection for all of the RELATIONSHIPS in our lives and with ourselves.

~ I AM reflecting on the RELATIONSHIPS in my life and choosing to rise to my essence.

~~~~~~~~

Blessings of Honor our sent to you today. May you shine your Light in every situation and in all your RELATIONSHIPS.

~~~~~~~~

Notes

Image captured by Susan Gossett.

Week 40
Genuine Self

~~~~~~~~

Blessings of Self–love are sent to you today. May your Genuine Self have compassion and forgiveness in all that you witness and experience.

~~~~~~~~

May we be faithful to ourselves as we walk the path of our lives and its many twists and turns. Our experiences bring us extraordinary strength and determination as we discover all that we know is our truth.

It is through the ins and outs of life that we become more proficient in our self-discovery. Each moment we learn to understand better the difference between that which we should place our attention on and that which does not resonate with the authenticity of who we are.

This is why each of our experiences are vastly different from one another. The choices that you and I make, and the feelings that we feel, will either lead us to make similar decisions or to stay clear of a particular scenario in the future.

286

Our differences in choices may vary because of our values or priorities. It is why we must be clear on our intentions and the outcome we desire in our journey. When you and I engage in tasks that are not in sync with our genuine self, our energy level suffers, and our heart, mind, and soul are no longer aligned as a unified force.

One of the many blessings of time is to evolve and expand into our true essence. Year by year, and experience by experience, we become clear on what we want more of in our journey and learn what steals our joy.

When we choose to go against our authenticity, and not to be genuine, we lead ourselves to moments of sadness, dissatisfaction, and eventually depression. We are here to be unique and authentic, to love others and ourselves thoroughly, and to create a world of compassion and empathy for all.

We can always recognize the path that leads us away from our purpose when we focus on the feelings we are experiencing. The signs are always there. Do you awaken with hope and excitement for what lies ahead in your day, or do you find yourself waking in a state of distress? Do you see yourself open to connecting with others, or do you want to call in sick and hide away? How many times a day do you feel joy? If that seems unrealistic, how many times a week, do you feel joy?

This is your journey, and it is your purpose to create a life filled with love and hope, and to discover that mere differences in opinions can lead to better outcomes, if we only keep an open heart with one another.

Let us be the curious souls that tune into our inner wisdom for guidance. Let us approach life with an inquisitiveness that awakens our joy. Let us stay true to our essence, our GENUINE SELF.

Be thy Light.

Day 1
CREATION~ You and I are a CREATION that is loved unconditionally by the Universe. We are unique beings that think, feel, and experience life through our individual perception. Each of us came here to create a one of a kind experience, to love, and to open our minds to the realm that we have around us. Let us be open to the contrast and to expand through that which we do not always comprehend. We are here to create, explore and to be

287

present with the CREATION of life. Let us find joy in the process, to see the beauty in that which we have in front of us, and to love ourselves in this moment unconditionally as the amazing CREATION that we are.

~ I AM embracing the CREATION of me, my gifts, and the unique journey that I share with the world.

Blessings of Light are sent to you today. May you witness the miracle of life's ever-expanding CREATION.

Day 2
HIGHER SELF~ There is a HIGHER SELF within each of us. This part is the one that chooses the highest thoughts of positivity and shares loving actions with the world. The HIGHER SELF feels the hope within the heart before the eyes see even a glimmer. This part of ourselves is manifested when we smile or open a door for a stranger, for it may be that one small act of kindness that provides a beacon of light and hope in that person's day. It is our decision in each moment to either voice the words of light and hope from our essence or to keep silent when there is nothing positive to say. In the latter circumstance, let us instead send a blessing to that which we do not understand. Let each of us live our lives from the HIGHER SELF and help create a more hopeful and loving world.

~ I AM striving to live my life from my HIGHER SELF in all that I do.

Blessings of Inner Light are sent to you. May you be empowered to live from your HIGHER SELF in every moment.

Day 3
EXTRAORDINARY~ Each of us is an EXTRAORDINARY being. There is no one like you or me in this entire Universe. Our looks, movements, voice, laughter, thought process, and viewpoints are unique to each of us; as well as

how we perceive the world around us. Let us acknowledge the EXTRAORDINARY uniqueness of who we are. Let us bask in the sun, smell the roses, sing a song, dance until our heart is pounding, laugh until the tears run down our cheeks, smile until our muscles hurt, and be the EXTRAORDINARY self of which we know we are capable. Let us not hide who we are but choose to shine our Light. Let us love beyond what we think we can and watch as the world reflects more love upon us than we thought possible. It is when we love unconditionally that the world around us becomes EXTRAORDINARY in every way.

~ I AM choosing to see the EXTRAORDINARY in every part of my life.

~~~~~~~~

Blessings of Inspiration are sent to you. May you be the EXTRAORDINARY Light you came here to be.

~~~~~~~~

Day 4

FAITHFUL~ We are radiant and beautiful beings that are experiencing life through the spirit that is residing in our body. Let us be FAITHFUL to who we are and to the love within us, which desires to be expressed in all of life's glory and light. You and I are ever-expanding in the ebb and flow of that which is within us and around us. Let us be FAITHFUL to the Universal Light that shines through us and the path that we walk. We are experiencing this world through the spirit that we are and are evolving to be. We are expanding in all that we see, hear, speak, touch, taste, and feel in the presence of each and every moment. We are connected to one another as we evolve into a place of love and Light. Let us be FAITHFUL to the highest good, to the possibilities of the seemingly insurmountable, and to a love that is unconditional toward all living things. Let us be FAITHFUL to who we are and who we are becoming.

~ I AM FAITHFUL to my highest self as I choose more joy, love, and compassion always.

289

Blessings of Creativity are sent to you today. May you be FAITHFUL to creating a better world through every experience, expanding into your true essence.

~~~~~~~

Day 5
GENUINE~ When each of us approaches life with the part of us that is GENUINE and true, our lives are enriched by the experiences and the epiphany moments along the way. It is when you and I are not functioning from our personal truth that we feel defeated and depleted in our journey. Each of us knows when we are operating from the GENUINE part of who we are - the essence of our highest self - and in the spirit of the unconditional love which we came here to share. Today, before we utter a word, let us check in with our heart, and may our words be GENUINE and true from our conscious state of being.

~ I AM communicating with others from the GENUINE and true essence of my being.

~~~~~~~

Blessings of Peace are sent to you today. May every word and action be GENUINE and authentic with your true self.

~~~~~~~

Day 6
INQUISITIVE~ Children explore the world around them with INQUISITIVE minds. They want to learn and understand, striving to know more. As you and I take steps in our lives, it is important to ask questions and explore life with an open heart. It is possible that a belief of yesterday was what was needed to persevere in the past. This same belief today may be holding us back from physical, mental, or spiritual growth. Let us not become stagnant and lose our passion for expanding into our higher selves. Let us be INQUISITIVE, bringing more Light into our thought processes and bringing more love into our world to dispel the fears of yesterday. Today

we will choose to be INQUISITIVE, expanding into our higher selves of unconditional love.

~ I AM walking through life as an INQUISITIVE being, expanding into my highest self.

~~~~~~~

Blessings of Joy are sent to you today. May you be INQUISITIVE as you approach all that is out of your comfort zone, expanding your world with endless possibilities.

~~~~~~~

Day 7

SELF~ The essence of each of us, and that which is residing in our unique body is SELF. We came here to participate in and witness a world of amazing possibilities. Along the way, we may have become disgruntled and negative because of things that we have witnessed. The SELF, in its earliest phases, can be vulnerable and does not always have the tools to overcome those moments through love and compassion. It is through time that we learn new tools to use that will help us become stronger and yet, kinder. We become more in tune with the wisdom, and it leads us to inner peace. Let us not become stifled in our journey by beliefs that no longer serve us. Let us choose to let go of the anger and negativity, the doubts and the fear that keep us from blossoming into our true SELF.

~ I AM living my life with an open heart that leads me to my true SELF.

~~~~~~~

Blessings of Consciousness are sent to you today. May you open your heart and awaken into your true SELF.

~~~~~~~

Notes

Image captured by Susan Gossett.

Week 41
Listening in Silence

~~~~~~~

Blessings of Peace are sent to you today. May your moments of Listening in Silence bring clarified answers to your questions.

~~~~~~~

It is in the silence that quietude comes to us as a welcoming gift that we may or may not have realized that we desperately needed. This hushed space gives us the solace we need to rejuvenate ourselves and to bask in the Universe's support and guidance.

We take a breath into our body, being mindful as it travels down through our lungs and into our diaphragm, replenishing our cells with energy through the awareness of our consciousness. As we breathe out, the tensions become apparent, and we are able to release that which no longer serves us out into the world. Over and over we bring in the energy that is needed and release that which does not resonate with the core of who we are here to be.

In between the in and out of our breath, there is a space within which we can choose to listen for the inner guidance. It will greet us, welcoming us back to the connection of our true essence, as we become at peace with the questions we are seeking from life.

In this space, we find refuge in the moment, where yesterday and tomorrow are no longer in our thoughts; there is only the presence of now. If the thoughts persist, we bless them and surround them in the Light of love and hope of a better world.

There is no need for frustration or disappointment because each experience is imperfectly perfect and you need only to be compassionate with yourself in each moment.

These experiences, that we graciously give ourselves in the silence, are what lead us to align our heart, mind, and soul. They bring us moments of synchronicity to tap into the Universal guidance of support and love.

It is not uncommon to have resistance to stillness, to avoid it at all costs, busying ourselves with laundry, television, phone calls, etc. All of our tasks seem vastly more important, but when you take the time, 5-minutes, 20-minutes, or 60-minutes of quiet reflection, you will open your eyes knowing that this was what you so desperately needed in order to align yourself with the present moment.

The silence always awaits you. It lingers for you in the trees that reach to the sky, or the grass that tickles your ankles. It whispers to you in the breeze or the calling of a bird's song. The universal calm is always waiting for you to take a moment and to connect with all that you came from and to assist you in where you are going.

Let us focus on the blessings as a listener and rejuvenate our journey by LISTENING IN SILENCE.

Be thy Light.

Day 1
SILENCE~ The truth that you and I seek is always found in the SILENCE. We often attempt to outrun the thoughts and feelings of yesterday's regrets, as well as our anxieties of tomorrow, but we know in our hearts that this cannot be done. When you and I are continually caught up in the busyness of life, and we don't take a moment of SILENCE to be centered, our hearts become frazzled, depleted and lost. Each of our lives is meant to be one of joy, and this comes from a place of surrender, acceptance and a willingness

to let the Universe lead the way. Peace and guidance are always waiting in the SILENCE for us to come home to the essence of our truth.

~ I AM always at one with my truth. I find peace and my truth in the SILENCE.

~~~~~~~~

Blessings of Openness are sent to you. May you seek the SILENCE and come home to your essence.

~~~~~~~~

Day 2
LISTEN~ You and I are an example to others in all that we say and do. Our lives are like no others that have come before us. Each of us is living experiences that differ in some way, and our example is a gift that we can choose to give to the world. It is when we open our hearts and LISTEN to the guidance of the Universe that our journey is enriched with love and joy. Whether our lives are filled with grandeur or simplicity, let us LISTEN to our intuitive thoughts and enhance our life experience by being present. We have been blessed with the gift of intuition. Let us be present, and LISTEN as the Universe guides us to our destiny.

~ I AM open to the Universal wisdom as I LISTEN for the guidance to fulfill my dreams.

~~~~~~~~

Blessings of Universal Wisdom are sent to you. May you LISTEN to the guidance that will lead you to create all that you imagine.

~~~~~~~~

Day 3
FAVORITE~ We all have a FAVORITE place where we feel at peace with everything around us. Where life is brighter and with more hope than just moments before we arrived. In this place we can be ourselves and talk about our hopes for tomorrow, but also feel safe to mention our fears and doubts. It is a safe place where you and I are loved and supported. That FAVORITE place may not be a physical space, but may instead be in the company of certain individuals who we treasure. It may be a place of quiet and serenity where we are surrounded by nature in all its beauty. Let us go to this

FAVORITE place for just a moment to experience it once again. Let us sit in silence, recalling the smells and how things felt to the touch of our fingers. Let us take a deep breath and feel the emotions that instantly arise when we return to this place.

~ I AM taking a moment each day to center my being in love, surrounded by the silence of my FAVORITE place.

~~~~~~~~

Blessings of Remembrance are sent to you today. May you find your FAVORITE place that will bring you many moments of serenity.

~~~~~~~~

Day 4
QUIETUDE~ It is in the QUIETUDE that we find the peace in our souls. Our heart opens further and allows more love to come and go in this space. The mind finds moments of silence, providing respite from the busyness of our thought patterns. The essence of who we are can take a long breath and reconnect with all that was, is, and will be. The QUIETUDE is where we rejuvenate and replenish the radiance of our Light, which may have become a bit dim. It is where the Universe fills us back up with all that we need to go forward with our journey. The QUIETUDE is where all the boundaries that separate us from each other disappear and we are one with all. Let us embrace and seek these moments in our life.

~ I AM enjoying the moments of QUIETUDE where I rejuvenate and replenish the Light within me.

~~~~~~~~

Blessings of Rejuvenation are sent to you. May you find moments of QUIETUDE to replenish your being.

~~~~~~~~

Day 5
SYNCHRONIZE~ Often as we take on challenges and accomplish the responsibilities of our lives, we neglect to align and SYNCHRONIZE our mind, body, and soul. It is important that we stay in sync with ourselves

emotionally, physically, and spiritually. Let us listen to our intuitive thoughts of what actions we need to take to SYNCHRONIZE with the world around us. Each of us can take a moment to sit in silence, to quiet the mind, to nourish our body, and to encourage the highest thoughts of love. These simple steps will soothe all that is currently swirling through our mind and assist us to SYNCHRONIZE with the world around us.

~ I AM listening to my intuitive thoughts as I SYNCHRONIZE my mind, body, and soul.

~~~~~~~~~

Blessings of Alignment are sent to you today. May you SYNCHRONIZE your mind, body, and soul into Oneness.

~~~~~~~~~

Day 6

LISTENER~ As we move through the day, let us be a LISTENER. May we attend to our hearts, for the answers that we seek are being revealed by words of wisdom within. These answers may come to us in an inner whisper or through the words of another. Let us truly be present to hear the truth that is offered, each of us being a LISTENER in every moment. When we are in tune with our inner voice or to that which is happening around us, the judgment can stay at bay. You and I can be open to the words, events, and messages that are being shared. Let us not assume where a conversation may lead but choose to be fully present as we communicate with one another, taking the time to hear the story that is being told. Let us be a LISTENER, hearing the wisdom within our own heart and in the hearts of others; for the heart whispers the truth to all of life's questions.

~ I AM available to the wisdom of the Universe, a LISTENER to that which is in the heart.

~~~~~~~~~

Blessings of Connection are sent to you today. May you consciously be the LISTENER in all your heart to heart connections.

~~~~~~~~~

Day 7

QUIET~ Let us each take a moment to sit in silence and find the QUIET within. Let us not concentrate on the thoughts that pass through our mind, but bask in the wonderful moments that lie between our thoughts. It is in this QUIET space that we regenerate our mind, body, and soul. It is here that we find the wisdom to create a life that is filled with grace, joy, and peace. We are beings with a voice, and our words are shared with those that surround us. Are we speaking words of love and Light? Let each of us tap into the QUIET space; the space that allows wisdom to enter into our mind and change our thoughts, words, and actions into ones that come from a higher and more loving space than we have ever been before.

~ I AM seeking moments where I connect with the QUIET space that renews my being.

~~~~~~~~

Blessings of Inner Wisdom are sent to you today. May you hear the guidance that waits for you in the QUIET space of solitude.

~~~~~~~~

Notes

Image captured by Tim Chinn.

Week 42
Shining Thy Light

~~~~~~~~

Blessings of Radiance are sent to you today. May you embrace Shining Thy Light for the entire world to see.

~~~~~~~~

Let us focus our thoughts, words, and action on shining our unique Light in the world. As we wake each morning, are we feeling gratitude for the opportunity of the day we are blessed to have? During mealtimes, are we conscious of the quality of the food we are choosing and placing into our bodies? How are you and I deciding to live consciously and to bring our Light to others?

There are many facets to the gem we are creating in this journey of our lives. We may differ from one another, but each experience is crucial to raising the world's consciousness. Together we can build all that we envision, to bring acceptance, compassion, and forgiveness to the planet for, not a selected few, but for all.

Let us shine through the smoke and mirrors of despair with the Light of

300

compassion and hope, reaching for the progress that leads us to a phenomenal world.

You may ask, 'How is it that with all of our differences we can find peace, harmony, and unity?' The answer lies within our perception, when each of us manifests from a space of abundance for all, the doors open from where once was hopelessness, unfolding into the endless possibilities of our tomorrows.

Most of the world is manifesting from the limited viewpoint of 'There is not enough for everyone; therefore, I will hold tightly to what I have accumulated.' This way of thought reinforces the misconception that there are limited resources.

Together we can create resources that have not yet been developed in order to satisfy the needs of food, water, shelter, and healthcare for every being that walks the planet. If these needs are met, there will be more energy to create more opportunities to use the talents and gifts of each person.

Each of us came here to contribute but, if our basic needs are not being met, it is difficult to create while in a state of hardship. If we are living in fear or doubt of our abundance, we reinforce situations where we are still living in a state of lack.

We choose every morning how we will contribute our Light to the world. Let us shine upon all that we encounter and radiate the Oneness that we came here to create. Let us be grateful to be walking this path with one another and shine our Light happily for all who witness and partake in this journey.

Let our actions and words be surrounded in love as we SHINE THY LIGHT wherever our path may lead us.

Be thy Light.

Day 1
FACETS~ There are many FACETS of a precious gem that enhance the way it sparkles in the sun. You and I also have many FACETS of our being that once buffed and shined, reveal the brilliance of who we are. Each of us experiences life, and that which is happening around us, with different perspectives and varying opinions. It is the Light within us that brings the hope into each and every situation. Let us each choose to reflect the Light of

301

who we are and are striving to be by allowing the experiences of life to buff and shine the FACETS of our being. Let us then shine our Light on the world with renewed hope and grace.

~ I AM embracing the experiences that buff the many FACETS of my being, for each of them allows me to shine.

~~~~~~~

Blessings of Unconditional Love are sent to you today. May you shine brilliantly from all the FACETS of your being.

~~~~~~~

Day 2
GRATEFUL~ Let us be GRATEFUL for every moment that has passed us by, and that lies before us. It is in this space, abounding with thankful thoughts and actions that we may be filled with peace. Let us be GRATEFUL for that which we have come to know as our truth, for the solace that resides within our hearts. We have been blessed with the gift of the sun that peeks over the horizon each day, the stars that twinkle in the sky, the wind that blows through the trees, and the rain that quenches the soil. It is through recognizing and expressing gratitude for these gifts that we may experience relief from the burdens upon our souls. It is at this moment, when we are GRATEFUL for all that is, was, and will be, that we may find peace.

~ I AM GRATEFUL for the lessons of the past, for my current wisdom, and for the gift of the future, in which to shine my Light upon the world.

~~~~~~~

Blessings of Openness are sent to you today. May you have a GRATEFUL heart for all of life's beautiful encounters.

~~~~~~~

Day 3
HAPPILY~ Let us awake HAPPILY as the sun rises for a new day. It is a blessed gift for each of us to be of service in the world and to be a Light to all whom we may encounter. Today, in every moment, let us be HAPPILY present, for dwelling on the thoughts of yesterday and tomorrow brings

worry and stress. This moment is a treasure, a gift that will be gone quickly and will not come again. Let us see the vivid colors that brighten the world, and hear the beauty in the words that are spoken and the music that is played. Yes, today we will be in tune to all that surrounds us, HAPPILY shining our Light as we journey out into the world.

~ I AM HAPPILY embracing all that I encounter today. My being is open to that which comes to me.

~~~~~~~~

Blessings of Joy are sent to you today. May you HAPPILY share the essence of all that you are with the world.

~~~~~~~~

Day 4

PHENOMENAL~ We are PHENOMENAL! There is no one in the whole world like you or me. Each of us is one of a kind; a unique being who is experiencing life through all of our senses. Let us recognize the PHENOMENAL beings that we are. You and I give beauty to the world just by embodying the essence of who we are. Let us not waste our time and energy being like everyone else; shine thy Light, be the star that guides others in moments of darkness, and be the sun that warms and brightens the path. Let us embrace our differences, as well as our similarities, for the colors of life, the notes within a melody, and the steps of a dance are what enrich the journey. All of that which we see and experience in life is what brings depth and meaning to this PHENOMENAL journey.

~ I AM a PHENOMENAL being, and I choose to live a life that is of greatness.

~~~~~~~~

Blessings of Courage are sent to you today. May you expand into the PHENOMENAL being that you came here to be.

~~~~~~~~

Day 5

PROGRESS~ Let us PROGRESS in the direction of more light and less darkness in the world in which we abide. When life brings us a new experience that is less than ideal, you and I can choose to see the positive point of view. When we hear a story of darkness on the news, let us choose to surround each of the individuals in the situation with Light and love. Let each of us continue to bring the Light to that which we do not understand. May we PROGRESS to be the best version of ourselves by shining the Light within each of our hearts. It is through raising our vibrations that we PROGRESS together, providing more hope, love, light, peace, and balance in the world in which we live.

~ I AM taking steps every day to PROGRESS in my journey to my highest self.

~~~~~~~~~

Blessings of Wisdom are sent to you today. May you PROGRESS with an open heart to create the miracles you wish to see.

~~~~~~~~~

Day 6

RADIATE~ You and I RADIATE our unique Light from the Universe. This Light is the sun that has been placed within each of us and that we came here to share with the world. Why do we question our worthiness when we have been given all that is needed to overcome every obstacle? What is it that we wait for as time keeps moving forward? We are perfect for what we came here to achieve. The experiences that we have been through have made us strong. We shall overcome all problems when we believe in the process of the journey and not just the outcome. Let us not compare ourselves to our brother and sister, but join together to create a world of compassion for all. Together you and I will RADIATE the love, hope, and peace upon the world. Our planet and all that encompasses our home; such as the trees, air, water, creatures, soil, seeds, and all beings need our Light to RADIATE upon them. Let us wait no more and walk forth sharing our essence with the world.

~ I AM one with all things, and I RADIATE my Light and love upon the world.

~~~~~~~~~

Blessings of Light are sent to you today. May you RADIATE your true essence out into the world brilliantly.

~~~~~~~~~

Day 7

SHINE~ In this moment, we have the power to SHINE our Light on the world. Each of us chooses with every breath how brightly to share our essence through the words that we speak to others. Our critical and condemning thoughts do not serve ourselves or the world around us. We can choose higher thoughts and instead share words of wisdom, love, and kindness, and allow our essence to SHINE through. Let us take a deep breath and feel the love that is within us, sharing it with all those that we encounter. Let us be the brightest Light we can be and SHINE brilliantly in the world.

~ I AM opening my heart to the Universe to SHINE my Light of love on the world through offering words of kindness and encouragement.

~~~~~~~~~

Blessings of Conscious Awareness are sent to you today. May you SHINE brilliantly with each word that you speak and action that you take.

~~~~~~~~~

Notes

Image captured by Susan Gossett.

Week 43
Soul Communication

~~~~~~~

Blessings of Connection are sent to you today. May your time with others be with the intention of Soul Communication.

~~~~~~~

When we focus our efforts on our communication with our true essence, the soul of who we are thrives with Universal support and guidance. Soul Communication is when we have aligned our heart, mind, and body; interacting with one another from a space of love and compassion, and making decisions for the highest good.

You and I are communicating in every moment, it may not be done consciously, but we are always placing thoughts, words, and actions out into the world, and directly to those around us. When we are with others, we are still using the tools of interpretation to hear what others are saying to us.

It is not just the spoken words that we hear. Much of our communication is non-verbal, through our body language and breathing patterns. Our facial expressions reflect what is happening in our thoughts and feelings. We even

307

tend to mirror similar emotions back and forth during our conversations to show understanding.

It is essential that we resolve our emerging issues or our interpretations in the future may become clouded by our past experiences. We need to be in tune to the situation, and bring our highest self to every moment, as we communicate heart to heart.

Even when we are hiding our emotions and trying to keep them under control, that energy is still being sent out into the world. You and I are in control of and responsible for our feelings. The more we are at peace, the more our world will be at peace.

Communication is a special gift that is received and given to the world. It is when we allow our soul to be open to the spirit of communication that magic happens, unconditional love unfolds, and we begin to see one another in our true essence.

Let us consciously uplift the way we communicate with one another in love, improving our connection with all that we encounter and witness.

It is through SOUL COMMUNICATION that we can raise our vibrations and assist with the energy around us. Let our actions, and the words that we convey to others, come from a space of love and compassion.

Be thy Light.

Day 1
COMMUNICATION~ COMMUNICATION with others is key in bringing either more joy or more pain into the relationships in our lives. We cannot effectively support one another without COMMUNICATION from the heart. It is true that each of us communicates differently, but our relationships are enhanced when we speak from the soul and listen with the heart. You and I cannot evolve into a place of love if we are not communicating with the intention of love and support for one another. Let us be empathetic, compassionate, loving, and without judgment, for this is how we all need and want to be heard. Let us keep the lines of COMMUNICATION open and witness the benefits to our souls and the world around us.

~ I AM listening and speaking to others with an open heart. My COMMUNICATION with others mirrors my soul intentions.

~~~~~~~

Blessings of Connections are sent to you today. May all your interactions and COMMUNICATION with others be from a state of compassion.

~~~~~~~

Day 2

INTERPRETATION~ It is through our INTERPRETATION of life, and the events that surround us, that we can fill ourselves up with joy or sorrow. We can choose to see the hope in the journey, or we can hinder our path with thoughts of doubt and hopelessness. You and I are the key to the life that we know we should be living. Life is not happening randomly around us; you and I make hundreds of choices every day. Let our INTERPRETATION be foundationally what brings more joy and fulfillment into the world. Choose to shift your INTERPRETATION at any point in time if it is not from your highest self. Let us begin today to interpret things with more joy, hope, compassion, and love. The Universe will respond by bringing more and more of those same things into our world.

~ I AM choosing the highest INTERPRETATION of thoughts for each of my experiences.

~~~~~~~

Blessings of Wisdom are sent to you today. May the INTERPRETATION of your life be through a veil of love without conditions.

~~~~~~~

Day 3

PLAYFUL~ Today let us choose to let go of the seriousness and fully embrace the PLAYFUL side of life. Let us lighten our hearts by letting go of the worries and concerns, laughing as children do; knowing that the Universe continues to guide our lives and all that we are striving to bring into the world. Today let us be PLAYFUL and watch the clouds drift by as if time is as light and free as the wind. We can let go of the hustle and bustle

309

and the deadlines that will no longer matter next week. Today we can choose to run until our side aches, and every cell in our body feels alive. Let us lay in the grass, grinning from ear to ear, thankful that our hearts are full of love, that our soul is deep with truth, and that the core of who we are is embracing the PLAYFUL side of life.

~ I AM being PLAYFUL in my actions today.

Blessings of Humor are sent to you today. May you embrace the PLAYFUL side of life and bask in the moments of laughter and joy.

Day 4

REACHING~ You and I must keep REACHING toward a state of joy by bringing more loving thoughts, and kinder words and actions to the world around us today. Now is our time that to create the environment in which we wish to live; to share our essence, reflect our Light, love without conditions, and be the hope that the world needs. We must be REACHING for the highest state of being and let our hearts be open to the depth of love that we should be sharing. Let our mind be open to all the opportunities to answer our most difficult questions. Let our soul be open to the wisdom that the Universe offers to guide our every thought, word, and action. Let us keep REACHING for the light and love in all things that we say and do.

~ I AM REACHING for the highest thought and sharing the words of hope with the world.

Blessings of Hope are sent to you today. May you keep REACHING for the highest thoughts, words, and actions with Universal guidance that surrounds you.

Day 5

SOUL~ When we stand in front of the mirror, are the thoughts kind and loving toward ourselves? Do we see the beauty of the capsule in which we reside and the miracle of this opportunity? Can we look beyond the physical image to our SOUL, which has a brilliance that cannot be contained? Each of us has enough light to fill the darkest of rooms when we live our truth. The miracle we came here to create is fueled by the love that we have to offer, and our SOUL is ever-expanding to bring our visions to reality. You and I are one with the Universe and contribute to the energy of our planet in every moment. We are each a SOUL of wisdom and infinite possibilities, who came here to be and share with the world. Let us see who we are as we look in the mirror. Let us feel who we are becoming as we allow ourselves to expand into our essence.

~ I AM an ever-expanding SOUL, living and contributing to the world around me.

Blessings of Courage are sent to you today. May you be in tune to the SOUL of who you are and shine your Light brilliantly upon the world.

Day 6

SPECIAL~ No one in the world has experienced life in the way that you and I have. It is a SPECIAL journey to which we have witnessed and contributed. It is our choice how we perceive the moments in the world. Are we choosing to see the joy and happiness? Are we sharing our talents with others? Let us minimize our doubts and fears that hinder our precious time in this SPECIAL body. This very day is a gift during which we can witness the beautiful sunrise with our eyes, breathe in oxygen with our lungs, and hear the sound of music in our ears. Each of us is SPECIAL; a gift that is given to the world. Let us love, live, and be who we came here to be.

~ I AM a SPECIAL creation of the Universe, and I AM sharing my gifts with the world.

311

~~~~~~~~

Blessings of Bravery are sent to you today. May you live the life you came here to create, this is your unique and SPECIAL opportunity to live fully in every way.

~~~~~~~~

Day 7

SPIRIT~ The SPIRIT within us cannot be contained in a vessel, or by walls of steel. It is always expanding and growing with life's changing experiences. The SPIRIT within us is pure and everlasting love. It is our responsibility to be in tune with this energy that inspires loving thoughts. When we take moments to connect with our highest self, we will feel the insight and wisdom that is guiding us. By breathing in the goodness of all that we see and feel, each of us will be open to the possibilities and have faith in that which appears impossible. Let us be in tune with the SPIRIT within us. It is here that miracles unfold before our eyes.

~ I AM in tune with the SPIRIT within me; listening for the continued guidance and support.

~~~~~~~~

Blessings of Possibilities are sent to you today. May you be in alignment with the SPIRIT of you and share yourself freely with all those around you.

~~~~~~~~

312

Notes

Image captured by Susan Gossett.

Week 44
Sacred Stillness

~~~~~~~~

Blessings of Intuition are sent to you today. May your moments in the Sacred Stillness be filled with a connection to the Divine.

~~~~~~~~

Our intuition is always nudging and guiding us to move in the direction of alignment with the Divine. We create space within ourselves to honor the sacred that waits for us in the solitude. It is in that solitude that we rejuvenate our physical and mental state to allow it to mingle with our spiritual essence.

It is the responsibility of each of us to take the time to create our own well-being, to find peace and ease within our body, to soothe the mind from stress and busyness, and to find the space between our thoughts where inner peace awaits us.

Let us focus our intention upon finding the sacredness within the stillness. It is here that we tune into the guidance that assists us along our journey.

I have found that the fastest way back to center is by being in nature. Even 10 minutes with my face towards to the sun or my feet in the grass brings me such peace and hope. One of my favorite things to do during the summer is to save the bees from my pool. I go out periodically throughout the day and scoop them up and place them on a flower to recuperate. It brings me hope to save a creature of the world, knowing that somehow my act of kindness is rippling out to the world.

I also go out at night with my dogs before we go to bed. As they do their business, I sing to the moon my praise and love for its assistance in keeping our world balanced. It is a beautiful way to greet the pillow each night with such a state of gratitude for the perfection of our place in the solar system.

These sacred moments, that we choose to create, can happen at any time and anywhere. Instead of being cranky when you wake in the middle of the night, you can lay in the silence and give thanks for all that you are grateful for in your life.

Sacredness takes place when we honor all of our yesterdays and reside in the present moment that we have been given. It is acknowledging the lessons that have guided our journey and the blessings that continue to surround you and me.

As we tune into the silence, let our conscious intention honor the SACRED STILLNESS that waits for us always.

Be thy Light.

Day 1
STILLNESS~ When we quiet our mind, sitting in the STILLNESS and tuning into the wisdom of the Universe, the answers will come. Our intuition will be heightened as we walk this journey, and we will become more aware of how we can contribute to the world around us. The guidance may come in an intuitive knowing, or through a whisper, as we embrace the STILLNESS. It is at this moment that the chatter within will begin to fade. It is when we embrace the guidance that we will begin to see, feel, and hear the support in everything that we do. Looking back, we will wonder why we didn't witness the guidance sooner, but it is all part of the process of our hearts opening to the journey that we walk in life. As we observe what may seem chaotic in the world, let us bring the love and peace of our souls to each and every moment. Let us be the STILLNESS and the world around us will begin to evolve into a more loving and supportive environment.

~ I AM one with the STILLNESS. My heart is expanding to the guidance of the Universe.

~~~~~~~

Blessings of Intuitive Guidance are sent to you today. May the STILLNESS bring you into alignment with your highest self.

~~~~~~~

Day 2

WELL-BEING~ It is important for our mental and spiritual WELL-BEING to embrace moments of silence. It is here in the stillness that the blessing of the Universe will guide us to the wisdom that we seek. Our thoughts are often thinking of all the things that we desire, the places we wish to visit, or the goals that we long to achieve. There is a time for this thinking, planning and doing. However, let you and I not forget to replenish our essence by greeting the present moment with consciousness and the grace that waits for us in the silence. Each of us has a spirit of love and joy that needs to reconnect with the Universe. The connection fills our minds, hearts, and souls that leads us to our WELL-BEING. It assists us in remembering our unique journey and all that we came here to share and be. The stillness renews our hope and the compassion of our spirit. Let us take a moment today to replenish our WELL-BEING.

~ I AM choosing that which replenishes my heart, mind, and soul of WELL-BEING.

~~~~~~~

Blessings of Stillness are sent to you today. May you consciously choose your actions that support your WELL-BEING.

~~~~~~~

Day 3

INTUITION~ Each of us has our unique INTUITION. We are intuitive beings, but not all of us have learned to recognize and honor the guidance. The decisions that we make along our journey can be guided by our INTUITION. That 'knowing' what is right, acting upon it, and recognizing that the decision belongs to each of us, not those around us. It is not uncommon for the best decision to be the one that brings us fear; for it is through stretching ourselves out of our comfort zones that we blossom into our essence. Let us reach for the stars and allow our INTUITION to guide us, leading us to our destiny. We are always supported by the Universe; let us know, believe, and live from that place of trust. We are wise beings with the answers within us if we trust in the intuitive guidance that is ours.

~ I AM open to my INTUITION, which is guided by the Universe.

~~~~~~~~~

Blessings of Guidance are sent to you today. May you be open to your INTUITION that supports you in every moment.

~~~~~~~~~

Day 4
SACRED~ Each of us must honor the SACRED space within us to allow the Light of who we are to shine through, even in the darkest moments. It is in the stillness that we allow for the regeneration of our soul and hear the whisper of wisdom seeping through to our consciousness. The SACRED part of you and me is what longs to connect with the Universe. The core of each of us is striving just to be. Let us remember to take moments in our journey to listen to the wisdom and guidance that is waiting to be heard. Let us find our moment today to connect with the SACRED part of who we are, and to open our heart to the continued guidance of that greater force.

~ I AM embracing moments of stillness to connect with the SACRED within me.

~~~~~~~~~

Blessings of Remembrance are sent to you today. May you find the SACRED moments to reconnect with your true essence.

~~~~~~~~~

Day 5
SOLITUDE~ Let us slip away for a moment of SOLITUDE; away from the ever-stimulating noises of cars whizzing by and voices rising in conversation. Let us leave our shoes on the ground and sit cross-legged as we take deep breaths, with our eyes closed. The chatter of the outside world

317

will begin to fade, and the inner chatter will start to rise in our minds. Let us take another deep breath, focusing on the SOLITUDE of this moment; this place of calmness that washes over us, engulfing us in all that we truly are, without the ego. We feel the love, peace, and joy flow over us, easing the stress within the body. Each of us must take the time to stay centered and in touch with our purpose. We are worthy of these moments of SOLITUDE to reconnect with our essence.

~ I AM taking moments of SOLITUDE, to ease the stress that is carried in my body and allow my essence to shine through.

~~~~~~~~

Blessings of Peace are sent to you today. May you seek out the moments of SOLITUDE to rejuvenate all that you are.

~~~~~~~~

Day 6

TIME~ Each of us has a relationship with TIME. When we have the belief that there are not enough hours in the day, our experiences will support this thought. Every moment that we are in this body is a blessing and a gift that has been given to us to create a life of love. The essence of TIME is our friend when we live in the present moment. It is like the wind moving around and through us; though it is not tangible, we know of its power in our lives. TIME is what we make of it, through our experiences and that which we give to the world. Let us ride it, enjoy it, and embrace all the things in life that it brings our way.

~ I AM embracing the power of TIME to create and experience the life I came here to share.

~~~~~~~~

Blessings of Inner Wisdom are sent to you today. May you value your TIME with heart to heart connections to enrich your journey.

~~~~~~~~

Day 7

SOOTHE~ Let us take a moment to SOOTHE our mind with a tranquil thought, to comfort ourselves in support, and to appreciate the amazing journey that we have walked thus far. Each of us needs to take a moment to SOOTHE our soul and to ground ourselves in the present, letting go of our judgment for yesterday and fear of our tomorrow. Let us take a deep breath and bask in the sunlight, feeling the rays upon our skin. Let the sounds of the birds comfort our mind as we gaze upon the world. Let us take this moment to SOOTHE away the hustle and bustle, embracing the calmness of the essence of who we are.

~ I AM letting go of yesterday and not thinking of tomorrow, for I SOOTHE my mind and body by being present with my heart.

~~~~~~~~

Blessings of Support are sent to you today. May you align your mind, heart, and soul to SOOTHE every aspect of your life in love.

~~~~~~~~

Notes

Image captured by Susan Gossett.

Week 45
Releasing Resistance

~~~~~~~

Blessings of Surrender are sent to you today. May you be open to Releasing Resistance from every aspect of your life.

~~~~~~~

Many of our greatest lessons come through the discovery that we need to let go of that which is outside of our control. It seems that our first reaction is often to shut down in sadness or to become angry with others or ourselves.

How can we be better equipped in the act of surrendering to the happenings of the world around us? How can we rise to greet our challenges with hope and trust?

We can begin by dissolving our walls, one brick at a time, to reveal our true vulnerability. It is here that resistance no longer has power; it is here that we may begin the healing process; it is here that we find our way to love without conditions.

When you find yourself wanting to resist, you hinder the flow of life's rhythm. Instead, let us embrace the grief, anger, disappointment, or sadness. These heavy emotions are not here to be your enemy; they are here to bring you a new or deeper understanding of all that you came here to experience in this journey.

These are the moments when clarity will come to you, just as the sun comes through dark clouds on a stormy day. These are the experiences that will lead you to discover better who you are and what you came here to do.

Let us surrender to the knowledge that we are always guided and supported in our journey. Let us acknowledge our fear and greet it with trust that all is unfolding in Divine timing. Let us assist ourselves in healing the scars we have received from going against life's flow.

May we be open to RELEASING the RESISTANCE, moving through the darkness into the Light amid a more aligned Universal timing. Let us release all that, which is no longer serving our journey.

Be thy Light.

Day 1
LETTING GO~ There are times in life when the 'to do' list should not be the priority. We must remember to nourish the spirit of who we are by LETTING GO of that over which we have no control over. Let us take a moment and place our toes in the grass or our hands in the dirt, becoming centered with Mother Earth. Let us breathe in deeply, allowing the air to fill our lungs and our senses to become in tune to that which is happening around us. Let us become centered, experiencing the present moment of now, releasing that which is not serving our journey. By LETTING GO of that over which we have no control, we allow the gates of joy to open and our hearts to accept the wave of blessings that the Universe brings. Let us not permit expectations of that which did not go as planned to steal our joy. Let us not grant a perceived failure to stop our hearts from receiving unexpected blessings. May we remain open to that which the Universe brings, LETTING GO of the preconceived notions regarding the way that things in life should or could have arrived.

~ I AM LETTING GO of all that does not serve my highest journey.

~~~~~~~~~

Blessings of Light are sent to you today. May you find the joy in LETTING GO of all that no longer serves you.

~~~~~~~~~

Day 2

RELEASING~ It is important that we do not hold on to negative thoughts, but allow ourselves the RELEASING of that which no longer serves us. Our physical bodies mirror what we are thinking and feeling. These amazing capsules that you and I reside in let us know, through aches and pains, when we are holding onto stress. There are times when you and I may become ill, and our bodies are simply communicating to us to slow down and to nurture ourselves through the RELEASING of past experiences. Today, let us be in tune with our physical being and let go of the thoughts that are not of our essence by RELEASING them and surrounding ourselves with the purity of love.

~ I AM RELEASING negative thoughts and experiences from my being and surrounding myself with unconditional love.

~~~~~~~~~

Blessings of Rejuvenation are sent to you today. May the process of RELEASING all that no longer serves your journey be with an open heart and mind.

~~~~~~~~~

Day 3

RESISTANCE~ You and I know that RESISTANCE to circumstances over which we have no control results only in continued dissatisfaction. Let us focus on that which we want more of in our lives. Let us complete the actions that we wish to see in others. We desire to see more love in the world, so let us choose to be an example and to be the person that acts in love. It is in the RESISTANCE, the struggle, and the internal fight that we become stifled. This turmoil is what is holding us back from the life that we should be living and experiencing. Let the process of letting go of the RESISTANCE, anger, frustration, and all that is not serving us, bring light and new-found energy into the essence of who we are. We are beings capable of unconditional love and Light that should be shared with the world.

~ I AM focusing on that which I want more of in my life. The RESISTANCE is dissolving from my world.

~~~~~~~~

Blessings of Courage are sent to you today. May you step through the RESISTANCE of doubt and fear into your true essence.

~~~~~~~~

Day 4
REVEAL~ You and I are a beacon of Light that is meant to shine the uniqueness of who we are upon the world. Let us not hide what makes each of us unique. Let us remove the veil that shields our Light, and REVEAL the heart and soul of our essence. Let us let go of the thoughts, habits, and belief systems of negativity and bask in the positivity of love and hope. It is through hope that more love will seep into our lives and REVEAL itself to us each and every day. Let us step through our fears, knowing that the path to our highest self will REVEAL our greatness.

~ I AM stepping through my fears to REVEAL my greatness.

~~~~~~~~

Blessings of Inner Strength are sent to you today. May you REVEAL your vulnerability to the world and connect heart to heart with others.

~~~~~~~~

Day 5
SURRENDER~ There are days that darkness creeps in and sadness overwhelms the spirit within us. These stressful moments bring tension and doubt. We forget to SURRENDER to the process of Universal timing. When you and I attempt to control things around us, it is similar to holding tightly to grains of sand. The tighter one grips, the more the grains slip through our fingers. Let us SURRENDER our need to control things to the Universe, living with faith that we are always supported on our journey. In these moments of despair that allow us to open our heart and SURRENDER to the

things that appear as impossibilities, knowing that miracles can transpire as we trust in the process.

~ I AM letting go of that which I cannot control. I SURRENDER to the process of the Universal timing.

~~~~~~~

Blessings of Faith are sent to you today. May you SURRENDER your heart, mind, and soul to the guidance of the Universe.

~~~~~~~

Day 6

TEACHINGS~ Our individual experiences are teaching us valuable lessons, and when our heart is open, we continue to expand into our essence. These personalized TEACHINGS are a gift for the path that each of us walks. Our spiritual tools continue to grow through the expansion of who we are becoming. We are now able to see and do things through the eyes of love. The lessons and TEACHINGS may at times seem difficult; but when we let go of attachment to the outcome, our burden will be lightened. Let us embrace the TEACHINGS with an open heart and expand into our full consciousness.

~ I AM embracing the TEACHINGS of my journey and expanding into consciousness.

~~~~~~~

Blessings of the Hope are sent to your today. May you embrace the TEACHINGS of life's moments that are leading you to your true self.

~~~~~~~

Day 7

UNBOUNDEDNESS~ The boundaries that each of us places on our lives keep us from achieving the dreams that we came here to share with the world. These boundaries that appear as insurmountable obstacles exist only in the realm of our limited thinking. We did not come here to be confined to belief systems that fail to serve the highest good, nor by fear which leaves us motionless. Let each of us believe in a life with UNBOUNDEDNESS; a life of opportunities with which to create from a loving heart, without fear of what others will say or think; to expand our minds to endless possibilities, knowing they will evolve further than what we can imagine. It is through our actions in UNBOUNDEDNESS, love, and joy that great things will unfold, that miracles will abound, and the lives of which we dream will come to pass before our eyes. Let us take away the mask of doubt, and allow the cape of all that is not serving the world fall from our shoulders. Let us embrace the UNBOUNDEDNESS that is available to each of us, and encourage our hearts to soar with the freedom of possibility.

~ I AM living each moment with UNBOUNDEDNESS as I offer love and compassion to the world.

~~~~~~~~

Blessings of Possibilities are sent to you today. May you be surrounded in the UNBOUNDEDNESS of life's opportunities.

~~~~~~~~

Notes

Image captured by Tim Chinn.

Week 46
Remembering Thankfulness

~~~~~~~

Blessings of Gratitude are sent to you today. May you be in tune with Remembering Thankfulness on your daily journey.

~~~~~~~

When you sprinkle gratitude around the world, joy is not far behind; they tend to follow each other around. The reverse is also true. I find it to be a bit like magic. Every time I go through a period where I can't seem to find my thankfulness due to life happenings, that realization allows hopelessness to settle in.

I basically, "fake it until I make it," as the saying goes. It is almost as if I must will the gratitude into existence, and then I am able to sprinkle joyfulness around once again.

On these occasions, I'll stand in front of the mirror and give myself a good pep talk. I remind myself of all that I have been blessed with in the past and present. I may even write myself a love letter of sorts, expressing all the thoughts and words that I need to hear, and somehow things start to shift. A

328

smile begins to rise up deep within, from my toes, into my heart, and all the way to my head.

There you are my gratitude-friend. I see you. I feel you. I remember you so deeply within my soul.

Each of us has moments of difficulty; regardless of your physical circumstances, being human and evolving into the highest version of you is a path filled with ups and downs.

We gain wisdom through time and acquire more spiritual tools to assist in our difficult moments, but each of us has our lessons to learn.

Gratitude brings hope and hope brings gratitude. If you don't have one, reach for the other, and both will lead you to more moments of joy. The world needs more joy, my friends. Let it be a part of our daily bread, for it feeds our souls with nourishment.

Let REMEMBERING THANKFULNESS be the foundation of our day. It is here that we will bring more Light into each and every moment.

Be thy Light.

Day 1

HAPPY~ You and I have the choice to be HAPPY, joyful, and grateful for everything in our lives. Let us be HAPPY in this very moment as we tune into our senses. May we observe all that is in front of our eyes, take a moment to feel that which touches our skin, pause and listen to the sounds that we hear with our ears, inhale the scents surrounding us through our noses, and savor the taste of food on our tongues. We cannot control that which happens around us, but we can control our reaction to those situations. Let us be HAPPY to be in this moment, present to all that is around us. May we be grateful for this day in which to fully experience this journey of life.

~ I AM so HAPPY, grateful and joyful for every experience in my life.

Blessings of Gratitude are sent to you today. May you consciously choose to be HAPPY and joyful in this journey of life.

~~~~~~~~

Day 2
JOYFUL~ Let us be JOYFUL at this moment, on this day that we have been given. Let us embrace the abundant blessings that surround us and are apparent in all that we see. Let us choose to greet all that we encounter today with a JOYFUL heart, and to send love and light to the world. You and I do not know the whys and hows of our tomorrows, or what the day will bring, but we can greet life with an open heart. Our smile and love will assist others as they embark upon their journey. Let us bring our blessings to the world with a JOYFUL and loving energy.

~ I AM going forth in each moment with a JOYFUL heart.

~~~~~~~~

Blessings of Inspiration are sent to you today. May you create many conscious JOYFUL moments in your life.

~~~~~~~~

Day 3
PERFECTION~ Often when we are in a stressful situation or having an experience that is less than ideal, it is difficult to see the PERFECTION of the moment. It is impossible to visualize how this moment will assist our journey in the future. It is only through time; a week, year, decade, or even longer, that we can see the PERFECTION of our past. It is through the experiences of life that we evolve into our true essence. Let us enjoy the journey, even when all may seem awry or in discord. Let us give thanks for the blessings of the day, even if the event was not surrounded by our highest choices. Let us keep walking with grace when all we see is impossibility. Let us keep reaching for love when we only see anger or bitterness. You and I must keep shining our Light, even when the world is at its darkest hour. The PERFECTION of our journey will come to pass despite all of life's perceived moments of imperfection.

~ I AM seeing my world with the view of love's PERFECTION and bestowing my Light on each situation.

~~~~~~

Blessings of Grace are sent to you today. May you see the PERFECTION of your amazing journey and all that it is teaching you.

~~~~~~

Day 4

OTHERS~ Life is not meant to be a journey that we take alone, but one that is accompanied by OTHERS. Along the way, we have relationships within our circles of family and friends. We receive guidance from teachers and mentors; there are cheerleaders who offer support; there are individuals who may be players in a contrasting situation; or encounters with animals and nature that bring our hearts back to a centering God-like place. Our journey is filled with OTHERS to provide more love, joy, grace, and peace, and the contrast assists us in reaching new levels of these qualities. Sometimes OTHERS even assist us in remembering those lessons that we have forgotten along the way. Today let us embrace all those in our current lives, express gratitude for those in the past who have crossed our paths, and to look forward to higher levels of love, joy, grace, and peace in our future.

~ I AM embracing and grateful for the accompaniment of OTHERS on my journey.

~~~~~~

Blessings of Patience are sent to you today. May you see the blessings of OTHERS and embrace the moments of true connection.

~~~~~~

Day 5

REMEMBER~ Let us REMEMBER the days when we were children and playing the games of 'Ring Around The Rosie' and 'Red Rover, Red Rover.' We use to pretend to play grown-ups, mimicking their world of obligations. It was fun to create a world of make-believe. We would giggle until our sides ached, run until our cheeks were rosy, and squeal with delight at the simple discovery of a fuzzy caterpillar. Today let us take a moment and REMEMBER the light-heartedness of life, the joy of feeling carefree, and the love that filled our hearts when we played with puppies and kittens. Let us REMEMBER and feel our hearts lighten, beginning our day from a place of gratitude and joy.

~ I AM taking a moment to REMEMBER the days of yesterday; my heart is filled with gratitude.

~~~~~~~~

Blessings of Clarity are sent to you today. May you REMEMBER the guidance that waits for you in every moment of your journey.

~~~~~~~~

Day 6
THANKFUL~ Each of us has much to be grateful for and, during the peaceful moments, it is easy to be THANKFUL for the blessings in our lives. It is during the chaotic moments that the feeling of gratitude is hard to express. Let us remember that we are always learning and growing and that the difficult moments also bring us gifts of clarity. May each of us express THANKFUL words and thoughts, even when the sadness overcomes us; for it is through gratitude that the light continues to shine through the darkness. Let each of us be THANKFUL for this moment to be residing in this body, with this mind and our ever-expanding soul.

~ I AM THANKFUL for this moment and all the blessings that life is teaching me.

~~~~~~~~

Blessings of Love are sent to you today. May you be THANKFUL and reach for the moments to surrounding your journey in gratitude.

~~~~~~~~

Day 7
VALUE~ Each of us determines what has VALUE in our lives. Many may believe that things such as gold, platinum, silver, pearls, and diamonds are of

importance, but we decide the VALUE of those things, as well as our relationships with one another and ourselves. You and I determine how we spend the commodity of time. That choice reflects what our priorities are, and this will differ for each of us. Let us consider how we spend our time and think about our priorities. The moments that we spend with our passion, relationships, and in nurturing ourselves should reflect what is important in our life. Let us begin by making conscious decisions about that which is important to us, aligning our time accordingly. Our life is filled with more joy when we VALUE that which enriches our lives and the world around us.

~ I AM aligning my priorities with my time and placing VALUE on that which brings my essence to the world.

~~~~~~~~

Blessings of Validation are sent to you today. May your journey reflect that which you place VALUE on and may those priorities bring much love and Light to the world.

~~~~~~~~

Notes

Image captured by Susan Gossett.

Week 47
Trusting in the Process

~~~~~~~~

Blessings of Faith are sent to you today. May you begin Trusting in the Process, that all is unfolding with Divine timing.

~~~~~~~~

There are certain times of the year when we find ourselves using our spiritual tools more frequently. It may be during certain seasons when the days are shorter, or on the anniversaries of painful happenings, or during celebration times when we are tempted by all the things that we tend to avoid, such as sweets or alcohol.

It is helpful to understand what our bodies and minds need to keep us in sync during life's changing moments. This varies from person to person, and sometimes from season to season, but it is essential to discover what you need to bring your brightest Light to the world.

You and I are always planting seeds in the world, and we have to nurture those thoughts, words, and actions for them to harvest in abundance. There must be a belief and trust that cultivates each seed, just as a real plant grows

335

with sun and water. You and I create our process, and if we lack faith in those tasks, our seeds will not produce an abundant harvest.

TRUSTING IN THE PROCESS is a reminder to check in frequently and to take the extra time to give yourself what you need to nourish your being. Each of us is a seed planter in the world. What are you harvesting? Is it hope, love, compassion, and joy, or fear, doubts, negativity, and hopelessness?

We are in this together my friends, and one conscious moment at a time will lead us to a world of higher consciousness for all.

Be thy Light.

Day 1
DIVINITY~ Let us feel the completeness of our being through the love and Light that we share with the world. Let us know that we are all one with the DIVINITY and that there is no separation. The DIVINITY is within our souls, in the things that we see, hear, touch and smell. It is through the belief that all we know is one, and there is nothing that cannot be accomplished with this unity. You and I need only to believe that the DIVINITY is always guiding and supporting us in our ever-expanding journey.

~ I AM one with the DIVINITY. The guidance and support is a constant in all that I do.

Blessings of an Open Heart are sent to you today. May you always embrace and welcome the guidance of the DIVINITY.

Day 2
HONESTY~ It is important to live each moment of our lives with HONESTY. When you and I speak our words and perform our acts with HONESTY, integrity and truth shine through. It is only through HONESTY that the wisdom of the Universe is able to guide us. When we allow fear to guide our journey, we are tempted to speak and act in a manner which is

insincere and lacking in love. It is only through HONESTY, with ourselves and others, that the truth can guide us and enrich every moment of our path.

~ I AM living my life with HONESTY, allowing integrity and truth to shine through.

~~~~~~~~

Blessings of Truth are sent to you today. May you speak and walk every moment in HONESTY throughout your journey.

~~~~~~~~

Day 3

PROCESS~ We often place our requests out into the world, through our thoughts and words, in both moments of insight and moments of distress. The energy of the request is released out into the world as a seed. It has the potential of being a catalyst in our life. If we think those thoughts or repeat those requests, again and again, continued energy nurtures the seed. If we take action when we are inspired, the added energy nurtures the seed, and it will start to sprout, and doors that were once closed will begin to open. What was once just a thought will become a thing, a place, or an event. You and I must trust the PROCESS and that we are an active part of bringing our request into reality. The PROCESS begins with our thoughts and words, and the belief that the Universe is conspiring to bring our request to the world. Let us be wise and, when inspiration beckons, act upon that energy. Let our thoughts and words be filled with love, joy, hope, and wisdom in creating this amazing journey. Let us believe in the possibilities and trust in the PROCESS.

~ I AM trusting in the PROCESS as the Universe conspires with me to bring my dreams to fruition.

~~~~~~~~

Blessings of Creativity are sent to you today. May you consciously create a life of joy and love that you came here to share with the world.

~~~~~~~~

Day 4

PROMISE~ Throughout our lives, we can experience what may seem to be a staggering amount of change. The myriad of thoughts about the things that have to be done can be overwhelming, but we must remember that after each storm, the sun will shine again. It is through the rays of the sun that the rainbow appears, bringing us the PROMISE of hope. It is with our trust and belief that everything is unfolding with the PROMISE of perfection by the Universe, that we are guided through every moment. Let us always remember the PROMISE that we are loved and supported always, in all things.

~ I AM walking through this path of life knowing that the PROMISE of support and love follows me always.

Blessings of Support are sent to you today. May you know the PROMISE of love and support that follow you always.

Day 5

REASSURED~ Let us be REASSURED that every one of us came here to love and to share that love with all the inhabitants of this planet. We are here to share our unique talents and gifts with this beautiful world, and to give with an open heart toward that which we understand and that which we do not. Let us be REASSURED that we are being guided through all that we see and do; that our actions of love are not just a drop of water, but they are the ripples that carry on, far beyond that which our eyes can see. Let us be REASSURED that the only thing that will stop us from achieving that which we desire, is if we lose hope and give up on what we know as our truth. Let us keep the faith, hope, and love, and move forward in our truth.

~ I AM REASSURED to follow my truth toward more love and compassion for the world, in every moment.

Blessings of Support are sent to you today. May you be REASSURED that you have the capabilities to be the Light in every situation.

Day 6

HONOR~ As a babe just entering the world, we were given a voice. Over time, as we heard the voices of others, we learned a language with which to communicate with all those around us. Through the years, our vocabulary and thoughts grew. We began to discuss those thoughts, which then turned into opinions and theories, often with passion and sometimes anger. Let us HONOR our truth with this voice that we have been given. Let us remember that each of us has our truth that may not coincide with each other's, and we should HONOR this also. It is when we can live from our highest state of consciousness that we HONOR all beings and creatures that reside on this planet.

~ I AM choosing to HONOR the truth within myself as I go out into the world today.

Blessings of Trust are sent to you today. May you HONOR your truth in every word that you speak and action that you take.

Day 7

TRUST~ Let us begin our day with an assuredness of TRUST that all is unfolding as it should. We do not know the hows and whys, only that we must be open to all things to hear the wisdom of the Universe. Each of us needs only to TRUST that we are always supported. We cause ourselves stress when we doubt that which we cannot see, heartache when we seek that which is not aligned with our truth, and sadness when our thoughts are ones of unworthiness. Each of us is made of that which we know as a miracle. Why would we not have faith that the miracles will pave the way for the alignment of the stars and the fulfillment of that which we came to achieve? Let us TRUST in the magic of today as we share our Light.

~ I AM living my life from a heart filled with TRUST that all is unfolding as it should.

Blessings of Miracles are sent to you today. May you TRUST fully that you are supported and loved in this journey of life.

Notes

Image captured by Susan Gossett.

Week 48
Authentic Truth

~~~~~~~

Blessings of Trust are sent to you today. May you be in tune with the Authentic Truth of all that you are and all that you create in the world.

~~~~~~~

As a writer, I have a passion for words. At times I fall in love with phrases, the way that the syllables sound or even the meaning behind a word. It is as if we begin to play a game of hide and seek, over and over they show up in various conversations, in magazine articles, billboards, etc. They flirt with me, building a relationship with my mind and heart.

I begin incorporating the word or phrase more frequently into my thoughts and conversations whenever possible, honoring them by speaking their name. They come into my life, and some are long-time friends, while others leave an impression but fade away with time.

Authenticity is a word that has come to stay and is never far from the thoughts I think or the words I write.

Being authentic implies that the words written by the author, the content that is spoken by the speaker, or the physical object being viewed is genuine and not portrayed fictitiously. Authenticity is being true to yourself, the spirit of all that you are, and following your inner guidance to lead you to create all that you came here to share with the world.

No one can take away your authenticity, except you. You may do this by giving your power away to others, denying actions you are called to because of doubts, or letting fear directly control your destiny by feeling paralyzed when trying to speak your truth.

Let's discuss truth and the meaning I intend with this word when I write about it. I resonate with the Merriam-Webster definition; when Truth is capitalized, it means a transcendent fundamental or spiritual reality.

Ultimately, your Authentic Truth is transcending into your genuine self within a spiritual reality.

That feels divine to me, and it is why I fully embrace this concept with my heart, mind, and soul. Let us transcend into our true spirit within a conscious spiritual reality, opening ourselves to living a life of AUTHENTIC TRUTH.

Be thy Light.

Day 1

KNOWING~ Let us lie in the grass, with the Earth beneath our skin, KNOWING that when we embrace the moment we can be in tune to the Universe. Does each blade of grass compare itself to its neighbor? No, for the blade of grass, as do all things in nature, grows effortlessly and with purpose. The flora and fauna of Mother Nature do not compare their unique journeys, for there is an intuitive KNOWING that all is perfect and as it should be. It often seems in life that humankind has lost their KNOWING; that we've lost sight of our purpose and the contributions for which we came into this world. We distract ourselves with the busyness of life, losing focus on the vision of the heart, the truth, and the unconditional love that we came here to share. Let us move through our day, KNOWING that each of us can live our truth by following the heart of who we are and sharing that with the world around us.

~ I AM living every moment, KNOWING that I am following my truth.

343

Blessings of Openness are sent to you today. May you be open to your soul's voice and the KNOWING that waits for you in the silence.

Day 2

TRUTH~ You and I have read the words of others, and many of their phrases have resonated TRUTH. We have listened to leaders speak from their hearts and have felt their passion as they spoke the words of inspired TRUTH. You and I have sat with like-minded souls and been in the presence of love and kindness, which are a reflection of the highest good. Only when we sit with an open heart; it is then that our deepest questions are answered. This sacred inner sanctum is given to us in love as a blessing by the Universe. It is in this place of serenity and guidance that we witness our TRUTH.

~ I AM in tune with the Universal TRUTH and embrace life from my essence.

Blessings of Guidance are sent to you today. May you speak and take action from your deepest TRUTH always.

Day 3

AUTHENTIC~ Today, as we go out into the world, let the AUTHENTIC you and I step forth with love, kindness, grace, and joy. As the thoughts form, let us pause and reflect that they are the words from the AUTHENTIC part of who we are. If the words are not of truth, then let us change the thought and the words that we speak to be from our highest self… love. We have many relationships in our lives, and each of those gives us the opportunity to shine and expand into the authenticity that we are striving to be. Let us be present today, to be in the moment and in tune to the AUTHENTIC being that we are and can be. Let us share from our hearts the unconditional love and light with the world.

~ I AM striving to become the AUTHENTIC being that I came here to be and share with the world.

Blessings of Courage are sent to you today. May you shine your
AUTHENTIC Light upon the world.

~~~~~~~

Day 4

DECLARE~ As we walk forward in our unique journey, you and I bring the
Light wherever we may travel. When we choose to live our lives from our
true selves, the Light within us shines brightly. This fully conscious state of
mind brings joy in the present moment. We become in tune with all that is
around us, and we share unconditional love with the world. Today let us
DECLARE that we will be a blessing to all that come into contact with us,
that we will bring the Light when we walk into a room, and that we will
reach for the thoughts of love and kindness. Let us DECLARE our truth and
walk in the direction of the Light.

~ I AM bringing my Light to the world in every moment, this I DECLARE.

~~~~~~~

Blessings of Compassion are sent to you today. May you DECLARE in
every moment that you are here to create a life filled kindness and love.

~~~~~~~

Day 5

DEVOTION~ Only when we make the conscious decision to live our lives
with a DEVOTION to our truth, can we find a sense of peace. It is in the
moments that you and I feel in discord that we need to reassess where we are
and reset our intentions. Let us go forth once more with the DEVOTION to
our truth; the DEVOTION to be the essence of who we are and to live in the
present moment, loving ourselves unconditionally in our personal journey.

~ I AM living my truth with a DEVOTION to love myself unconditionally.

Blessings of Consciousness are sent to you today. May you surround yourself with a DEVOTION to your truth and sharing your essence with all that you experience.

~~~~~~~

Day 6

ENLIGHTENMENT~ Let us take away the blindfold that hinders the truth that lies deep within each of us. Let us open our hearts, that we may see the grace of all that is alive within us. Let us be open to ENLIGHTENMENT, shining our Light through the darkness and differences that we witness. May the essence of who we are come forth and may we find grace in reaching the path of true ENLIGHTENMENT. It is possible to create a better world, a home of compassion and harmony. Let us choose the higher thoughts, the words of love, and the actions of ENLIGHTENMENT.

~ I AM open to the guidance of unifying my heart, mind, and soul to discover my path of ENLIGHTENMENT.

~~~~~~~

Blessings of COMPASSION are sent to you today. May you unify your heart, mind, and soul to discover the path to ENLIGHTENMENT.

~~~~~~~

Day 7

TRUTHFUL~ Our souls are longing for us to be TRUTHFUL with ourselves. They are calling for us to stop with the tasks that are stealing our joy and lowering our vibrations, and that fail to provide contentment or peace. Our essence does not care about the latest craze surrounding a TV show. It is begging for us to walk in the grass and to reconnect with Mother Earth. Let us open our hearts and be TRUTHFUL when our thoughts and actions are not stemming from our highest self. Each of our souls is ready to listen to the Universal wisdom. Let us return to our essence by being TRUTHFUL with ourselves and seeking guidance to lead a life of our highest calling.

~ I AM allowing the Universe to guide me on a path that is TRUTHFUL to my highest calling.

~~~~~~~~

Blessings of Hope are sent to you today. May you be TRUTHFUL to the essence of who you are in every thought, word, and action.

~~~~~~~~

Notes

Image captured by Susan Gossett.

Week 49
Unity Collaboration

~~~~~~~~

Blessings of Connection are sent to you today. May you take action from a space of Unity Collaboration.

~~~~~~~~

More and more my path shows me the importance of connecting with the Higher Power, Mother Nature, Father Time, myself, and with one another.

I have learned that true connection begins with listening from a heart that is open. It speaks with a compassionate tongue. It gives the gift of time to do both with the grace of the Divine.

Life without connection leads an individual into hopelessness and despair. Fear feeds on every wayward thought and our darkest emotions; such as hatred, revenge, and bitterness, creating an ugliness that may appear to be a living hell.

It is when we take the time to truly connect to what is really happening in our lives and relationships, that we see the blessings of everyone's unique path upon this Earth.

This connection with each other is Oneness, and it brings unity. We begin to cheer each other on to 'be' and to 'create' that which each of us came here to share. It becomes so clear how important it is for you and me to bring our unique gifts to the world.

Think of each of our lives as a strand in the beautiful web of life. A collaboration that combines love, abundance, and unity will bring peace to our world and create our heaven on Earth.

One strand is not more important than another, for a web cannot be formed with a single strand, only by an arrangement of many. It is the collectiveness that creates the strength and beauty of the web.

Let us place our intentions upon UNITY COLLABORATION. It is a time to focus upon the collective we. Together we can create miracles for our Earth, including every being and every creature that inhabits her, bringing us into a consciousness of well-being for all.

Be thy Light.

Day 1
ARISE~ Let us ARISE in assisting the world around us, giving of ourselves to the beings and creatures that call this planet home. You and I did not come here to leave nothing for the future, but to assist in creating a better and brighter tomorrow. Do not get swept up in the negativity, that there is no hope or that we cannot make a difference with our actions. ARISE today, making a conscious choice to make decisions that are the best for our planet. This choice may not be the easiest, but it is a positive step for our future. Check in with your highest self on how you can make a difference today in everything that you do. As we envision our tomorrows, see them through the Universal rays of light, the energy of hope, the possibilities of love, and ARISE to the conscious choices of the highest good.

~ I AM consciously making choices that are for the highest good. Through conscious decisions, I ARISE to the energy of unconditional love.

Blessings of Awareness are sent to you today. May your heart be open and ARISE to the loving all without conditions.

Day 2

BLESSED BE~ BLESSED BE to all who see that believing is the key to moments of unity and harmony. Blessings to all who are living with purpose and with a passion for fulfilling our destiny. BLESSED BE to this home called Earth and her patience with us as we tread upon her resources, which she gives so graciously. Can we not make more loving and compassionate choices, that give more and take less of this world? Yes, this is key. A blessing to each of us that we become more than we currently are and that all we dream comes to fruition. A species of grace, giving, and peace with all the inhabitants of land and sea. Let us be more than takers. Let us begin today to end the lack that we currently behold, by being more and giving back abundantly. BLESSED BE to you, to me, and to an encompassed we.

~ I AM giving more to the world than I am taking. BLESSED BE that all I touch is with unconditional love.

Blessings of Grace are sent to you today. May your journey be filled with the beauty of miracles, BLESSED BE to all that you are sharing with the world.

Day 3

COLLABORATION~ It is through COLLABORATION that the Universe assists with the momentum of bringing our dreams into reality. If each of us shares our gifts, the COLLABORATION of a group effort produces a higher result and a greater sense of accomplishment for our tasks. When we work together toward solutions, pondering ideas that may be out of our comfort zone, the results will be more powerful than we thought possible. Our world is empowered through COLLABORATION with others. This step towards unity has an energy that builds momentum. This is where miracles can begin to take place.

~ I AM open to working in COLLABORATION with others to assist in bringing my dreams to fruition.

~~~~~~~~~~

Blessings of Unity are sent to you today. May you bring the highest version of yourself to each moment of COLLABORATION.

~~~~~~~~~~

Day 4
CONNECTION~ It is when we are present in the moment that the CONNECTION with everything around us is apparent. You and I are one with one another in the Universal Light, and we are experiencing life in these separate, amazing bodies. It is through our unique experiences that we expand and rediscover the oneness of this CONNECTION. When we live in the anxiety of the future or the depression of the past, it is here that we lose our hope and see more darkness than light in the world. It is through our trust and the belief that all is unfolding as it should, that the Light within us continues to shine. Let us take this moment to be present and restore our CONNECTION to the space of love and hope, peace and light, joy and harmony.

~ I AM living in the present moment, witnessing the CONNECTION that all things are one.

~~~~~~~~~~

Blessings of Harmony are sent to you today. May your heart, mind, and soul be aligned with your CONNECTION to others as you honor their journey

~~~~~~~~~~

Day 5
DIFFERENCES~ Often in life we focus on the similarities that you and I have in common. This action is what bonds us together, but it is the DIFFERENCES that bring diversity and moments of expansion. Our contrasting views and opinions bring color to our world. What would a rainbow look like with just one color? It would be a beautiful streak of violet across the sky, but a prism of all the colors brings the joy of diversity and

magnificence. Our past experiences have led us to different conclusions, but it is possible that future experiences may bring an expansion that aligns our truths. The conversations of our DIFFERENCES must be from an open heart, and with the intention to bring more Light into our world. If we embrace one another from a place of higher consciousness and unconditional love, acceptance brings us together, raising the vibration of our planet. Let us go out into the world with an open heart, mind, and spirit, embracing the colors of life and the DIFFERENCES between you and I.

~ I AM consciously choosing to see the beauty of our DIFFERENCES.

~~~~~~~~

Blessings of Alignment are sent to you today. May you be open to the beauty of our DIFFERENCES and love without conditions.

~~~~~~~~

Day 6
UNIQUE~ Each of us is a UNIQUE being who came here to experience life within the vessel of our individual bodies. Our perceptions of what we see and experience write the story from which we gain our inner wisdom. The creatures and plants in this world are also UNIQUE; they, too, came here to fulfill their purpose. Although we are each UNIQUE, the one thing that we have in common is that we are each striving to fulfill our soul's purpose. Let us not step on one another in competition or dominate those who are unable to protect themselves. Let us choose to walk through the world with love and compassion. Let us embrace our essence with the intention that each footprint we leave bears the mark of a united truth.

~ I AM a UNIQUE being who shares my love and compassion with the world around me.

~~~~~~~~

Blessings of Courage are sent to you today. May you bring your UNIQUE Light out into the world for you are always supported and loved unconditionally.

~~~~~~~~

Day 7

UNITY~ The controversy of today will bring more clarity for tomorrow. Together, in UNITY, we can bring more light to the darkest of moments. There are times when things may appear unfair, and we want to lash out at those who seem to be causing this havoc in our lives. Let us quiet the ego and soothe our pride with unconditional love. It is during these moments that we must reach higher for feelings of hope and seek our inner wisdom for more love. It is only through UNITY with one another that our world will become one that is full of compassion. Let us focus on the higher thought; the one of UNITY and togetherness for the highest good.

~ I AM living each moment with the guidance of my inner wisdom, which is in UNITY with the world.

~~~~~~~~~

Blessings of Compassion are sent to you today. May you bring UNITY in every conversation and connection, shining your Light brightly upon the world.

~~~~~~~~~

Notes

Image captured by Susan Gossett.

Week 50
Warrior Strength

~~~~~~

Blessings of Courage are sent to you today. May your movements be from a space within, your inner Warrior Strength.

~~~~~~

Each of us has the strength of a warrior inside of us. Do you know your warrior's voice? It is the thoughts that no one else hears, the commentary inside your being from the time you wake in the morning until you fall asleep at night.

My inner warrior has genuinely become my biggest cheerleader. She encourages me to speak and write when I need to be supported to do so. She comforts me by saying loving words of encouragement when I am tired from life's journey and sometimes too exhausted to move any further.

She encourages me to love Big, to live a life of adventure, and to explore that which may be out of my comfort zone. She is always nudging me to dream bigger and not to underestimate what I am capable of doing in this lifetime.

356

Now let me say that we weren't always 'friends', but somewhere along the journey, this inner voice and I came to an understanding that we were in this together. We realized that unkind thoughts and criticism were not going to build a life of love and Light. This inner warrior and I became a unified team to create, to be, to see, and to do more with the precious time that I have here.

If your inner thoughts are still critical and possibly your most prominent critic, it is time for you to connect with your inner warrior. Take some time to redefine what you need to hear, the kind of encouragement that you need to succeed in your life. This is an opportunity to allow your inner warrior to help you shift fear into courage and guide you to tackle your doubts, step out of your comfort zone, and do that 'something' you know you should be doing.

Let us step into being the warrior of our destiny. Our voice needs to be heard speaking the truth, doing that which we came here to create, loving others, and loving yourself fully and completely without conditions.

Let the inner and outer critics fade away and allow a new focus of kindness and compassion in all that we think, say, and do.

We came here to shine, to overcome obstacles, to strive to be the uniqueness of who we are, and to be love and truth in our WARRIOR STRENGTH.

Be thy Light.

Day 1
ADVENTURE~ Let us look at life as an ADVENTURE, embarking on life's journey with the enthusiasm of a child. Let us explore and ask questions about what you and I see or hear. Our life should not be a monotonous undertaking, but one to embrace with excitement for the things, places, and people that we have yet to discover. An ADVENTURE does not have to be to a foreign land or across vast distances; it can be to the neighborhood park, exploring a new place, or attending an event. Let us renew the energy within us by expanding our hearts to the endless possibilities of something new; stretching our minds to touch the hope of our souls; creating situations that will bring more enthusiasm, excitement, and expansion of our personal

journey. Embrace and create the ADVENTURE that is awaiting our discovery.

~ I AM renewing the ADVENTURE within my being.

~~~~~~~~~

Blessings of Bravery are sent to you today. May you step out of your comfort zone and create a life filled with ADVENTURE.

~~~~~~~~~

Day 2

DECLARATION~ Let us choose a personal DECLARATION to go out and embrace the day before us. It may be a silent vow to bring more love and light to everyone that we see. It may be a demand for our actions, that we will overcome the fear that is hindering our journey. No matter if it is said silently, or out loud to someone else, each of us has a DECLARATION that mirrors our belief system. Let us ask if it is serving our journey. Do you and I need to shift our thoughts, words, or actions to reflect the true essence of who we are? Let us embrace a DECLARATION of love, compassion, grace, and harmony with ourselves and with the Universe.

~ I AM choosing a DECLARATION of love, compassion, and grace for myself and all those in the world.

~~~~~~~~~

Blessings of Courage are sent to you today. May you align your belief system with a daily DECLARATION that you are living a life of consciousness.

~~~~~~~~~

Day 3

EXPLORE~ Let us choose to EXPLORE the many possibilities of our unique path and be a bit more adventurous. It is by exploring new opportunities that we bring new people and places to our experience, which enables us to expand our perceptions of the world. We may see something spectacular, that will bring a bit more joy to our day. Let us choose to EXPLORE life with an open heart and mind. Let us bring the childlike joy back into our day and vibrancy into our world. Let us be present and aware of all that is happening around us and to EXPLORE all that comes into our lives.

~ I AM present and aware of my world, and I EXPLORE all that life is presenting to me.

~~~~~~~~

Blessings of Opportunities are sent to you today. May you EXPLORE all that waits for your unique journey with a heart and mind that are open.

~~~~~~~~

Day 4

OVERCOME~ As we walk along the path of life, blessing those that bring joy and wisdom into our lives, it is always difficult to say goodbye to those we love. The grief may overwhelm us emotionally and physically, for we long for more moments with them. How does one OVERCOME this grief? We often feel anger for the loss and ask "why?" in regards to that which we do not understand. As the tears fall, let us remember the moments of laughter; and as our hearts ache, let us remember the gifts of love that our cherished ones brought into our lives. You and I are loved. We always have been and always will be. We are always supported in our efforts to OVERCOME the obstacles that enter our lives. In our hearts, we know this to be true. Let us breathe in all that was and bask in these days of love; and then breathe out all that will be, knowing that tomorrow will bring continued love into our world. We have been given the tools to conquer these periods of grief that pass through our lives. We will OVERCOME these moments of sadness.

~ I AM allowing the guidance of the Universe to flow through me. I have been given the tools to OVERCOME all obstacles.

Blessings of Faith are sent to you today. May you OVERCOME all the obstacles that will lead you to the highest version of you.

Day 5

STRENGTH~ Hush now and let us listen with the intent to hear our inner wisdom speak over the chatter of our ego. Let us breathe deeply, filling our lungs with life energy that feeds our soul. May we become aware of the inner STRENGTH of the spirit that resides in this temple of a body. The knowing of who we are, the essence of you and I, becomes manifest in this moment of silence. Let us take this moment and just be, breathing out the doubts and fears that hinder our journey to a joyful life. The chitter-chatter of our mind does not serve the highest good; it weakens the STRENGTH within us that is capable of all things. Let us feel the STRENGTH that we were given to share our gifts with the world. Let us share our true essence with all whom we encounter today.

~ I AM in tune with my inner STRENGTH, and I move forward in my actions to fulfill my dreams.

Blessings of Miracles are sent to you today. May you know your own inner STRENGTH and honor all that you are capable of doing.

Day 6

STRIVE~ Let us take a moment to check in with the essence of who we are. Let us tune into the spirit that resides within our Earthly body--that which does not fear rejection or allow insecurities to prevent us from doing what we came here to do. Each of us can achieve great things in this lifetime. We can STRIVE to make the world around us a better place by loving one another and being an example of compassion. Our journey can support all the inhabitants of the Earth; from humankind to the creatures, to those living beings that do not have a voice. Through our highest actions and choices, we can make a difference for the planet that each of us calls home. Let us STRIVE to be better than yesterday and choose that which is for the highest good. Each of us co-exists with one another. Let us not be short-sighted and deplete our world to ruin, but instead, let us STRIVE to give back and replenish the Earth for the lifetimes of tomorrow.

~ I AM living a life of compassion. I STRIVE for my actions to be from my highest self.

~~~~~~~~

Blessings of Alignment are sent to you today. May you STRIVE to be connected to your highest self, creating actions for the highest good.

~~~~~~~~

Day 7

WARRIOR~ The obstacle that stands in our way is only the mountain or the vast canyon that we have created in our minds. Despite these seemingly insurmountable barriers, you and I have the capability to reach our goals. Within each of us is a WARRIOR; we have the ability, the wisdom, and the guidance of the Universe to accomplish all that we dream. Let us not lower our head in defeat or give up because we feel that it is too difficult. Let us tap into the spiritual WARRIOR that makes us want to roar and climb that mountain. Let us dig deep into our soul to find a way across the canyon. Let each of us tap into our inner strength, light, and love, all of which are bigger than the mountains and deeper than the oceans. Let us create a journey filled with love and be the WARRIOR that shares Light with the world.

~ I AM a WARRIOR of love, sharing my Light with the world around me.

~~~~~~~~

Blessings of Connection are sent to you today. May you be the WARRIOR that you came here to be, creating a life of miracles.

~~~~~~~~

Notes

Image captured by Susan Gossett.

Week 51
Honoring Wisdom

~~~~~~~~~

Blessings of Grace are sent to you today. Together we are Honoring the
Wisdom that surrounds our journey to love and Light.

~~~~~~~~~

You and I are born from that which can only be called miraculous. Our
fingerprints and DNA are uniquely our own among millions
of others; truly amazing are these bodies that we experience our journey in.

We are also blessed to have Universal wisdom that resides within each of us;
our thought patterns, experiences, and all that we witness are how you and I
navigate and determine what we want
to create and be in this lifetime.

There is no doubt that you are part of my family on this planet, and I am
your sister. I know this from deep within the heart of me. Everything is
connected far beyond what our body senses, there is a deeper connection in
the space where our souls kindly show us the sacred wisdom.

Let us honor this wisdom through the words we speak and the actions that we take, understanding that we came from love, compassion, and grace. Even when we do not agree, let us be respectful of one another and speak with kindness. Together we can communicate with an intention to understand each other's viewpoint, instead of trying to force our opinions on one another.

Let us approach our differences with curiosity for a mystery we do not yet understand. I will listen to your words without anger, because together we can create a world of more depth and compassion. As I speak, you need not take my words personally, for my viewpoint is from my own life's experiences. It is here, where we connect heart to heart, that we honor the wisdom of yesterday in order to bring love to the present moment.

Let us be the hope, share our essence of love, and HONOR the WISDOM that lives in each of us. May we shine our unique beauty in the world.

Be thy Light.

Day 1

ADAPTATION~ We don't always get to choose what enters into our lives; often we would make a different choice if given the opportunity. It is important to remember that we are here to expand and grow, to become wiser through the process and the contrast. It is when we learn the tool of ADAPTATION in all things that we find peace within our hearts, even in the most difficult times. ADAPTATION is not necessarily accepting behavior that is unkind or ruthless, but it is sending love and blessings to those that have lost their truth. We have all read the stories of history and can even witness current events that are filled with hatred. These negative emotions cannot be met with the same energy, for we all know that nothing loving comes from this dark place. Only when hatred is met with love, forgiveness, acceptance, and hope, can it evolve into sadness, remorse, vulnerability, and ultimately become love. Let us embrace the tool of ADAPTATION into our daily lives and become a haven of tolerance and love for all sentient beings.

~ I AM the ADAPTATION of love and compassion to all things that I encounter today.

Blessings of an Open Heart are sent to you today. May you experience the spiritual tool of ADAPTATION through the veil of compassion to create a world of peace.

Day 2

HONORED~ Oh little leaf that floats in the breeze, you were once a bud of vibrant green. Now you are withered and brown as you lie on the ground. Do not shed a tear, for your purpose in life is HONORED. Yesterday you provided shade in the beauty of summer's green. Now you are HONORED and will become one with the Earth, nurturing her soil for future needs. May we embrace our truth in this path of life at each stage that we encounter; from the energy of our youth and the focus of middle age, to the wisdom that accompanies our later years. All stages of our journey have a purpose, and each is HONORED for what they bring to our world.

~ I AM HONORED by the ebb and flow of this journey, and embrace the wisdom that is imparted.

Blessings of Forgiveness are sent to you today. May you be HONORED by the blessing of each moment as you expand into your true essence.

Day 3

BECOMING~ You and I are BECOMING wiser through our experiences; just as the rainbow appears after the rain, the butterfly soars after emerging from the cocoon, and spring arrives after the harshest of winters. You and I grow through the experiences of our lives. It is the expansion of who we are BECOMING and where we are going. The trials and tribulations will pass. The laughter and joy will fill life once again. The wisdom of yesterday will be the gift we receive. Let us believe in the rainbows of our tomorrow. Let us fly like the butterfly, and trust that spring is waiting to greet us after the winter. We are consciously choosing higher thoughts, words of compassion, and a heart filled with love. We are BECOMING that which we choose to be.

~ I AM BECOMING that which I came here to be - the essence of me.

365

Blessings of Courage are sent to you today. May you consciously choose the higher thoughts and actions that lead you to BECOMING all that you came here to be and do.

Day 4

EXPERIENCES~ Life is a journey of EXPERIENCES, and we evolve through that which we encounter. There are moments of joy, anger, bliss, and sadness, and each of them has a lesson from which you and I can gain wisdom. The world around us is always changing; this is the one constant in our journey. In every instance, it is our decision as to how we choose to perceive the changes that happen in our lives. Will we react with love and compassion, or will we close our hearts and lose our faith? Let us choose to be ever-expanding through life's EXPERIENCES, reaching for higher thoughts and acts of kindness. This journey is a gift that has been given to each of us. Let us move through the EXPERIENCES of life with an open heart.

~ I AM reaching for the wisdom in all of the EXPERIENCES of my journey.

Blessings of Love are sent to you today. May you embrace the gift of life's EXPERIENCES with your inner wisdom.

Day 5

PATIENCE~ It is with PATIENCE that the irritation and anger toward others no longer appears. Having patience truly is the answer to many of the problems that we see around us, and it is a choice that we can make each and every day. When you and I live with a compassionate heart, the virtue of PATIENCE enters into our world. As we step forward today, let us envision a planet with more compassion and embrace the PATIENCE within us. It is in this space that the Universe unfolds its wisdom and guidance for us.

~ I AM living each moment with a heart filled with compassion and PATIENCE for the world around me.

Blessings of Compassion are sent to you today. May you be surrounded with PATIENCE and love through the most difficult moments.

~~~~~~~~

Day 6

HONORING~ Each day, as we begin our journey, we tell ourselves a story. Images flash through our minds of what needs to be done and with whom we will converse with throughout the day. These thoughts are often accompanied by waves of emotions that may determine a positive or negative state of mind. Today as those images begin to form, let us consciously choose to see them through a veil of love, HONORING the essence of all those who enter into our world. It is through HONORING our intentions that we hone in on love and can walk through feelings of fear and anxiety. By always HONORING the truth within us, and initiating our intentions with love and Light, we will raise the consciousness of the world around us.

~ I AM HONORING my thoughts today and initiating my intentions with love and Light.

~~~~~~~~

Blessings of Intention are sent to you today. May you begin each day by HONORING your truth consciously and sharing your essence with the world.

~~~~~~~~

Day 7

WISDOM~ We are one with all things; this truth is manifested through the essence of our being. It is evidenced by the inner WISDOM that radiates through our words and actions when we are in tune with this Oneness. Let us choose to seek the guidance of the Universe as we go throughout our day. Our lives will become aligned with that which we came here to do, and the WISDOM will assist each of us through times of joy and difficulty. We are always supported; we need only to listen and quiet the fearful thoughts. Let us be in tune with the inner WISDOM that radiates through us each day.

~ I AM in tune with the inner WISDOM and guidance of the Universe in every moment.

~~~~~~~~

Blessings of Love and Light are sent to you today. May your heart be open to your inner WISDOM and the guidance of the Universe in every moment.

~~~~~~~~

Notes

Image captured by Tim Chinn.

Week 52
Witness of Wonder

~~~~~~~

Blessings of Unconditional Love are sent to you today. May you Witness the Wonder of all that you are and all that surrounds you.

~~~~~~~

There are miracles that happen all around us. We have the opportunity to witness these wonders, if only we choose to open our hearts and minds to these phenomenal events.

The final week of our 365 days together is upon us, and I knew I wanted to place our intentions on seeing the marvels that surround our days, allowing us to be in awe of the synchronicities of life, and encouraging us to admire the many wonders of our world.

My sincerest hope is that the words of *Be thy Light* have encouraged you to step through your doubt and fears and into your own power to create all that you came here to share. No one else can place your unique footprint on the world. We so need your Light, my friend.

Together we can be the generosity, the encouraging word, the smile of kindness, the heart of love, and the shoulder of support that we wish to see in the world. When we recognize a need, let us take actions of hope, kindness, and compassion towards a positive outcome. Indeed these are the gifts that we can choose to give in every moment.

Let us open every cell of our being to Witness the Wonder of the world we live in, to be a part of the creation of miracles, and to consciously begin changing our planet into a place of unity and peace.

You and I can choose to incorporate more peace in our souls, relationships, communities, and throughout this amazing world. Let us live our lives with the intention of becoming a WITNESS OF WONDER, for these moments are everywhere. We can also create them, using our unique gifts, by shining our Light for all to see.

Be thy Light.

Day 1
EXAMPLE~ Our lives are an EXAMPLE to the world around us of our values and beliefs. Others view our journey by the words that are spoken and in the actions that are taken. They witness whether we shine light upon the world or spread darkness. Let us choose to be an EXAMPLE of love, kindness, peace, and hope. Let us be the Light when all is dark, the calmness in the storm, and the EXAMPLE that the world needs to witness for the possibilities of a better tomorrow.

~ I AM an EXAMPLE of Light and love; which I share unconditionally with the world.

~~~~~~~~~

Blessings of Hope are sent to you today. May you be an EXAMPLE of love and compassion in every moment.

~~~~~~~~~

Day 2
MOMENTS~ Our lives are just a series of MOMENTS that seem quite small when we think of how long humanity has existed. You and I are here experiencing all that is around us. We are learning from these experiences

371

and are always desiring a bit more of this or less of that. We each partake of MOMENTS that are both high and low. We laugh and cry over the ups and the downs of the life that we lead. It is through all of these experiences that we create the story of our journey. Let us be present, thankful, and enjoy all the MOMENTS that we are given.

~ I AM embracing the MOMENTS that I have been given in gratitude and joy.

~~~~~~~

Blessings of Joy are sent to you today. May you embrace all MOMENTS with a heart filled with love and compassion.

~~~~~~~

Day 3
OBSERVER~ Each of us is an OBSERVER to that which occurs in the world around us. What we do with those experiences could harden our hearts, close our minds, or dampen our enthusiasm for life. It does not serve us to hold back our love, or to live life in a negative state of mind. Let us be an OBSERVER of the beauty in life, and share our love, so that others can witness our light in times of darkness. Let us be an OBSERVER that shares with an open and compassionate heart to the world around us.

~ I AM an OBSERVER of life, who sees the good in all things. I share my love and compassion with the world.

~~~~~~~

Blessings of Wisdom are sent to you today. May you see the truth of each moment, as an OBSERVER of the world witness all through a compassionate heart.

~~~~~~~

Day 4
STORYTELLER~ Each of us is the STORYTELLER of our journey; there is a plot that thickens through the various scenes, the narration is in the words that we speak, and the hero has many battles to conquer throughout the ever-evolving story of our lives. We choose our allies during our

interactions with, and through our reactions to, the many players in our world. You and I will never rid the world of that which we disdain or don't want in our lives. We can only align our mind, body, and soul with the story we create, by following our hearts and being the STORYTELLER of our truth. May each of us think thoughts of love, speak words of compassion, and take actions of peace for a better world. May we be the STORYTELLER of a journey of love, peace, and joy that is told for generations to come.

~ I AM a STORYTELLER that shares the stories of love and compassion for all to hear.

Blessings of Clarity are sent to you today. May you align every cell of your being to the STORYTELLER that is within you; thinking, writing, speaking, and being the Universal truth.

Day 5

TODAY~ Let us choose to find the good in all that we witness. May we choose higher thoughts, surrounded in compassion, rather than judgment for what we experience. TODAY let us be present to the true miracle that we are in our essence. Let us treat the stranger, friend, and relative with love and acceptance. TODAY let us shine for the whole world so that all may see the Light that is within our being. We have only this moment to share that which we came here to give. Let us not wait for tomorrow, but choose to take action TODAY.

~ I AM choosing to be present TODAY, and to find the good in all things that I witness.

Blessings of Presence are sent to you today. May you be in the moment of TODAY, living each moment in the awareness that surrounds you.

Day 6

VALIDATE~ Each of us is walking this path of life and experiencing the trials and tribulations that enter into our world at times. We lean on those we love to VALIDATE the emotions and feelings that arise. As we listen to others describe their challenging moments, let us support them with compassion; for we are not here to cast judgment, fix, rescue, or enable one another. Being there for one another means to VALIDATE that we all have moments of adversity and that we are always guided by the Universe in our journey to gain more wisdom. When we communicate, we assist one another through the fearful thoughts to a place of more hope and faith. Let us continue to VALIDATE one another in this journey of life, as we move past the darkness and into the light.

~ I AM supporting all on their journey of life. I VALIDATE their moments of darkness with Light from my essence.

~~~~~~~~~

Blessings of Support are sent to you today. May your presence bring hope to the words and actions of others to VALIDATE the love and Light of who we came here to be.

~~~~~~~~~

Day 7

WONDER~ Let us be a witness to the WONDER of life today. It surrounds us always, but often in the busyness of our days, we forget to look around and observe the miracles that are taking place in every moment. Let us see the dust on a butterfly's wings and hear the flutter of the hummingbird in flight. Let us open our hearts to the love that flows through us when a newborn baby sleeps, or when a rainbow appears with the promise of hope and trust for tomorrow. Life is filled with the magic of WONDER and mystery; it is abundant in all things through our faith and wisdom. We can make the choice in every moment to see our life through love and to share that love with everyone around us. Let us see the WONDER and magic of all that is and be a part of the miracles that surround us.

~ I AM recognizing the WONDER in all that I witness by being present in the moment.

~~~~~~~~

Blessings of Miracles are sent to you today. May you bring the magic and WONDER to each and every moment through your true essence.

~~~~~~~~

Notes

Image captured by Tim Chinn.

Bonus

PEACE~ The sun shines down on thee, light breeze touches thy hair, the scent of honeysuckle fills the air, and PEACE abounds in all that we see. In every moment, may our hearts be full of love, flowing to everyone that we meet, and bless them with the PEACE that resides within our hearts. May the joy of who we are, guide the words that we speak. May PEACE surround the world in which we live and guide all the actions that you and I place into the world.

~ I AM at PEACE with myself and all that I encounter. I send blessings and unconditional love to all whom I encounter today.

~~~~~~~~

Blessings of Love are sent to you today. May you be aligned in your heart, mind, and soul as you have the opportunity to bring PEACE and love to the world.

~~~~~~~~

Shine Brilliantly

The journey of *Be thy Light* has been more than I could have imagined. I feel blessed to have been the vessel that these words have manifested through to find their presence in the world.

I began writing these daily intentions over thirteen years ago. At the time, I did not realize they were intentions; they were just my way of sharing hope with the world around me.

Over time they have evolved and morphed into an app, and now an EBook. I am not sure if they will continue to expand or if they have fully blossomed into their final season. Either way, I am always open to the call, if they seek to be shared in a different medium.

Be thy Light is designed to be used year after year. You will find that what resonated with you last year will be different in the coming year because we are continually expanding into our true essence.

I hope that the words have guided you to live a compassionate life of intention. They have been created to bring you guidance when all seems lost. They will assist you in becoming the highest version of yourself, embracing forgiveness, and creating a more mindful way of living through your awakened consciousness.

We are One, truly connected to all things, a family here on this beautiful planet. Let us come together and create a life of intention, leading to a world of compassion and joy for all.

The words at the beginning of *Be thy Light* were the following, and I feel it is only appropriate to end with them as well:

> 'You are here to shine your Light upon the world. You are a unique being with thoughts, experiences, and gifts that only you can give to those that witness your journey.'

Be thy Light.

When you and I shine our unique Light in all that we do,
we create a world of compassion for all.

~Kim Christin

Kim Christin is the creator of *365 Intentions to Inspire App*. She is a spiritual healer and inspirational writer, supporting others in their journey to true awareness and connection through her inspirational words of Light. She lives with her significant other and their three dogs near San Diego, California.

Notes

Notes

Notes

385

Index

Abundance	15	Blessed	51
Acceptance	210	Blessed Be	351
Accountability	267	Bliss	226
Achieve	139	Blossoms	204
Achieving	266	Bold	81
Acknowledge	29	Brave	81
Action	267	Bravery	268
Activate	232	Breath	196
Adaptation	364	Brilliance	227
Admiration	15	Calmness	260
Adventure	357	Capable	246
Adventurous	88	Carefree	14
Aligned	6	Catalyst	66
Allowing	204	Certainty	163
Always	161	Challenge	163
Answers	161	Change	205
Appreciate	273	Choices	22
Appreciated	117	Circumstances	154
Arise	350	Clarify	182
Arising	176	Clarity	177
Ask	162	Collaboration	351
Aspiration	185	Colors	155
Aspire	37	Communication	308
Attention	154	Compassion	67
Attitude	16	Complete	275
Authentic	344	Confidence	164
Authenticity	225	Connection	352
Awaken	24	Conquer	82
Awakened	225	Conscious	75
Awakening	22	Contemplate	206
Aware	226	Contribution	155
Awareness	29	Conviction	247
Balance	6	Courage	80
Be	38	Courageous	83
Be Fulfilled	66	Cradle	252
Beauty	146	Creation	287
Becoming	365	Creative	88
Beginning	176	Creativity	91
Beliefs	167	Creator	238
Believe	44	Declaration	358

Declare	345	Fears	140
Deliverance	275	Feel	30
Desire	177	Feelings	184
Destination	97	Flow	132
Destiny	96	Flowing	7
Devotion	345	Focus	184
Differences	352	Focusing	8
Divine	239	Forever	119
Divinity	336	Forgiveness	68
Effortless	206	Freedom	111
Embrace	175	Fulfillment	185
Emotions	67	Gathering	281
Empower	68	Generosity	156
Empowering	268	Genuine	290
Encouraging	118	Gift	124
Enjoy	213	Giggles	213
Enlightenment	346	Given	52
Enriched	189	Glorious	52
Enthusiasm	211	Glory	17
Envision	183	Goodness	23
Essence	224	Grace	147
Eternity	233	Graciously	149
Everything	148	Grateful	302
Evolving	131	Gratitude	153
Example	371	Greatness	38
Excitement	212	Growth	133
Exhilaration	212	Guidance	160
Expanding	133	Guide	59
Expansion	23	Guided	140
Experience	131	Happily	302
Experiences	366	Happiness	261
Explore	358	Happy	329
Extraordinary	288	Harmonious	168
Facets	301	Harmoniously	281
Faith	139	Harmony	171
Faithful	289	Heart	178
Family	280	Higher Self	288
Fascination	253	Honesty	336
Favorite	295	Honor	339
Fearlessness	83	Honored	365

Honoring	367	Light	228
Hope	182	Limitless	239
I Am	39	Listen	295
Imagination	8	Listener	297
In Sync	197	Listening	31
In The Beginning	253	Living	17
In Tune	207	Love	232
Incredible	74	Loved	125
Infinitely	74	Loving	234
Initiative	111	Lovingkindness	220
Inner Voice	141	Magic	247
Inquisitive	290	Magnificent	119
Inseparable	282	Manifest	240
Insight	189	Manifestation	218
Insightful	125	Manifesting	32
Inspiration	53	Mantra	218
Inspire	190	Master	240
Inspired	45	Masterpiece	89
Instinctively	31	Meaning	76
Integrity	269	Meaningful	24
Intention	75	Miracle	246
Intentions	178	Mirror	234
Interpret	283	Moments	371
Interpretation	309	Moonbeams	53
Interpreter	233	Movement	76
Intuition	316	Music	89
Intuitive	276	Mysterious	248
Joy	211	Mystery	59
Joyful	330	Narrating	96
Just Be	36	Narrator	120, 254
Kind	69	Nature	9
Kindness	217	Nurture	255
Knowing	343	Nurturing	126
Laughter	254	Observer	372
Lean In	142	Open	134
Legacy	283	Openness	198
Lessons	17	Others	331
Letting Go	322	Our-Self	77
Liberty	31	Overcome	359
Life-Giving	134	Passion	126, 197

Patience	366	Relationships	284
Peace	260, 377	Release	61
Perception	248	Releasing	323
Perfect	127	Remember	331
Perfection	330	Renew	61
Perseverance	269	Renewed	191
Persevere	97	Resilience	112
Persistence	84	Resilient	142
Perspective	198	Resistance	323
Phenomenal	303	Responsible	112
Playful	309	Reveal	324
Pleasure	90	Rise	113
Poetry	91	Rising	99
Positive	199	Sacred	317
Possibilities	9	Sacredness	249
Potential	261	Seeds	191
Power	45	Self	291
Powerful	25	Serenely	147
Praise	54	Shift	62
Preciousness	219	Shine	305
Present	274	Silence	294
Proactive	241	Similarities	262
Process	337	Smile	120
Progress	304	Solitude	317
Promise	338	Song	192
Prosperity	242	Soothe	319
Purpose	58	Soul	311
Quiet	298	Spark	121
Quietude	296	Sparkle	40
Radiate	304	Special	311
Reach	156	Spirit	312
Reaching	310	Spontaneity	192
Realization	98	Spontaneous	199
Reassured	338	Step by Step	46
Receptive	203	Stillness	315
Recognize	98	Story	262
Reflect	39	Storyteller	372
Reflection	60	Strength	360
Rejoice	54	Strive	360
Rejuvenate	255	Supported	46

Surrender	324	Undoing	169
Synchronize	296	Union	170
Teachings	325	Unique	171, 353
Thankful	332	Unity	354
Thankfulness	276	Unstoppable	149
Thrive	114	Validate	374
Time	318	Value	332
Today	373	Vibrant	235
Together	263	Vitality	103
Transform	47	Voice	103
Transition	48	Warrior	361
Triumph	219	Well-Being	316
True	127	Whispers	104
Truly	220	Wisdom	367
Trust	339	Within	104
Truth	344	Witness	274
Truthful	346	Wonder	374
Twilight	148	Worthy	105
Unboundedness	325	Yield	106
Uncertainty	169	You	106

Made in the USA
San Bernardino, CA
17 September 2019